MOUS Essentials
Excel 97 Proficient

Jane Calabria

Dorothy Burke

Michele Reader

An Imprint of Macmillan Computer Publishing

MOUS Essentials: Excel 97 Proficient

Library of Congress Catalog No: 98-066766

ISBN: 1-58076-054-6

01 00 99   4 3

Interpretation of the printing code: the rightmost double-digit number is the year of the book's printing; the rightmost single-digit number, the number of the book's printing. For example, a printing code of 98-1 shows that the first printing of the book occurred in 1998.

Screens reproduced in this book were created using Collage Plus from Inner Media, Inc., Hollis, NH.

This book was produced digitally by Macmillan Computer Publishing and manufactured using computer-to-plate technology (a film-less process) by GAC/Shepard Poorman, Indianapolis, Indiana.

Composed in *Stone Serif* and *MCPdigital* by Que® Education and Training

Publisher:
Robb Linsky

Executive Editor:
Randy Haubner

Acquisitions Editor:
Jon Phillips

Director of Product Marketing:
Susan L. Kindel

Managing Editor:
Caroline Roop

Development Editor:
Nancy D. Warner

Production Editor:
Susan Hobbs

Copy Editor:
Cliff Shubs

Acquisitions Assistant:
Ken Schmidt

Technical Editor:
Ed Metzler

Cover Designer:
Nathan Clement

Book Designer:
Louisa Kluznick

Production Team:
Kim Cofer
Cheryl Lynch
Chris Barrick

About the Authors

Jane Calabria has authored 13 Macmillan Computer Publishing books. As a consultant, Jane works on a national level with large corporations and training organizations, developing user training programs and modeling help desk support structures. As a trainer, Jane teaches Microsoft desktop applications, operating systems, and Lotus Notes and Domino. She is a Certified Lotus Notes Professional (Principal level) and a Certified Microsoft User Specialist.

Jane and Dorothy Burke have teamed up successfully on several MCP books, including the *Certified Microsoft Office User Exam Guide for Microsoft Word 97, Microsoft Excel 97* and *Microsoft Power Point 97*. They also co-authored *Microsoft Works 6-in-1, Microsoft Windows 95 6 in 1, Microsoft Windows 98 6 in 1, Using Microsoft Word 97,* and several Lotus Notes books.

Dorothy Burke has traveled a few career paths before becoming a computer instructor and consultant. She has worked as a magazine editor for an engineering trade magazine, in customer service and management in the home medical equipment industry, and in a management consulting firm as an office manager and editor of its newsletter and catalogs. Dorothy is a Certified Lotus Instructor and a Certified Lotus Professional in Lotus Notes. With a strong background in graphics and desktop publishing, Dorothy develops applications in Lotus Notes and for Domino Web sites. Writing with Jane Calabria, she has contributed to the *10 Minute Guide to Lotus Notes Mail 4.5* and *Lotus Notes 4.5 and the Internet 6-in-1* published by Que Corporation. She is also a contributing author to Que's *Special Edition Using PowerPoint 97* and is the co-author of the *10 Minute Guide to Lotus Notes Mail 4.6, 10 Minute Guide to Lotus Notes 4.6, Microsoft Works 4.5 6 in 1, Microsoft Windows 95 6 in 1, PowerPoint 97 Exam Guide, Word 97 Exam Guide, Excel 97 Exam Guide,* and *Using Microsoft Word 97*.

Michele Reader has taught courses on personal computing for more than nine years. She teaches courses in the Continuing Education Department at the College of DuPage, and has worked as a technical writer and computer trainer. Michele holds a B.A. from North Central College in Naperville, Illinois. Some of the books she has authored for Que include *WordPerfect 7 for Windows 95 SmartStart, Windows 95 SmartStart,* and *Windows 3.1 SmartStart.* Michele has also served as the technical editor of several books. Michele lives in Wheaton, Illinois with her husband Gary, and their daughters, Rachel, Amy, and Lydia.

Trademark Acknowledgments

All terms mentioned in this book that are known to be trademarks or service marks have been appropriately capitalized. Que Education and Training cannot attest to the accuracy of this information. Use of a term in this book should not be regarded as affecting the validity of any trademark or service mark.

Preface

Que Education and Training is the educational publishing imprint of Macmillan Computer Publishing, the world's leading computer book publisher. Macmillan Computer Publishing books have taught more than 20 million people how to be productive with their computers.

This expertise in producing high-quality computer tutorial and reference books is evident in every Que Education and Training title we publish. The same tried-and-true writing and product-development process that makes Macmillan Computer Publishing books bestsellers is used to ensure that educational materials from Que Education and Training provide the most accurate and up-to-date information. Experienced and respected computer application instructors write and review every manuscript to provide class-tested pedagogy. Quality-assurance editors check every keystroke and command in Que Education and Training books to ensure that instructions are clear, accurate, and precise.

Above all, Macmillan Computer Publishing and, in turn, Que Education and Training have years of experience in meeting the learning demands of students across all disciplines.

The "MOUS Essentials" of Hands-On Learning

The *MOUS Essentials* are appropriate for use in both corporate training and college classroom settings. They can be used effectively as computer-lab applications modules to accompany any of Que Education and Training's computer concepts text or as stand-alone texts for an applications-only course. The *MOUS Essentials* workbooks enable users to become self-sufficient quickly; encourage self-learning after instruction; maximize learning through clear, complete explanations; and serve as future references.

The *MOUS Essentials* series uses the following elements to get the most out of the material:

Objectives list what students do and learn from the project.

Required Activities are the objectives as they relate to the Microsoft Office User Specialist exams.

"Why Would I Do This?" shows students why the material is essential.

Step-by-Step Tutorials simplify the procedures with large screen shots, captions, and annotations.

If you have problems...anticipates common pitfalls and advises students accordingly.

Inside Stuff provides tips and shortcuts for more effective applications.

Key Terms are highlighted in the text and defined in the margin when they first appear, as well as in an end-of-book glossary.

Jargon Watch offers a layperson's view of "technobabble" in easily understandable terms.

Exam Notes provide information and insight on topics that are covered on the MOUS exam and that should be reviewed carefully.

Checking Your Skills provides true/false, multiple choice, matching, and completion exercises.

Applying Your Skills contains directed, hands-on Practice exercises to check comprehension and reinforce learning, as well as self-directed Challenge exercises requiring students to use critical thinking skills.

CD-ROM contains files for the text's step-by-step tutorials and end of project exercises.

Annotated Instructor's Edition

If you have adopted this text for use in a college classroom, you will receive, upon request, an Annotated Instructor's Edition at no additional charge. The manual contains suggested curriculum guides for courses of varying lengths, teaching tips, answers to exercises in Checking Your Skills and Applying Your Skills sections, test questions and answers, and data files and solutions for each tutorial and exercise. Please contact your local representative or write to us on school or business letterhead at Macmillan Computer Publishing, 201 West 103rd Street, Indianapolis, IN 46290-1097, Attention: Que Education and Training Sales Support.

Microsoft Office User Specialist Exams

In order to validate your skills using Office, Microsoft has created the Microsoft Office User Specialist program. The Specialist Program is available for many Office 95 and Office 97 applications at both Proficient and Expert User levels.

The Specialist designation distinguishes you from your peers as knowledgeable in using Office products, which can also make you more competitive in the job market.

The *Microsoft Office User Specialist exams* are for anyone who:

■ Wants to expand their skills.

■ Is seeking certification in a particular software.

■ Wants to learn or reference tasks in short, concise lessons.

■ Is an instructor or trainer preparing groups of people for the Microsoft Exams.

Que Education & Training Certification Resource Center

To keep up to date on the Microsoft Office User Specialist program exams, check the following Web sites:

```
www.queet.com/certification
www.mous.net
www.microsoft.com/office/train_cert
```

MOUS PinPoint® Training and Testing Software

MOUS PinPoint training and testing software is designed to supplement the projects in this book. It aids you in your preparation for taking and passing the *Microsoft Office User Specialist* exams. The MOUS PinPoint software consists of:

■ Trainers

■ Evaluations

Each **trainer** asks you to perform specific tasks that were covered in a particular project of this book. If you don't know how to perform a particular task, you can watch a demonstration (**SHOW ME**) of the task. Immediate feedback (concerning the correctness of performance) is given after each task in each trainer. Each **evaluation** consists of the same questions that were given in the trainer. However, with an evaluation, you may not view demonstrations and you do not receive feedback after trying each task. After performing a **trainer** or **evaluation**, you can view a report of your overall performance.

Preparing to Install the MOUS PinPoint Training and Testing Software

To install the MOUS PinPoint training and testing software, we recommend following these steps:

1. Check to see if your computer meets the minimum requirements (see Table I.1).

2. Perform a full installation of Office 97 on your computer if you have not already done so (see the section "Installing Office 97").

3. Install the MOUS PinPoint testing and training software (see the section "Installing the MOUS PinPoint Training and Testing Software").

Using the MOUS PinPoint Training and Testing Software

To use the MOUS PinPoint training and testing software, we recommend following these steps.

Study the projects in this book. After reading each project:

1. Run the **trainer** for the project (see the section "Running the MOUS PinPoint Software"). Then view a report on your performance (see the section "Viewing Reports").

2. Run the **evaluation** for the project (see the section "Running the MOUS PinPoint Software"). Then view a report on your performance (see the section "Viewing Reports"). Note: Some projects may not have a corresponding MOUS PinPoint trainer and evaluation.

After you have finished reading this book, take the MOUS PinPoint Final Exam:

1. Run the **evaluation** for the Final Exam Part 1. Final Exam Part 1 covers material included in the first half of this book.

2. Run the **trainer** for the Final Exam Part 1. Only the items missed in the trainer will be set to run.

3. Run the **evaluation** for the Final Exam Part 1 (again) as a final check.

4. Repeat the steps 1–3 given for Final Exam Part 2. Final Exam Part 2 covers material from roughly the second half of this book.

5. When you are finished using the MOUS PinPoint software, you can remove it from your computer (see the section "Removing the MOUS PinPoint Training and Testing Software").

Running MOUS PinPoint Testing and Training Software Requirements

The system components in Table I.1 are required to run the MOUS PinPoint Testing and Training Software.

Table I.1	System Component Requirements	
Component	Minimum	Recommended
CPU	Pentium 90	Higher than Pentium 90
Operating System	Windows 95 or NT 4.0 Note: You must have an Administrator's or Power User's login if you are working on a Windows NT workstation.	N/A
Installed Apps	Office 97 (full installation)	N/A
RAM	16 MB	32 MB or higher

continues

Table I.1 (continued)		
Component	Minimum	Recommended
Hard Drive	Adequate space for installation, Office 97, and for MOUS PinPoint training and testing software.	N/A
CD-ROM Drive	2X speed	4X speed or faster
Pointing Device	Windows-compatible mouse or pointing device.	N/A
Video	Color VGA video display	N/A

Installing Office 97

Important: It is necessary to do a complete installation of Office 97. This means installing *all* components.

To perform a full installation of Office 97, complete the following steps:

1. Start Windows 95 or Windows NT 4.0 and close any applications that are running (other than Windows).

2. Insert the Office 97 CD and run **setup.exe**.

3. Click on the **Add/Remove** button, as shown in Figure I.1 (if a previous installation of Office 97 is already on your computer). If you do not have a previous installation of Office 97 on your computer, select **Custom** installation from a different screen.

Figure I.1
The Microsoft Office 97 Setup dialog box.

4. Click on the **Select All** button (see Figure I.2).

5. Click on the **Continue** button.

6. Continue with the installation until it is finished.

Figure I.2
Choosing the Select All button will install *all* Office 97 components to the system.

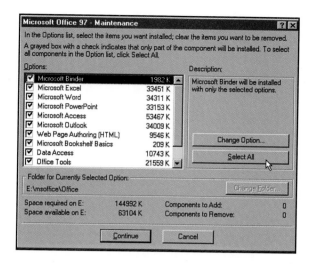

Installing the MOUS PinPoint Training and Testing Software

To install and run MOUS PinPoint trainers and evaluations on a single-user computer, you must first install the MOUS PinPoint **Launcher** by running a setup program from the MOUS PinPoint CD.

Installing the MOUS PinPoint Launcher

To run the setup program for the MOUS PinPoint Launcher:

1. Start Windows 95 or Windows NT 4.0 and insert the MOUS PinPoint CD into the CD-ROM drive.

2. Select **Start/Run** from the Windows desktop.

3. Enter (or browse to) **[Drive Letter]:\SETUP.EXE** (where **[Drive Letter]** is the assigned drive letter of the CD-ROM (see Figure I.3).

Figure I.3
Indicating the location of the setup.exe executable.

4. Click on **OK**. The setup program runs.

5. Answer the questions that appear during the installation.

6. When the dialog box in Figure I.4 displays, choose **Normal Single-User Installation**.

Figure I.4
The MOUS PinPoint
Network Installation Setup
dialog box

7. Click **Yes** when you are asked if you want to install MOUS PinPoint modules to your hard disk. The dialog box in Figure I.5 appears. The installation program is getting ready to install the **Launcher** to your computer. It needs to know the directory where you would like it installed.

Figure I.5
The default location
Destination Folder is
shown.

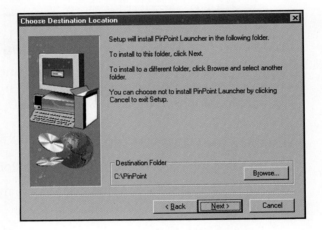

8. To install the **Launcher** to the default location, click on the **Next** button. Otherwise, enter a new path for the **Launcher** and then click on the **Next** button.

9. Confirm the installation location by clicking on **Yes** in the dialog box in Figure I.6.

Figure I.6
The destination folder
requires confirmation.

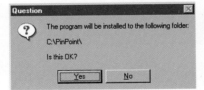

10. When Figure I.7 appears, click on Next.

A **PinPoint Training** group window is created (see Figure I.8). You can close this window. It is not necessary to use this window to start the PinPoint Launcher in the future since you can always select Start/Programs/PinPoint Training/PinPoint Training from your desktop.

Figure I.7
Creation of the Program Folder.

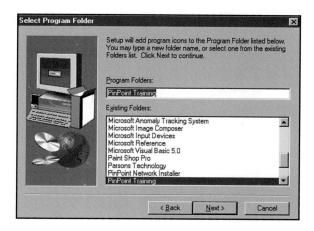

Figure I.8
The PinPoint Training group window that is created.

The PinPoint **Launcher** is used to:

- logon with your **UserID** and **Password**.
- install your MOUS PinPoint training and testing software for *an exam*.
- run your MOUS PinPoint training and testing software for *an exam*.
- view reports after you have run the MOUS PinPoint training and testing software.

To install the MOUS PinPoint training and testing software for *an exam*, continue with the next section.

Installing the MOUS PinPoint Software

To install the MOUS PinPoint training and testing software:

1. Start the Launcher by selecting Start/Programs/PinPoint Training/ PinPoint Training (see Figure I.9).

2. Click on the **Installer** button (see Figure I.10).

3. Install your MOUS PinPoint software by selecting the specific module (for example, **Microsoft Excel 97 Proficiency Custom ME**) from the **Available Modules** list box and clicking on the **Install** button. (Do not install the **Launcher**. It's already installed!)

4. Answer the questions that appear during installation. You are asked to verify the location where the MOUS PinPoint software will install to your hard drive (see Figure I.11)

Figure I.9
The Home screen of
the Launcher.

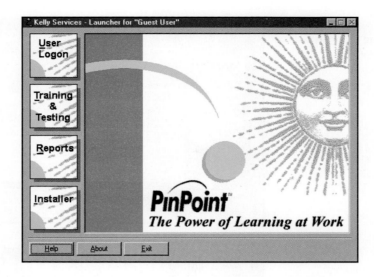

Figure I.10
The **Installer** screen.

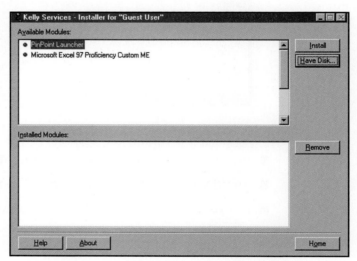

Figure I.11
The default location
Destination Folder is
shown.

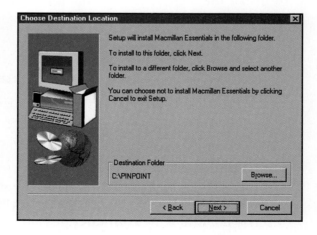

5. Make changes as necessary by clicking on **Browse** and selecting a different destination folder. Important: The MOUS PinPoint software for *the specific exam* and the PinPoint **Launcher** must be installed under the same main directory (for example, **C:\PinPoint**) in order to work properly.

6. Click on **Next**.

7. Accept the subdirectory (for example, **xl8prome**) where the MOUS PinPoint software will be placed. You do not have a choice concerning the name of this subdirectory.

8. Click on **Yes.**

9. If you would like to view a README file concerning MOUS PinPoint software, click on **Yes** in the dialog box in Figure I.13. Otherwise, click on No.

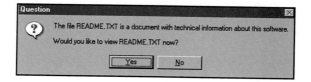

A PinPoint Training group window is created (see Figure I.14).

Close this window. It is not necessary to use this window to start the PinPoint **Launcher** in the future since you can always select Start/Programs/PinPoint Training/PinPoint Training from your desktop.

If you want to run the MOUS PinPoint software that you just installed, don't exit from the **Launcher**. Continue on with step 3 in the next section.

To exit from the **Launcher** to Windows, click on the **Exit** button.

Running the MOUS PinPoint Software

To run the MOUS PinPoint software, it is necessary to start the PinPoint **Launcher**. Important: Shut down all applications.

To run the MOUS PinPoint software:

1. Shut down all applications (except Windows and the Launcher) that are running, including any shortcut bars (such as Microsoft Office

shortcut bar). If the Office 97 exam application is running, shut it down.

2. Start the Launcher by selecting Start/Programs/PinPoint Training/PinPoint Training from the Windows desktop.

3. Click on the User Logon button (see Figure I.15). Logging on under your name allows the **Launcher** to keep track of your personal progress. This enables the **Launcher** to reconfigure a module the next time you take it. It also enables the **Launcher** to create a report containing information about your training or evaluation sessions.

Figure I.15
The **User Logon**
screen.

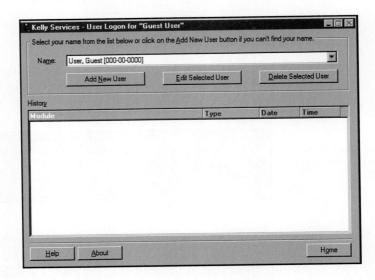

4. Select your name from the drop-down list in the **Name** combo box in Figure I.16:

   ■ You may need to use the scroll bar to find your name.

   ■ If your name is not in the list, go to step 5.

   ■ If you found your name, skip to step 8.

Figure I.16
Specify your logon
name.

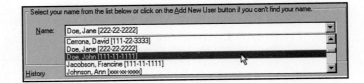

5. If this is your first time running MOUS PinPoint software, your name will not be in the list. If that is the case, create a user account for yourself by clicking on the **Add New User** button.

6. Enter your personal data, tabbing between fields in Figure I.17:

   ■ Enter all five data items. If one or more of the data items are missing, the **OK** button will remain grayed out (disabled).

   ■ Your **User ID** and **Password** may both consist of up to fourteen characters and are both case sensitive.

■ After entering your **Password** in the **Password** field, you must confirm this **Password** by entering the identical **Password** again in the **Confirm Password** field.

7. Click on **OK**. Your account is created and you are logged on. You are ready to move to the **Training & Testing** screen.

8. Click on the **Home** button to move to the **Home** screen.

9. Click on the **Training & Testing** button (see Figure I.18).

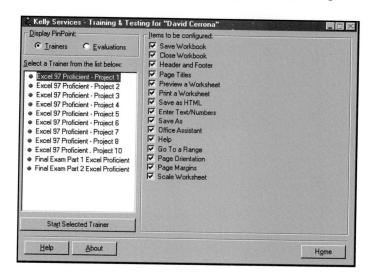

10. Select **Trainers** (or **Evaluations**), depending on which you would like to run (see Figure I.19). A list of trainers (or evaluations) displays.

11. Select the particular trainer or evaluation that you would like to run. Each trainer and evaluation is named by the project that it covers. Trainers may be configured. That means you can select the tasks that you would like to run. The first time you run a trainer, all tasks will automatically be selected. (Note: Evaluations may not be configured.)

12. If you are running a trainer, configure it by selecting or deselecting tasks in the **Items to be configured** section:

■ A check indicates that the task will run.

■ No check indicates that the task will not run.

You are now ready to start (launch) the trainer or evaluation for the project.

Figure I.20
Select the tasks you
want to configure.

13. Click on the **Start Selected Trainer** button if you are starting a trainer or the **Start Selected Evaluation** button if you are starting an evaluation. Before the trainer or evaluation runs, you are asked to confirm (see Figure I.21).

Figure I.21
Confirm the running
of the trainer or
evaluation.

14. Click on **Yes** to confirm. While running the trainer or evaluation, you may use the controls in Figure I.22.

Figure I.22
Controls available while
running the trainer or
evaluation.

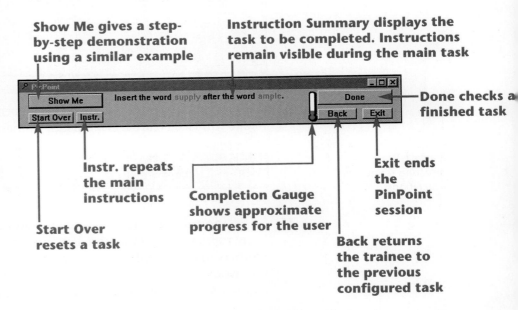

Show Me gives a step-by-step demonstration using a similar example

Instruction Summary displays the task to be completed. Instructions remain visible during the main task

Done checks a finished task

Instr. repeats the main instructions

Completion Gauge shows approximate progress for the user

Exit ends the PinPoint session

Start Over resets a task

Back returns the trainee to the previous configured task

After running a trainer or evaluation, the **Training and Testing** screen reappears. You can continue to run other trainers or evaluations for other projects. When you are finished studying the whole book, you can also run the trainers and evaluations for the final exams.

To view reports for each trainer or evaluation that you ran, click on the **Reports** button (see the section "Running the MOUS PinPoint Software").

To exit from the **Launcher**, first move to the **Home** screen by clicking on the **Home** button. Then click on the **Exit** button.

Viewing Reports

In the **Launcher**, you can view two kinds of reports after running a MOUS PinPoint trainer or evaluation:

To display reports in the Launcher:

1. Start the **Launcher** and log on.

2. Click on the **Reports** button (see Figure I.23). This report displays a line (record) of data for each instance that you have run a MOUS PinPoint trainer or evaluation:

   ■ **Accuracy** is the number of tasks you performed correctly

   ■ **Maximum** is the total number of tasks that were configured to run

   ■ **Time** is the total elapsed time in minutes (from the moment you started running the trainer or evaluation to the moment that you exited the trainer or evaluation)

Figure I.23
The Reports screen appears, displaying the first kind of report.

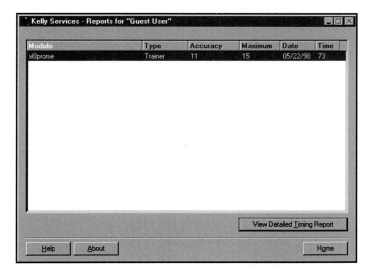

3. The second kind of report is the **Detailed Timing Report** (see Figure I.24). If you wish to view this report, select the record for which you would like the timing report and click on the **View Detailed Timing Report** button.

Figure I.24
Select the specific record.

Module	Type	Accuracy	Maximum	Date	Time
xl8prome	Trainer	11	15	05/22/98	73

Figure I.25
The **Detailed Timing Report**.

Timing results of xl8prome for Guest User

Item No.	Item	Actual	Optimal	Correct	Did Show Me
1	Save Workbook	2	10	No	No
1	Save Workbook	8	10	Yes	No
2	Close Workbook	2	10	Yes	No
21	Header and Footer	130	30	No	No
21	Header and Footer	1	30	No	Yes (1)
26	Page Titles	23	25	No	No
26	Page Titles	21	25	No	Yes (1)
26	Page Titles	29	25	Yes	Yes (1)
35	Preview a Worksheet	8	20	No	No
35	Preview a Worksheet	24	20	No	Yes (1)
35	Preview a Worksheet	7	20	No	Yes (1)
35	Preview a Worksheet	7	20	No	Yes (1)
35	Preview a Worksheet	1	20	No	Yes (1)
36	Print a Worksheet	26	20	No	Yes (1)
41	Save as HTML	12	45	No	No
44	Enter Text/Numbers	58	30	No	No
44	Enter Text/Numbers	66	30	Yes	No
45	Save As	12	30	Yes	No
49	Office Assistant	24	25	Yes	No
50	Help	13	30	Yes	No
51	Go To a Range	10	10	Yes	No
53	Page Orientation	12	15	Yes	No
54	Page Margins	27	20	Yes	No
55	Scale Worksheet	36	10	Yes	No

Close   Print

4. To print the **Detailed Timing Report**, click on the **Print** button:

   ■ **Actual** is the time, in seconds, you used to complete the task. This time is considered the "involved time," the time that was taken from the moment that you clicked with the mouse (or entered something on the keyboard) to the moment that you clicked on the **Done** button. It does not count the "thinking time" before you first moved the mouse (or used the keyboard), and it does not count the time used to run and view a SHOW ME demonstration.

   ■ **Optimal** is a reasonable amount of time, in seconds, required to perform a task by an efficient method

   ■ **Correct - Yes**, if the you performed the task correctly; **No** if you did not perform the task correctly

   ■ **Did Show Me - Yes**, if you viewed a SHOW ME demonstration for the task; **No**, if you did not view a SHOW ME demonstration for the task. The **Did Show Me** column appears only if the timing report contains data for a **trainer** and not for an **evaluation**. (Evaluations do not have SHOW MEs.)

5. Close the **Detailed Timing Report** window by clicking on the **Close** button. The **Reports** screen of the **Launcher** returns.

Removing the MOUS PinPoint Training and Testing Software

When you are finished using the MOUS PinPoint training and testing software, you can remove it. Be sure to follow the following procedure.

To remove your MOUS PinPoint training and testing software:

1. Start the **Launcher**.

2. Click on the **Installer** button.

3. Select the exam module from the **Installed Modules** list.

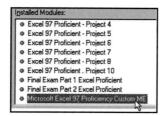

4. Click the **Remove** button.

5. When the **Confirmation** dialog box appears, click **Yes.**

6. When the **Remove** dialog box appears, click the **Yes** button.

7. An **"Uninstall complete"** message appears.

8. Find the MOUS PinPoint directory on your computer and delete it.

Troubleshooting

Table I.2 lists a few problems that can arise while running the MOUS PinPoint training and testing software. For each problem, a solution or explanation is given.

Table I.2	MOUS PinPoint Training and Testing Software Problems and Solutions
Problem	Explanation or Action
A task is grayed out and not selected on the Training and Testing screen in the Launcher program (see Figure I.27).	A particular component has not been installed. Exit the Launcher and perform a full installation of Office 97 (see section "Installing Office 97").

Your computer crashes (locks up or exits ungracefully) while running the MOUS PinPoint training or testing.	Start you computer again and rerun the desired MOUS PinPoint training or testing. Exit the trainer or evaluation in the normal way. It is important to do this, even if you have no desire to run a trainer or evaluation. By running any trainer or evaluation, you will insure that your computer's registry is reset to normal.

continues

Table I.2	(continued)
Problem	Explanation or Action
You see a message that says **"program was left in an unfinished state"** AND you have deleted the MOUS PinPoint directory (or one of its key components).	The problem is that your Windows Registry was changed by running the registry and needs to be set back to the state it was in before you started the MOUS PinPoint training and testing. Do the following: 1.Go to the **Windows** directory and find the following files: **OFC97.PIN** **OFC971.PIN** **OFC972.PIN** **OFC973.PIN** **OFC974.PIN** 2. Delete the **OFC97.PIN** file. 3. Rename the other four **.PIN** files so that they have a **.REG** extension. 4. Double-click on each of the .REG files to run them. This will reset your Registry.

Microsoft Excel Proficient Specialist User Skills

The skill areas covered in the exam and the required tasks for those skill areas are listed in Table I.3.

Table I.3 Proficient User Skills			
Skill Set	Required Activity	Project	Lesson
Create workbooks	Open electronic workbooks	2	1
	Enter text and numbers	1	5
	Enter formulas	3	1, 2
	Save workbooks	1	7
	Close workbooks	1	10
Modify workbooks	Delete cell contents	2	4
	Delete worksheets	8	3
	Revise text and numbers	1	6
	Rotate and indent text	5	4
	Revise formulas	3	5
	Copy and move data	2	6, 7
	Insert, modify, and delete rows and columns	2	4
	Use references (absolute, relative, and mixed)	3	4
	Sort data	2	8
Print workbooks	Preview and print worksheets	1	9
	Print the screen and ranges	4	3
	Print headers and footers	1	8

Skill Set	Required Activity	Project	Lesson
Format worksheets	Modify cell size and alignment	5	2, 3
	Apply general numbers formats	5	5
	Apply font formats	5	1
	Apply outlines	5	6
Create and apply ranges	Create and name ranges	4	1
	Clear and format ranges	4	4
	Copy and move ranges	4	5
Use functions	Use the AVERAGE, MIN, and MAX functions	4	7
	Use worksheet functions	4	6
Use draw	Create and modify lines and objects	7	3, 4
	Create and modify 3D shapes	7	6
Use charts	Create, format, and modify charts	6	1, 2 3, 4
	Preview and print charts	6	5
Save spreadsheets as HTML	Save spreadsheets as HTML documents	1	7

Table of Contents at a Glance

Table of Contents

Conventions Used in This Book

The *MOUS Essentials* series uses the following conventions to make it easier for you to understand the material:

- Text that you are to type or that appears onscreen appears in a **special font**.

- Underlined letters in menu names, menu commands, and dialog-box options are the shortcut keys. Examples are the File menu, the Open command, and the File name list box.

- Key terms in *italic* the first time they are discussed and are defined in the margin as soon as they are introduced.

- On-screen text and messages appear in a `special font and color`.

Project 1 — One

Getting Started with Excel

Creating a List of Office Expenses

Objectives   **Required Activities**

In this Project, you learn how to

➤ Start Excel

➤ Use the Excel Window

➤ Get Help

➤ Move Around the Worksheet

➤ Enter Data ... ...   Enter Text and Numbers
                                                            Revise Text and Numbers

➤ Save a Worksheet ... ...   Save Workbooks
                                                            Save Spreadsheets as HTML

➤ Prepare for Printing ... ...   Print Headers and Footers

➤ Print a Worksheet ... ...   Print and Preview Worksheets

➤ Close a File and Exit Excel ... ...   Close Workbooks

Why Would I Do This?

Computer spreadsheet software is the application software that started the personal computer revolution. That's because electronic spreadsheets, such as Microsoft Excel, are versatile tools for both personal and business use. As you work through the projects in this book, you will find that spreadsheet technology enables you to calculate and display your business applications easily and flexibly. Spreadsheets, as you will see, aid your thought processes and save you time.

Basically, spreadsheet software turns your computer into a business analysis tool. Many people compare spreadsheets to pocket calculators, but spreadsheets have capabilities that are many times more powerful than even a high-tech calculator. At the most basic level, Excel enables you to decide what *data* you want to see and how it is to be displayed—a capability no pocket calculator can duplicate. You will explore these features of Excel first.

Exam Notes

The Microsoft Excel 97 Proficient User exam is designed to help you create budgets, marketing and sales reports, expense reports, invoices and purchase orders, basic financial statements such as profit and loss, and creating spreadsheet information for use on the Internet or an intranet. Familiarizing yourself with these types of documents, many of which are used as examples in these lessons, will help you complete your certification.

Data
The information that you work with in a spreadsheet, including text, numbers, and graphic images.

In this project, you begin to learn how spreadsheets work and what you can do with them by starting the software and taking a tour of the Microsoft Excel screen. You also get a taste of how spreadsheets can help you by creating a list of office expenses. After you create the list, you learn how to revise your worksheet, save your work, prepare the list for printing, and, finally, print it.

Lesson 1: Starting Excel

Workbook
An Excel file that contains one or more worksheets.

The first thing you need to know about Excel is how to start the software. Windows 95 must be running on your computer before you can start Excel. If you are not familiar with Windows 95 or using the mouse, ask your instructor for assistance.

Worksheet
One page of your work in an Excel 97 workbook.

When you first start Excel, the program displays a blank *workbook* titled Book1, which displays a blank *worksheet*, titled Sheet1. In Project 2, "Building a Spreadsheet," you learn to create a new worksheet and work on an existing worksheet. In this lesson, you use the blank *default* worksheet supplied by Excel.

Default
The settings a program uses unless you specify another setting. For example, in an Excel 97 worksheet, the default column width is 8.43 characters. Generally, you can change a default setting.

To Start Excel

❶ Turn on your computer and monitor.

If Windows 95 is installed on your computer, the computer should automatically start Windows 95, and the Windows desktop should appear on your screen, as shown in Figure 1.1. (Your screen may appear slightly different, depending on how Windows is set up on your computer.) When you see the Windows desktop, you are ready to start Excel.

Figure 1.1
The Windows 95 desktop.

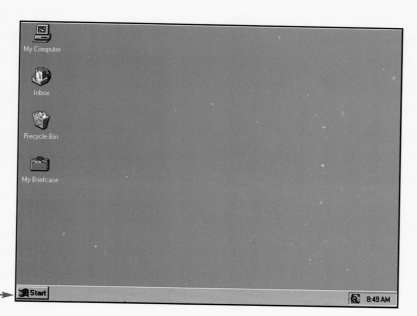

Start button ───────→

Submenu
A list of options that appears when you point at some menu items in Windows 95 and in applications designed for use with Windows 95. A small, right-pointing arrowhead appears to the right of menu items that have submenus.

❷ Click the Start button on the Taskbar (see Figure 1.1).

The Start menu opens on the desktop (see Figure 1.2). From the Start menu, you can start programs and open documents, get help, find files or folders, change settings, and shut down Windows 95. For more information on using the Start menu or the Taskbar, ask your instructor.

❸ Move the mouse pointer to the Programs item at the top of the Start menu.

A *submenu*, listing the programs installed on your computer, appears on the desktop to the right of the Start menu, as shown in Figure 1.2.

If you have problems...

Because you can customize Windows 95, your desktop may look different from the one shown in the illustrations in this book. Your Programs menu may be different from the menu illustrated in this book, depending on the programs that are installed on your computer. For example, you may have to point at the Microsoft Office item on the Programs submenu to display another submenu from which you can select Microsoft Excel.

continues

To Start Excel   (continued)

Figure 1.2
When you move the mouse pointer to the Programs item on the Start menu, a submenu of installed programs appears.

The Programs submenu

Point here to see a list of programs

Click here to start Excel

The Start menu

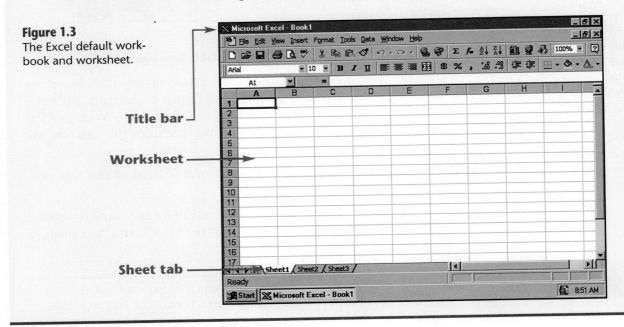

❹ **Choose Microsoft Excel from the Programs submenu.**

Excel starts, and the Excel screen appears with the default workbook and worksheet displayed, as shown in Figure 1.3. Now you can begin using Excel.

Keep this worksheet open to use in the next lesson.

Figure 1.3
The Excel default workbook and worksheet.

Title bar

Worksheet

Sheet tab

If a Microsoft Excel icon appears on the Windows desktop, you can double-click it to start Excel. If you have the Microsoft Office suite of applications installed, you may have an Office toolbar in the upper right-hand corner of your screen. If the Office toolbar appears, you can click the Microsoft Excel button to start Excel.

The very first time you start Excel 97, the Office Assistant may appear in the upper right-hand corner of your screen. The Office Assistant is an animated graphics image included with Microsoft Office 97. (By default, it assumes the appearance of a paper clip called Clippit.)

The Office Assistant is designed to help you learn how to use the Microsoft Office applications quickly and easily. If the Office Assistant appears when you start Excel 97, simply click the button next to the statement, `Begin working in Excel 97 right away`. The Office Assistant will close, and you can continue using Excel. You learn more about using the Office Assistant in Lesson 3 of this project.

Lesson 2: Using the Excel Window

Now that Excel 97 is running on your computer, it's time to learn about the Excel window. You may recognize some of the elements from other Windows programs, such as the minimize and maximize buttons, the control menu icon, scroll bars, the title bar, the menu bar, and so on. Other elements of the window are features of Excel that will help you complete your work quickly and efficiently. The formula bar, sheet tabs, and toolbars are convenient tools that you will use in most of the projects throughout this book. To get to know the elements of the Excel window, take a look at Figure 1.4.

Figure 1.4
As you work through the projects in this book, you'll use many of these Excel screen elements.

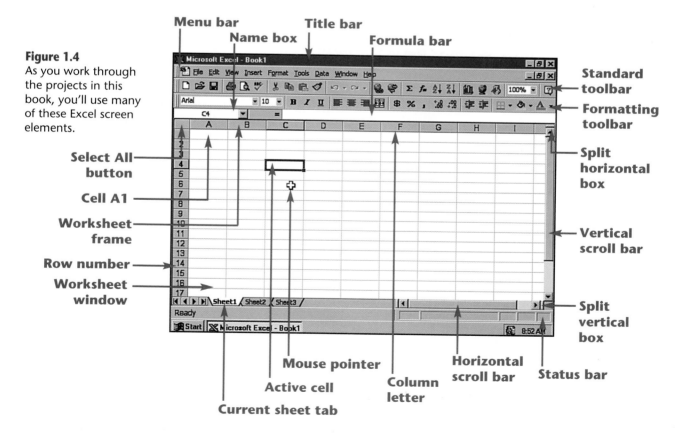

In the following exercise, you practice finding your way around the Excel screen on your computer. (If you need help, refer to Figure 1.4.)

To Use the Excel Window

① Using the mouse, click File on the menu bar.

This opens the File menu. Notice that Excel menus appear the same as menus in any Windows program. In Excel, you can open menus and choose commands to perform actions. You can cancel a menu by clicking the menu name again, by clicking anywhere in the window outside of the menu, or by pressing Esc. Press Esc again to deactivate the menu bar.

② Click the word File again to cancel (close) the menu.

③ Move the mouse pointer to the title bar.

The title bar contains the names of the program and the workbook, and other common Window 95 elements, such as the maximize, minimize, and Close buttons, and the control menu icon.

④ Move the mouse pointer to any cell of the worksheet, and then click the left mouse button.

An outline appears around the **cell** to indicate that the cell is the **current** or **active** cell. The cell's **address**—such as A1 or B1—appears in the **Name Box** to let you know which cell is **selected**. The cell address refers to the row and column that intersect to form the cell. The selected cell is where any typing or new action takes place.

⑤ Move the mouse pointer around the edges of the selected cell.

Notice that the mouse pointer changes from a white plus sign to an arrow when you are near the cell boundary. In later projects, you will see that as you perform different actions on the selected cell, the mouse pointer assumes different shapes.

⑥ Click the column letter for column A.

The entire column becomes selected. Every cell in the column, except for the first (cell A1) is highlighted. You can select any column or row by clicking the column letter or row number in the worksheet frame. You select a column or row to perform an action—such as copying or deleting—on the information in the selected area. When you select more than one cell, such as a column or row, the entire **range** is highlighted, but the first cell is still the active cell; data that you type is entered into the active cell.

⑦ Click cell B1 (the first cell in column B).

Cell B1 is now the active cell, and column A is no longer highlighted. To **deselect** cells, simply click outside the highlighted area.

⑧ Move the mouse pointer to the Bold button on the Formatting toolbar.

The fourth line of the Excel screen is the **Formatting toolbar**. **Buttons** on the toolbars are small pictures that represent actions you can perform—generally, the most common actions you perform or menu commands you choose when using Excel. If you click a button only once, you trigger the action that the button represents. Remember, you need only single-click the toolbar buttons, not double-click.

Leave Excel open on your computer. In the next lesson, you learn how to get help with common Excel features while you are working.

Inside Stuff   To find out what any button does, position the mouse pointer over the button and leave it there for a moment. In a second or two, a ScreenTip appears that contains a description of that button.

If you have problems...   If the ScreenTips don't appear, you must enable them. Open the <u>V</u>iew menu and point at the <u>T</u>oolbars command to display the Toolbars submenu. Click Customize to open the <u>C</u>ustomize dialog box. In the dialog box, click the <u>O</u>ptions page tab and then click the Show Screen<u>T</u>ips on toolbars check box. Choose Close to clear the dialog box from the screen. The ScreenTips should now appear when you point at a toolbar button.

Jargon Watch   Key words and phrases are defined for you throughout this book where they are first used. Words and phrases that are important for you to know are shown as bold in the text and then defined in the Jargon Watch sections. This should help take some of the mystery out of the words.

In this lesson, you have had to wade through a lot of computer jargon. Because you have just been introduced to a number of spreadsheet basics, Table 1.1 lists and describes all the screen elements that are shown in Figure 1.4, and defines all the key terms used in this lesson.

Table 1.1 Parts of the Microsoft Excel Screen	
Element	Description
Active cell	The selected cell where the next action you take, such as typing or formatting, happens.
Address	Describes which column and row intersect to form the cell; for example, A1 is the address for the first cell in the first column (column A) and the first row (row 1).
Cell	The intersection of a column and a row.
Cell A1	The first or top-left cell on a worksheet
Column heading	Lettered *A* through *Z,* then *AA* through *AZ,* and so on through *IV,* up to 256 columns.
Formatting toolbar	Represents various shortcuts to the F<u>o</u>rmat menu commands, such as Font, Bold, Italic, Underline, Alignment, Numeric display, and so on, in button form.

continues

Table 1.1 (continued)	
Element	Description
Formula bar	Displays the address and contents of the current or active cell.
Menu bar	Contains common menu names that, when activated, display a list of related commands; the Edit menu, for example, contains such commands as Cut, Copy, Paste, and Clear.
Mouse pointer	Selects items and positions the insertion point (cursor).
Name Box	Displays the cell address of the current (selected) cell or a named range.
Range	Multiple adjacent cells.
Row heading	Numbered 1 through 65,536.
Scroll bars	Enable you to move the worksheet window vertically and horizontally so that you can see other parts of the worksheet.
Sheet tab	Displays tabs representing each sheet in the workbook. Click a sheet tab to quickly move to that sheet.
Select All button	Selects all cells in the current worksheet.
Split horizontal box	Enables you to split the worksheet window horizontally to display two window panes of the same worksheet so that you can view two different areas at the same time.
Split vertical box	Enables you to split the worksheet window vertically to display two window panes of the same worksheet so that you can view two different areas at the same time.
Standard toolbar	Represents various shortcuts to menu commands, such as Open File, Save, Print, Cut, and so on, in button form.
Status bar	Contains information about options you have on or off, such as NUM (Num Lock) and CAPS (Caps Lock).
Title bar	Displays the name of the software and the name of the active workbook—either a default name, such as Book1, or a saved file.
Workbook	An Excel file that contains one or more worksheets.
Worksheet frame	The row and column headings that appear along the top and left edge of the worksheet window.
Worksheet window	Contains the current worksheet—the work area.

Lesson 3: Getting Help

By now you have probably realized that you may run into problems as you work with your computer and Excel. If you find that you need a quick solution to a problem, you can use any one of Excel's help features. For example, you can use the Office Assistant to help you find the answer to a specific question or when you can't remember how to complete a task. You can use the Help Contents or Index to find additional information about any of Excel's features, or you can use the What's This? pointer to display a description of any feature on the screen. In this lesson, you use the Office Assistant to learn more about getting help while working with Excel.

To Get Help

❶ Click Help on the menu bar.

The Help menu displays a number of options that you can use to get help information.

❷ Choose the Microsoft Excel Help command.

The Office Assistant appears (refer to Figure 1.5). A balloon instructs you to Type your question here, and then click Search. The balloon may also include a list of topics.

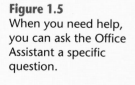

If you have problems...

Sometimes the Office Assistant opens, offering you a list of topics. This is because it tries to establish what you need answered before you actually ask. Don't worry if your Office Assistant opens and looks different from the one in Figure 1.5—the steps work the same.

❸ Replace the text in the text box by typing Get Help and then click the Search button.

Office Assistant displays a new balloon that lists related topics, as shown in Figure 1.5. You can select a topic, type a different question, display more topics, display tips or options, or close the Office Assistant without getting any help.

Figure 1.5
When you need help, you can ask the Office Assistant a specific question.

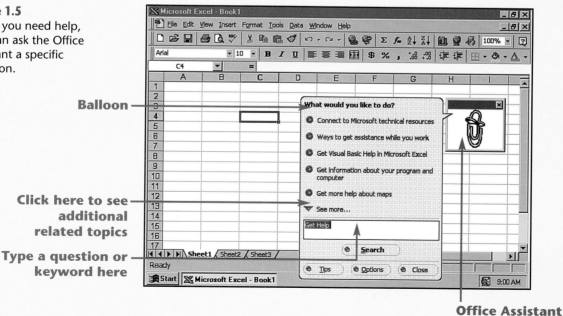

Balloon

Click here to see additional related topics

Type a question or keyword here

Office Assistant

continues

To Get Help   (continued)

If you have problems...

A balloon appears if the Office Assistant can't find topics related to a question you have asked. Check to be sure you typed the question correctly, or try to be more specific, and then click Search again.

❹ **Click See more and then click the topic** `Get Help, tips, and messages through the Office Assistant`.

The Excel Help program starts, and a Help Topics window is displayed on your screen, as shown in Figure 1.6. This window provides information about the many ways you can use the Office Assistant.

Figure 1.6
Help information is displayed in a separate window.

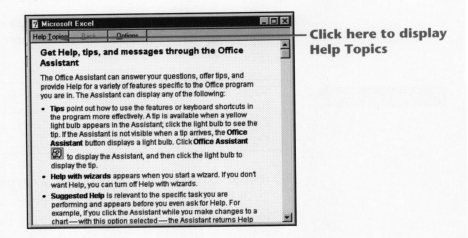

Click here to display Help Topics

❺ **Click the Help Topics button in the Help window.**

The Excel Help Topics dialog box appears (see Figure 1.7). Here you can choose from three Help functions to help find the information you need: Contents, which displays a list of general topics; Index, which displays a comprehensive, alphabetical list of all topics; and Find, which enables you to search through all topics for a word or phrase.

❻ **Click the Contents tab to make sure the Contents page is displayed.**

Clicking the Contents tab ensures that the list of general help topics is displayed (see Figure 1.7). The help information in the Contents tab is similar to a book with chapters—you display the chapter and read the pages.

❼ **In the list of topics, click Getting Help and then click the Open button.**

This opens the topic Getting Help. Specific tasks related to getting help appear in the topic list, as shown in Figure 1.8.

Figure 1.7
Excel offers many ways to access useful help information.

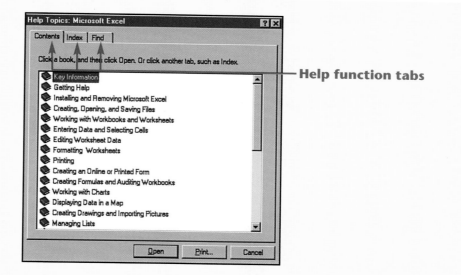

Help function tabs

Figure 1.8
You can click any topic for more information

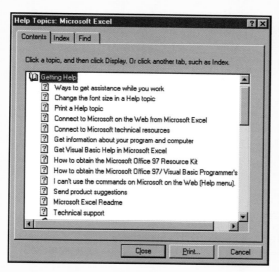

⑧ Click the topic Ways to get assistance while you work, **and then click the Display button.**

A Help screen appears, providing access to information about how to get assistance while you work in Excel (see Figure 1.9). Some help topics, like this one, provide at-a-glance information as well as labels that you can click for more information.

⑨ Click the label ScreenTips.

A help box appears, providing information about how to use the Excel ScreenTips feature while you work, as shown in Figure 1.10. Notice that when you move the mouse pointer to a label, the pointer becomes a hand with a pointing finger. This mouse pointer indicates that more information is available. Click any label on the Help screen to get information about using that feature.

continues

To Get Help   (continued)

Figure 1.9
In some Help screens, you can click labels for additional information.

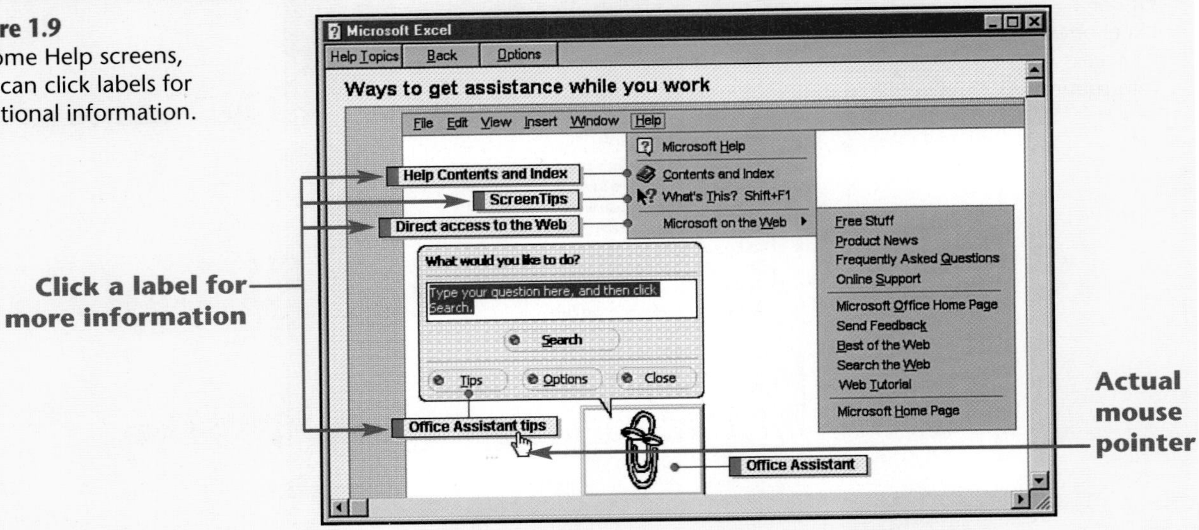

Click a label for more information

Actual mouse pointer

Figure 1.10
Excel displays the specific information you require.

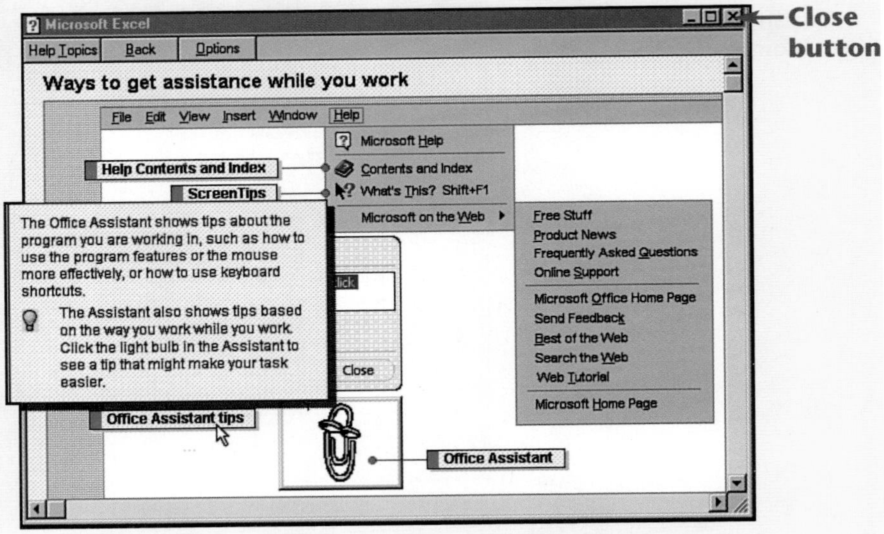

Close button

⑩ Click the Close button at the right end of the Help Topics window's title bar.

This closes Help and returns you to the worksheet. If necessary, click the Close button in the Office Assistant to clear it from the screen. You are now ready to continue learning about how to use an Excel worksheet.

Inside Stuff

To quickly open the Office Assistant, press F1 at any time or click the Office Assistant button on the Standard toolbar. If the Office Assistant icon is on the screen, simply click it to open the balloon where you can type a question.

To change the icon used to represent the Office Assistant, click the Options button in any Office Assistant balloon, choose the Gallery tab, and click Next to display a series of available icons. Select from The Dot, The Genius, Hoverbot, Mother Nature, Power Pup, Scribble (the cat), Office Logo, and Shakespeare and then click OK.

To quickly open the Help Topics dialog box, choose <u>H</u>elp, <u>C</u>ontents and Index. To print a topic from the Help Topics window, choose <u>P</u>rint. If you open a topic window and want to print the contents of the window, choose <u>O</u>ptions and select Print Topic from the menu.

To use the What's This pointer to display a ScreenTip about anything on the screen, choose <u>H</u>elp, What's <u>T</u>his, or press [⇧Shift]+[F1]. When the pointer resembles a question mark with an arrow, point at the item for which you need information.

In the Help program, keywords and phrases that appear highlighted in green and underlined are glossary terms. When you point at a glossary term, the mouse pointer changes to a hand with a pointing finger. When you click on a glossary term, Excel displays additional information.

Lesson 4: Moving Around the Worksheet

Format
To change the appearance of text or numbers.

To use Excel, you need to learn how to move from one part of a worksheet to another. You can move around a worksheet using either the keyboard or the mouse. You probably will use a combination of these two methods.

When you move around the worksheet, you usually go to a specific cell. When you get to that cell, it becomes the active cell so you can enter or edit information, *format* information, or otherwise change the contents of the cell.

Exam Notes

Become familiar with Excel, the parts of the worksheet windows, and how to move around the worksheet. The Microsoft Excel 97 Proficient User exam is a timed exam. It not only tests your competency, but your productivity as well. The longer it takes you to complete a task, the less time you have to complete all the activities in the exam, which affects your score. You are allowed to use Help during the exam, but the time you spend consulting Help will slow you down.

Now use the default worksheet on your screen to practice moving around Excel.

To Move Around a Worksheet

❶ Move the mouse pointer to cell A9 and click the left mouse button once.

The border of cell A9 is highlighted in bold to indicate that it is the active cell (see Figure 1.11).

❷ Press [↑] three times.

This moves the highlighting three rows up, making A6 the active cell.

❸ Press [→] three times.

This moves the highlighting three columns to the right, making D6 the active cell.

continues

14   Getting Started with Excel

To Move Around a Worksheet   (continued)

Figure 1.11
The address of the active cell appears in the Name Box in the formula bar.

Cell address

Column A

Row 9

Vertical scroll bar

Click here to scroll down

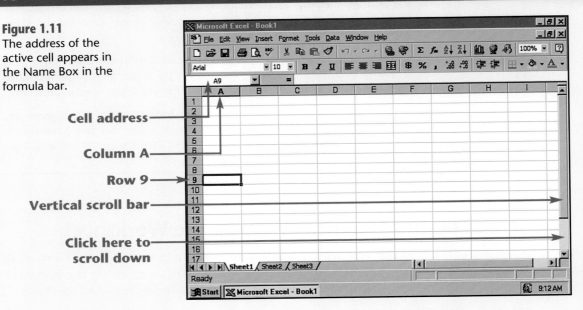

4 **Use the mouse to click in the vertical scroll bar below the scroll box (see Figure 1.11).**

Your view of the worksheet changes so you can see rows that appear further down. Use the vertical scroll bar to move up and down in the worksheet; use the horizontal scroll bar to move left and right. No matter which view of the worksheet is displayed on-screen, if you begin typing before you click a new cell, the text you enter appears in the last active cell—in this case, cell D6.

5 **Click cell A19.**

Cell A19 becomes the active cell.

6 **Press Ctrl+G.**

The Go To dialog box appears, as shown in Figure 1.12. In the Go To dialog box, you can specify the exact cell that you want to make active. The key combination Ctrl+G means that you press and hold down Ctrl while you press G. This convention is used to show key combinations throughout this book.

7 **In the Reference text box, type r12 and press ↵Enter.**

The active cell is now R12.

8 **Press Ctrl+G again.**

The Go To dialog box appears. When you open the Go To dialog box again, the address of the last active cell appears in the Go to list box, with dollar signs ($) added before the row number and column letter. To go back to a cell that you had been working in earlier, simply click it in the Go to list and choose OK.

Figure 1.12
Use the Go To dialog box to make a specific cell active.

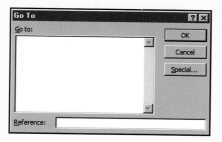

❾ In the Reference text box, type aa6 **and choose OK.**

Cell AA6 becomes the active cell. As in other dialog boxes, you can also choose OK in the Go To dialog box to make the specified cell active.

❿ Press Ctrl + Home **.**

Your view of the worksheet changes and A1—the first cell in the worksheet—becomes the active cell again.

Keep this worksheet open for the next lesson, in which you begin entering data. Table 1.2 lists other keystrokes for moving around a worksheet.

Table 1.2 Moving Around a Worksheet Using the Keyboard	
Press	**To Move**
↑, ↓, ←, and →	One cell in the direction of the arrow (up, down, left, or right).
PgUp or PgDn	One screen up or down.
Home	To the first cell of the current row.
Ctrl + Home	To the first cell of the active worksheet: A1.
Ctrl + →	To the last or first cell in a range of contiguous cells—to the right—stopping at Column IV (256 columns).
Ctrl + ←	To the first cell in a range of contiguous cells—to the left—stopping at Column A.
Ctrl + ↑	To the first cell in a range of contiguous cells—to the top—stopping at Row 1.
Ctrl + ↓	To the last cell in a range of contiguous cells—to the bottom—stopping at row 65,536—(the bottom row).
Ctrl + PgUp	To the preceding worksheet. You can also click the Sheet tab.
Ctrl + PgDn	To the following worksheet. You can also click the Sheet tab.

Lesson 5: Entering Data

Now that you have had a chance to find your way around the Excel window, it's time to create your own worksheet. **Values, text,** and **formulas** are referred to as data and can be entered in the cells of your worksheet. Each cell can hold up to 32,000 characters. In this lesson, you set up a simple worksheet to track office expenses. You also use a formula, one of the most powerful features of Excel, to find the total amount of the expenses.

 Jargon Watch

If you are not used to working with numbers, you may not be familiar with some of the terms used to describe spreadsheets. **Values** and **formulas** are terms borrowed from math that apply to even the simplest work that you do with a spreadsheet.

The formal terms are used here simply to let you know what they are and what they mean. A value is a number you enter in a cell of a worksheet. **Text** is any word or label you enter in the spreadsheet. A formula is a specific calculation that Excel performs, such as adding or subtracting two numbers.

To Enter Data

❶ In the default worksheet (Book1) that you used in the previous lesson, click cell A2.

A2 becomes the active cell. Information you that type will appear in this cell. You can now enter the first item on your office expense worksheet.

❷ Type Rent.

Insertion point
A blinking vertical line that appears on screen at a location where you can enter data. The insertion point is sometimes called a cursor. Characters that you type appear to the left of the insertion point.

As you type in the cell, a blinking vertical cursor, or *insertion point*, appears, indicating that you are in edit mode. Characters that you type appear to the left of the cursor. Also, as you type in the worksheet cell, the word also appears in the formula bar (see Figure 1.13). You can type directly in the formula bar by selecting the cell where you want the data entered and then clicking in the formula bar.

Notice that when the mouse pointer is positioned within the formula bar or within the cell while you are typing, it changes to an I-beam. You can use the I-beam to position the insertion point for entering or editing data.

Notice that three buttons appear on the formula bar. The red *X* is the Cancel button. Clicking the Cancel button is the same as pressing Esc when you are typing data into a cell; that is, Excel stops accepting the entry and the cell's previous contents reappear. The green check mark is the Enter button. Clicking the Enter button accepts the data you entered as complete. The equal sign is the Edit Formula button, which you learn about in Project 3, "Creating Formulas."

Figure 1.13
You can type directly in the cell or in the formula bar.

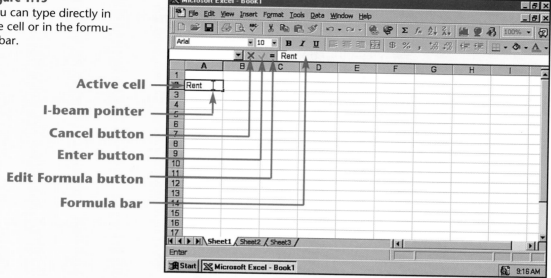

Active cell

I-beam pointer

Cancel button

Enter button

Edit Formula button

Formula bar

If you have problems...

If you make a mistake while typing, press → to delete the error and then continue typing. If you discover a mistake after you've moved to another cell, select the cell and type the correct data. The new text you enter replaces the cell's previous contents.

❸ **Press ↓.**

The text you typed is entered in cell A2, and A3 becomes the active cell. You can now enter the other expenses in your worksheet. You can also press ↵Enter to enter information and move to the next cell down the column, or you can click the Enter button on the formula bar to enter the information and remain in the same cell.

❹ **Enter the following additional expenses in your worksheet. Press ↓ or ↵Enter after typing each word to enter the data and move to the next cell down the column.**

Supplies

Phone

Cleaning

Insurance

Total

Each time you press ↓ or ↵Enter, the text is entered in the active cell and the cell below becomes the active cell. By default, text appears flush with the left border of the cell. Don't worry if it looks as if there is not enough room in the cell for the text. You can enter up to 32,000 characters in each cell! If the column is not wide enough to display all of the characters, the characters are simply hidden; they are not erased. You learn how to adjust cell width in Project 4, "Calculating with Functions."

continues

To Enter Data   (continued)

You have now entered row labels (headings) for all the various expenses you will track in this office expense worksheet. The word Total should appear in cell A7 and cell A8 should be active. Now you can enter the amount paid for the rent last month.

⑤ Click in cell B2, type 1200, **and press** ⬇.

Be sure to press ⬇ or ↵Enter to enter the information. Now enter the amounts for the rest of your expenses. (Don't worry that your numeric entries don't show dollar signs right now; in Project 5, "Improving the Appearance of a Worksheet," you learn how to format numbers to show dollar signs.)

⑥ Type each of the following amounts, and press ⬇ **or** ↵Enter **to enter them into the worksheet:**

300

150

80

75

You have now entered a record of your expenses into the worksheet. To see how useful a spreadsheet can be, try entering a simple formula to find the monthly total for the expenses in this example.

⑦ In cell B7, type =b2+b3+b4+b5+b6.

You have now typed the formula for adding all the expenses in column B. The equal sign identifies the information as a formula rather than data to be entered in the cell, and the plus signs are the mathematical operators that tell Excel to use addition. (Notice that as soon as you type the equal sign, the Functions button replaces the Name Box on the formula bar.) This formula tells Excel to add the contents of the five preceding cells in column B. Because the formula is entered in cell B7, the total is displayed there as well.

⑧ Click the Enter button (the green check mark) on the formula bar to enter the formula.

You can also press ↵Enter or ⬇ to enter the formula. Excel adds the numbers and displays the result in cell B7 with the total for the expenses. Notice that as long as cell B7 is active, the formula—not the actual numerical total—appears in the formula bar (see Figure 1.14). If necessary, click cell B7 to make it active so you can see the contents of the formula bar.

The true power of Excel resides in formulas. If several of your expenses change next month, you can find the new expense total simply by entering the new information in the correct cells. The formula in B7 automatically calculates a new total for you.

Try changing one of the expense values now.

Figure 1.14
The formula appears in the formula bar, while the formula's results appear in cell B7.

Formula

Result of formula

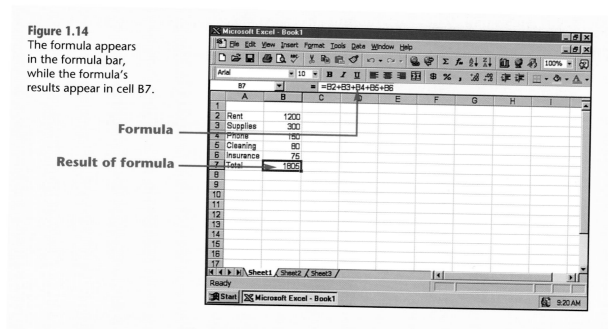

⑨ **Click cell B4.**

This makes cell B4 the active cell. Its contents appear in the Formula bar.

⑩ **Type 100 and press** ⏎Enter.

Notice that when you enter the new amount in cell B4, the total automatically changes in cell B7.

Keep this expense worksheet open for the next lesson, where you learn how to revise the text and numbers you entered.

Lesson 6: Revising Text and Numbers

The labels, numbers, and formulas you enter in a worksheet are subject to change as new information becomes available or as you detect errors in your entries. Although you can easily click on a cell and enter new contents, there are times when editing the contents works better.

To Revise Your Text and Numbers

❶ **In the worksheet you used in the previous lesson, click cell A2.**

A2 becomes the active cell. The word Rent appears in the cell and in the formula bar.

❷ **Click the formula bar.**

As your mouse pointer moves over the formula bar, it changes to an I-beam. After you click, an insertion point appears on the formula bar.

continues

Excel

To Revise Your Text and Numbers   (continued)

❸ Move the insertion point to the beginning of the word Rent **and type** Monthly **followed by a space.**

To move the insertion point on the formula bar, use the → and ← or click in the appropriate spot to place the insertion point there. Note that the text you typed in the formula bar also appears in cell A2.

❹ Click the Enter button (the green check mark) on the formula bar.

When you edit data, you must click Enter or press ⏎Enter. You can't use the ↑ or ↓ like you do when entering data in the worksheet to accept your entry and move to the next cell. However, using Tab⇄ or ⬆Shift+Tab⇄ does accept your changes and moves to another cell. Don't worry if you can't read the entire entry in cell A2. You learn how to adjust the width of columns in Project 5, "Improving the Appearance of a Worksheet."

If you have problems...

If you start to edit a cell and realize you don't want to change its contents after all, press Esc.

❺ Double-click B3.

Double-clicking a cell puts it into edit mode. An insertion point appears in the cell (see Figure 1.15).

Figure 1.15
When a cell is in edit mode, the insertion point appears in the cell. You type to enter characters or delete any unnecessary characters.

Cell in edit mode ———

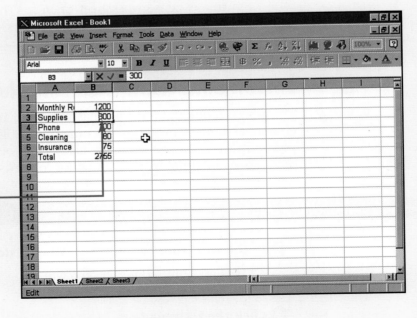

❻ Change the value in B3 to 1300.

Move the insertion point using → or ←. Type to add characters. Use →| or Del to remove characters.

❼ Press ⏎Enter.

After you turn on the edit mode, you must press ⏎Enter or click the Enter button to have Excel accept your changes. You can also press Tab⇆ or ⇧Shift+Tab⇆ to have your changes accepted and then move to another cell.

❽ Click cell A3 and press F2.

Pressing F2 has the same effect as double-clicking the cell—the edit mode is turned on and the insertion point appears in the cell.

❾ Move to the beginning of the word Supplies **and type** Office **followed by a space.**

❿ Press ⏎Enter.

Keep this expense worksheet open for the next lesson, where you learn how to save your work.

Lesson 7: Saving a Worksheet

Up to this point, none of the information that you have entered in your expense worksheet has been safely stored for future use. At the moment, your worksheet and the workbook that contains it are stored in the computer's **random-access memory (RAM)**. If your computer were to crash or shut down for any reason, you would lose your expense worksheet.

For this reason, it is important to save your work every 10 to 15 minutes. You can save your work to the **hard disk** inside the computer or to a **floppy disk** that you insert and can take with you. You may already be familiar with the concepts and terms described here. If not, see the Jargon Watch later in this lesson.

When you save a workbook, or *file*, you assign the file a name and location on a disk. Later, you can retrieve the file, and add to, edit, and print it. So that you don't lose any of your valuable work (and your valuable time), save your expense worksheet now.

To Save a Worksheet

File
Information you enter in your computer and save for future use, such as a document or workbook

❶ Choose File from the menu bar.

The File pull-down menu opens.

❷ Choose the Save command.

The Save As dialog box opens, as shown in Figure 1.16. The first time you save a file, choosing either Save or Save As opens the Save As dialog box. Notice that the text in the File name text box is highlighted; this is the temporary file name that Excel assigns to your workbook.

continues

To Save a Worksheet   (continued)

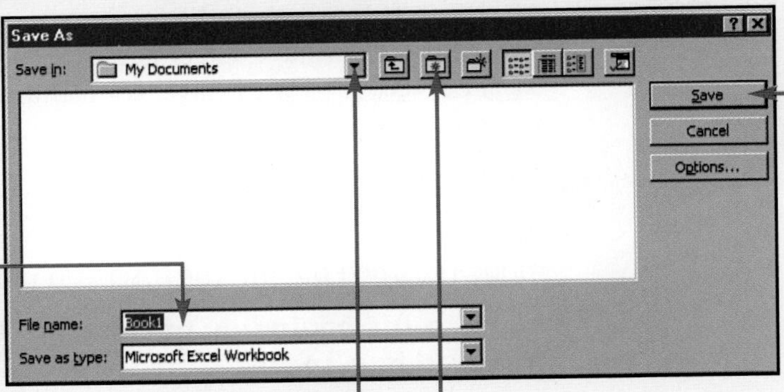

Figure 1.16
Enter the name of the file and select the location where you want it stored in the Save As dialog box.

Type a new file name here

Click here to save the file

Click here to choose a different disk drive or folder for storing the file

Click here to create a new folder

❸ **Type** OffExp **in the File name text box.**

The name you type replaces the temporary name assigned by Excel.

You can type any name you want using Windows 95's file-naming rules. You can include spaces as well as upper- and lowercase letters. Excel automatically stores the file in the default Excel 97 file format, adding the XLS file extension, but by default, Windows 95 does not show file extensions.

❹ **Click the Save in drop down arrow and click the drive or folder where you want to save your workbook.**

In the Save As dialog box, Excel automatically proposes to save the workbook on the current drive (usually C:) and in the default folder, My Documents. Ask your instructor where to save the files you create during this course. If you want to save to a different drive, such as a floppy disk, select the drive from the Save in list. If you want to save the file in a different folder, select the folder from the Save in list or click the New Folder button to create and name a new folder.

If you have problems...

If you try to save to a floppy disk and get an error message, check two things: First, be sure to select the correct disk drive—most likely drive A. Second, be sure that you are using a formatted disk. If this is the problem, you should see an error message that tells you the disk you selected is not formatted. The error message may ask you if you want to format the disk now. If this is the case and you want to format the disk so you can save files to it, click the Yes button and follow the instructions until the disk formatting is complete.

Be careful when formatting disks and make sure that you don't format your hard disk drive. When you format a disk, all information stored on the disk is erased. If you have any questions about formatting or disk drives, don't hesitate to ask your instructor for help.

5 **Choose Save.**

This saves a copy of your workbook containing the worksheet data as a file named OffExp. The Save As dialog box closes, and the new file name appears in the workbook window title bar. Now practice a shortcut method for quickly saving a file that already has a name, drive, and folder.

6 **Click the Save button on the toolbar.**

This method quickly saves your workbook. Alternatively, you can press Ctrl+S. If you want to save an existing workbook with a different name or to a different drive or folder, choose Save As from the File menu. See the following Exam Note for more information about saving files.

Keep the OffExp workbook open for the next lesson, where you learn how to prepare a worksheet for printing.

If you need to publish your worksheet data on a Web site (so it's available via the Internet) or on your company's intranet, you can convert your worksheet to HTML format. HTML is the language in which Web pages are written.

1. After you've saved your file first as a workbook, click on the first cell of the data you want converted to HTML and drag to the end cell (this is selecting the cells by highlighting them).

2. Click File on the menu and select Save as HTML.

3. The Internet Assistant Wizard appears. Click Next.

4. Select Create an independent, ready-to-view HTML document and click Next.

5. Enter a title for the document in the Title text box and any header text you want to include in the Header text box.

6. The last date you modified the worksheet data and your name should automatically appear in the Last Update on and By text boxes. If you want to add an e-mail address to the HTML document, enter one in the Email text box.

7. Click Next.

8. Click Save the result as an HTML file and enter the location where you want the file stored in the File path text box (or click Browse to select a location).

9. Click Finish.

In this lesson, a number of technical terms have been used to describe how computers save information. **RAM** stands for **random access memory**, which simply means the temporary storage space the computer uses for programs and data it's currently working with.

continues

Header
Text or graphics that appear at the top of every page.

Footer
Text or graphics that appear at the bottom of every page.

Page setup
The way data is arranged on a printed page.

When a computer crashes, it means that an error—either in a program the computer is running or in the hardware or power supply—has caused the computer to stop working. Everything stored in RAM is lost when a crash occurs. Remember, it's important to frequently save your work to a hard disk or a floppy disk.

Floppy disks are small disks that you can carry around with you. Although 3 1/2-inch floppy disks have hard outer cases, the disk inside is flexible. Your **hard disk** is built into your PC and is made up of several rigid platters that look similar to the CDs that you buy in music stores. The bulk of the programs and information that your computer uses is stored on the computer's hard disk.

Lesson 8: Preparing a Worksheet for Printing

With Excel, you can quickly print a worksheet using the default *page setup*. However, you can improve the way the worksheet looks when it is printed, and you can add useful information to the printed page by changing the page setup. For example, you can add *headers* and *footers* to help identify the contents of the printed page, and you can adjust the page margins. Now, use Excel's Page Setup features to make sure your worksheet is ready for printing.

To Prepare a Worksheet for Printing

❶ In the OffExp **worksheet, open the File menu and choose Page Setup.**

The Page Setup dialog box appears (see Figure 1.17). Use this dialog box to adjust the page setup before you print your worksheet. This dialog box provides a wide range of options from which you can choose to customize your printed worksheet. By default, the Page options are displayed. These options enable you to select features pertaining to the actual page on which the worksheet is printed, such as the correct paper size and orientation. For this example, you want to change the margins, center the worksheet on the page, add a header and a footer, and choose to display gridlines for the printed worksheet.

Figure 1.17
The Page options in the Page Setup dialog box lets you set page size and orientation.

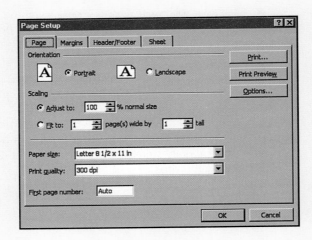

② Click the Margins tab in the Page Setup dialog box.

This displays the Margins options. The default top and bottom margins are 1-inch. The default left and right margins are 0.75-inch.

③ In the Top text box, click the up arrow twice.

This changes the top margin to 1.5. Notice the preview page in the dialog box shows you the changes.

④ In the Bottom text box, click the down arrow once.

This changes the bottom margin to 0.75.

⑤ In the Center on page area, select both the Horizontally and Vertically check boxes.

The worksheet is now centered horizontally between the left and right margins and vertically between the top and bottom margins. You can see how the changes affect the preview page in the dialog box, as shown in Figure 1.18.

Figure 1.18
The Margins options in the Page Setup dialog box enable you to set the page margins as well as the alignment of the worksheet on the page.

Set margins here ————

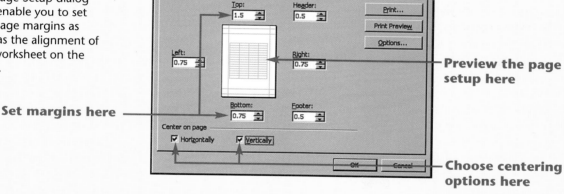

—— Preview the page setup here

—— Choose centering options here

⑥ In the Page Setup dialog box, click the Header/Footer tab.

The Header and Footer options let you specify information to print in the header and footer area of each page. You can choose from pre-defined headers and footers, or you can create your own.

⑦ Click the drop-down arrow next to the Header text box and then scroll down through the list of pre-defined headers and select Prepared by {YOUR NAME} MM/DD/YY, Page 1.

This header will print the words "Prepared by" followed by your name and today's date in the center of the header and the page number on the right side of the header.

continues

To Prepare a Worksheet for Printing   (continued)

8 **Click the drop-down arrow next to the Footer text box and select OffExp.**

This footer prints the current file name in the center of the footer area.

9 **Click the Sheet tab in the Page Setup dialog box.**

On this page, you can choose options that affect the way the data in the worksheet is printed.

10 **Select the Gridlines check box.**

When this option is selected, the gridlines between rows and columns are printed. You have now finished setting up the worksheet page for printing.

11 **Choose OK.**

The Page Setup dialog box closes.

12 **Click the Save button on the Standard toolbar.**

This saves the changes you have made to the OffExp worksheet file. Leave OffExp open. In Lesson 9, you learn how to preview and print the worksheet. See the following Exam Note for additional information about page setup.

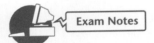

Exam Notes

On the Page tab of the Page Setup dialog box, the default page orientation is Portrait. In Portrait orientation, your worksheet prints so the top of the page is the narrow edge of the paper. For example, if you choose Letter as your Paper size, the page is 8.5 inches wide and 11 inches long. To have your worksheet print on the page so the top is 11 inches wide and the page is 8.5 inches long, select Landscape as your page orientation. Printing Landscape is useful when you have worksheets with several columns that don't fit on a page that's 8.5 inches wide.

When you have a worksheet that doesn't fit on one page, use the scaling options on the Page tab of the Page Setup dialog box to shrink your text to fit. Choose either Adjust to and specify a percentage in the spin box (either click the up and down arrows to change the percentages in small increments or enter the number directly in the box), or click Fit to and then specify the number of pages wide and the number of pages tall on which you want your worksheet to print.

When adding a custom header or custom footer to your worksheet, you may not be satisfied with the choices Excel provides. Click Custom Header or Custom Footer on the Header/Footer page of the Page Setup dialog box to create your own header or footer. Text boxes for the left, center, and right sections allow you to enter text so it aligns correctly. Use the page number, date, time, filename, or tab name buttons to insert that information in the header or footer.

Lesson 9: Printing a Worksheet

Now that you have saved your workbook and worksheet and have adjusted the page setup, you can print a copy of your worksheet for your files or to review while you are away from the computer.

Current worksheet
The worksheet containing the active cell.

It's a good idea to save documents immediately before printing them, as you did in Lesson 8. It's also a good idea to preview on your screen the way the worksheet will look when it is printed. That way, you can make adjustments to the page setup before you print. Now, preview and print your expense worksheet—the *current worksheet*.

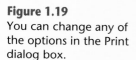

To Print a Worksheet

Online
Directly connected to a computer and ready for use.

❶ Make sure that the printer is turned on, has paper, and is *online*.

You can't print if the printer is not turned on, if the printer is out of paper, or if the printer is not online. Printers often have a light that shows whether the printer is online or receiving commands from the computer. If the printer is not online, Excel displays an error message.

❷ From the File menu, choose Print.

The Print dialog box appears, as shown in Figure 1.19.

Figure 1.19
You can change any of the options in the Print dialog box.

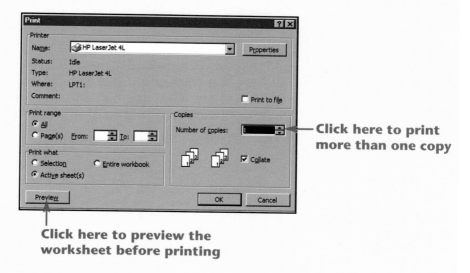

Click here to print more than one copy

Click here to preview the worksheet before printing

❸ In the Number of copies spin box, click the up arrow once.

This changes the number of copies to be printed to 2. You can also change other options in the Print dialog box. After the printer is ready, you should check the worksheet you are going to print.

continues

Figure 1.20
View the worksheet as it will look when printed to decide if you need to make changes.

Click here to print

Click here to open the Page Setup dialog box

Click here to close Print Preview

Header

Footer

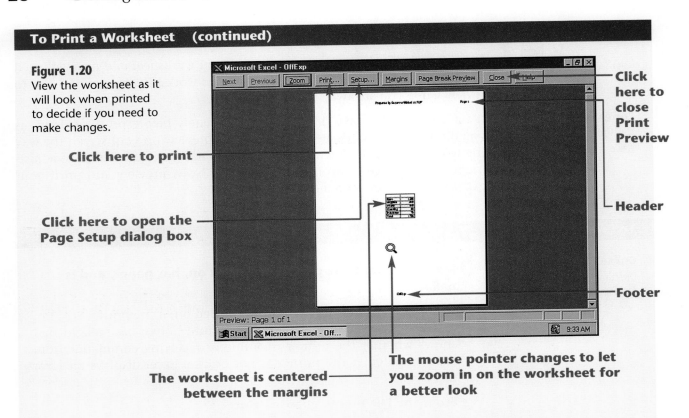

The worksheet is centered between the margins

The mouse pointer changes to let you zoom in on the worksheet for a better look

❹ **Click the Preview button in the Print dialog box.**

The worksheet now appears in the Print Preview window, which enables you to see how the entire worksheet will look when printed (see Figure 1.20). In Print Preview, you can see the effects of the changes you made to the page setup, including the header and footer you have added to the page, as well as the gridlines. When the mouse pointer changes to a magnifying glass, you can click within the window to increase the size of the document being displayed.

❺ **Click anywhere in the worksheet.**

Your view of the worksheet becomes enlarged so that you can more easily read it, but you can't see the entire page. You can click the worksheet again to go back to the view of the whole page. If you decide you want to make a change in the worksheet before you print it, click the Close button to close the view and return to the worksheet in Excel, or click the Setup button to open the Page Setup dialog box.

❻ **Click the Print button on the Print Preview toolbar.**

Excel sends two copies of your worksheet to the printer. The Print Preview window closes and the OffExp worksheet is displayed in Normal view. Leave the worksheet open in Excel. In the next lesson, you learn how to close it and exit the program.

To quickly open the Print dialog box, press Ctrl+P.

To quickly print the current worksheet without opening the Print dialog box, click the Print button on the Standard toolbar.

To change to Print Preview without opening the Print dialog box, click the Print Preview button on the Standard toolbar, or choose Print Preview from the File menu.

Lesson 10: Closing a File and Exiting Excel

Before you turn off your computer, you should first close the file you have created and exit Excel so that you don't lose any of your work. Complete this project by closing your file and exiting the Excel and Windows program.

To Close a File and Exit Excel

1 Choose File, Close.

If you haven't saved your work, Excel displays a dialog box that asks if you would like to save your work. Choosing Yes saves the file and closes it. Choosing No closes the file and erases any work you have done since the last time you saved.

2 Choose File, Exit.

Excel closes. If there are any files left open, Excel displays a dialog box that asks if you would like to save your work. Choosing Yes saves all open files and closes the program. Choosing No closes the program without saving the files; any work you have done since the last time you saved is erased. After you close Excel, the Windows desktop appears if no other software applications are running.

If you have completed your session on the computer, proceed with Step 3. Otherwise, continue with the "Applying Your Skills" section at the end of this project.

3 To exit Windows, click the Start button on the Taskbar and choose Shut Down from the Start menu.

The Shut Down Windows dialog box appears, asking you to confirm that you are ready to shut down Windows and your computer.

4 Verify that the Shut Down the Computer? option button is selected and choose Yes.

Windows closes and prepares your computer for shut down. When a message appears telling you it is safe to shut off your computer, you may do so.

continues

To Close a File and Exit Excel (continued)

You have now completed the lesson on getting started with Excel. If you want to continue with the "Checking Your Skills" and "Applying Your Skills" sections at the end of this project, restart your computer and Excel using the information you learned in Lesson 1.

 **Inside Stuff**

To exit any file or program you are currently using, you can also click the Close button at the right end of the window's title bar. For example, clicking the Close button of a workbook closes the workbook, and clicking the Close button in the Excel title bar closes Excel. Again, you are prompted to save unsaved work before you close any file or software.

Project Summary

To	Do This
Start Excel.	Click the Start button on the Windows Taskbar, point at Programs on the Start menu and then choose Microsoft Excel from the Programs submenu.
Make a cell active.	Click it.
Get help.	Open the Help menu and choose Microsoft Excel Help to start the Office Assistant, or choose Contents and Index for general information.
Move to cell A1.	Press Ctrl+Home.
Enter data in a cell.	Click the cell, type the data, and press ↵Enter.
Enter a formula in a cell.	Click the cell, type an equal sign, type the formula, and press ↵Enter.
Edit the contents of a cell.	Double-click the cell or click on the cell and press F2, make your changes, and press ↵Enter.
Save a worksheet.	Choose File, Save. If necessary, type the file name in the File name text box, choose a disk drive and folder from the Save in list and choose Save.
Change page setup	Choose File, Page Setup, select options and choose OK.
Print a worksheet.	Click the Print button on the Standard toolbar.
Preview a worksheet before printing.	Click the Print Preview button on the Standard toolbar.

Checking Your Skills

True or False

For each of the following, check *T* or *F* to indicate whether the statement is true or false.

__T __F **1.** The formula bar of the Excel screen displays the contents of the current cell and the cell's address.

__T __F **2.** Pressing F10 starts the Office Assistant.

__T __F **3.** The only way to move around a worksheet is by using the mouse.

__T __F **4.** You can have up to 65,536 rows in a worksheet.

__T __F **5.** You can press Ctrl+S or click the Save button on the toolbar to save changes to a file that has already been named.

__T __F **6.** When you click a glossary term in the Help program, Excel takes you to a location on the Internet that provides additional information.

__T __F **7.** If you make a mistake while typing, press Shift+Tab to delete the error.

__T __F **8.** Until you save a worksheet, it is stored only in the computer's random-access memory (RAM).

__T __F **9.** You cannot include spaces in an Excel file name.

__T __F **10.** You can publish your spreadsheet data on a Web site by saving it in HTML format.

Multiple Choice

Circle the letter of the correct answer for each of the following.

1. Which of the following is not a part of the Microsoft Excel screen?

  a. ruler line

  b. sheet tab

  c. status bar

  d. toolbar

2. Which of the following is a valid cell address?

  a. b-12

  b. B:12

  c. B12

  d. B/12

3. What is the address of the top-left cell in a worksheet?

  a. T1

  b. L1

  c. B1

  d. A1

4. Which of the following is an example of an Excel formula?

  a. $240

  b. =B2+B3+B4

  c. January

  d. 1/21/94

5. Which of the following is a method of getting help in Excel?

    a. Office Assistant

    b. Directory Assistance

    c. Help Assistant

    d. Excel Assistant

6. Menu items that have sub-menus are indicated by

    a. an ellipsis (...) .

    b. a small, right-pointing arrowhead.

    c. a small, left-pointing arrowhead.

    d. the letters **sm**.

7. The active cell is indicated by

    a. an outline around the cell.

    b. highlighting within the cell.

    c. shading within the cell.

    d. a red border around the cell.

8. To select an entire column,

    a. drag the mouse pointer down all the cells visible on the screen.

    b. click the column letter.

    c. right-click the column letter.

    d. choose Select, Entire Column from the menu bar.

9. You can have _____ columns in a worksheet.

    a. an unlimited number

    b. 200

    c. 256

    d. 150

10. Double clicking a cell

    a. puts it into Edit mode.

    b. deletes the contents of the cell.

    c. applies default formatting to the cell.

    d. opens the Help menu.

Completion

In the blank provided, write the correct answer for each of the following statements.

1. Data is entered in the _____ cell.

2. To use a button on the toolbar, you _____ the button.

3. The Name Box in the formula bar displays the _____ _____.

4. You can add a header or footer to a worksheet using the _____ _____ dialog box.

5. To print a worksheet, open the _____ menu and choose Print, or click the Print button.

6. A _____ displays a description of a toolbar button.

7. To quickly select all the cells in a worksheet, click the _____ button.

8. If you use the _____ dialog box, you can quickly move to a specific cell in your worksheet.

9. Values, text, and formula are referred to as _____ in your worksheet.

10. Clicking the Cancel button on the formula bar is the same as pressing _____.

Matching

In the blank next to each of the following terms or phrases, write the letter of the corresponding term for phrase.

a. floppy disk

b. Formula

c. Text

d. Value

e. Data

f. footer

g. hard disk

h. header

i. cell

j. Insertion Point

_____ 1. A number that you enter in a cell of a worksheet

_____ 2. Any word or label you enter in the spreadsheet

_____ 3. A specific calculation that Excel performs

_____ 4. Information entered into a worksheet

_____ 5. A blinking vertical cursor that indicates you are in Edit mode

_____ 6. A disk that is built into your PC

_____ 7. A small disk that you can carry around with you

_____ 8. The intersection of a column and row

_____ 9. Text or graphics that appears at the top of every page

_____ 10. Text or graphics that appears at the bottom of every page

Applying Your Skills

Practice

The following exercises enable you to practice the skills you have learned in this project. Take a few minutes to work through these exercises now.

Creating an Employee List

Imagine that you are the owner and hands-on business manager of a new gourmet coffee shop. With Excel, you can keep track of the employees you hire and plan to hire. You can list hire dates, starting salaries, and pay raise information.

To create an employee list, follow these steps:

1. Start Windows and then start Microsoft Excel.

2. Use the default worksheet.

3. Enter the following row labels, starting in cell A3 and moving down to cell A6:

Office Manager

Sales Clerk

Stock Clerk

Cashier

4. After you have finished setting up the row labels, enter the following column labels, starting in cell A2 and moving to the right to F2 by pressing `Tab⇆` to move from one column to the next:

Position

Description

Salary

Employee name

Start Date

Next Review Date

5. Enter the following data into the Salary column, starting with cell C3 and ending with cell C6:

35000

20000

18000

17000

6. Enter a formula in cell C7 to calculate your total projected salary costs.

7. Enter the following employee names in column D, beginning with cell D3 and ending with cell D6:

Gary Edwards

Lydia Johnnson

Rachel Smit

Amy Hoffman

8. Save the file as `Job List`. Leave the file open for the following exercise.

Revising an Employee List

You realize that you made some errors when you created the employee list in the previous exercise. In this exercise, you will edit the data in the list to correct your errors.

To revise an employee list in the `Job List` worksheet you created, make the following corrections:

1. Delete one letter `n` in the name `Johnnson`.

2. Add an `h` to the end of the name `Smit`.

3. Change Rachel Smith's salary to `18500`.

4. Save the file again, using the same file name.

Adding Headers and Footers to the Employee List

To keep track of revision dates of your Job List worksheet, you decide to use headers and footers.

To add headers and footers to the employee list in the job list worksheet, add headers and footers as described in the following exercise:

1. Access the Page Setup dialog box.

2. Click the Header/Footer tab to access this section of the dialog box.

3. Click Custom Header to add your own text to a header.

4. Type the word Confidential in the Center section of the dialog box.

5. Click Custom Footer.

6. Type the word Revised in the Center section of the dialog box.

7. Press the Spacebar and then click the date button to automatically enter the current date.

8. Save the file again and then leave it open for the following exercise.

Previewing and Printing a Worksheet

Now that you have completed the Job List worksheet, you are ready to preview and then print it.

To preview and print a worksheet, follow these steps:

1. In the Job List worksheet, choose File, Print. The Print dialog box displays.

2. Click the Preview button at the bottom of the dialog box. The worksheet displays in the Print Preview window.

3. You decide that the worksheet would look better printed sideways, so you want to change to Landscape mode. Click the Setup button at the top of the Print Preview window. The Page Setup dialog box displays.

4. Click the Page tab and choose the Landscape option button.

5. Click the Margins tab and choose the Horizontally option button to center the worksheet between the left and right margins.

6. Choose OK to return to the Print Preview window.

7. Click the Print button to print a copy of the worksheet.

8. Leave the worksheet open for the following exercise.

Saving a Worksheet as HTML and Closing the File

You need to post a copy of the Job List worksheet on your company's intranet, so that it will be accessible by your Human Resources Manager.

To save a worksheet as HTML and close the file, follow these steps:

1. In the Job List worksheet, drag from cell A1 to cell F7 to select the worksheet data.

2. Click File on the menu and then select Save as HTML.

3. The Internet Assistant Wizard appears. Click Next.

4. Select Create an independent, ready-to-view HTML document and then click Next.

5. Enter the document title `Employment Listing` in the Title text box.

6. The last date you modified the worksheet data and your name should automatically appear in the Last Update on and By text boxes. Click Next.

7. Click Save the result as an HTML file and enter the location where you want the file stored in the File path text box (or click Browse to select a location).

8. Click Finish.

9. Choose File, Close to close the workbook.

Challenge

The following challenges enable you to use your problem-solving skills. Take time to work through these exercises now.

Creating an Inventory Worksheet

You decide that another good use for an Excel worksheet would be to keep track of the inventory for your coffee shop.

To create an inventory worksheet, follow these steps:

1. Create an Inventory worksheet for the coffee shop that includes the following column headings:

   Item

   Amount in Stock

   Min. Stock Required

   Unit

   Cost per unit

2. Under the Item column heading, type the following items:

   Arabica coffee

   Kona coffee

   Columbian coffee

   Blueberry muffins

   Apple cinnamon muffins

3. Under the Amount in Stock column heading, type the following quantities:

   20

   15

   18

   24

   12

4. In the Minimum Stock Required column, type:

   18

   15

   15

   15

   15

5. In the Unit column, type `lb` for all the coffees and `dozen` for all the muffins.

6. In the Cost per Unit column, type the following prices:

   1.99

   1.79

   2.09

   1.50

   1.50

7. Save the file as `Coffee Shop Inventory` and leave it open for the following exercise.

Editing the Inventory Worksheet

Now that you have entered the preliminary data into the `Coffee Shop Inventory` worksheet, you need to make some changes.

To edit the inventory worksheet, make the following changes:

1. Change `Arabica` coffee to `French Roast`.

2. Change the `Price Per Unit` of the Columbian coffee to `2.59`.

3. Change the `Amount in Stock` of the Apple Cinnamon muffins to `20`.

4. Save the file again and then leave it open for the following exercise.

Adding Headers and Footers to the Inventory File

To provide additional information, you decide it would be useful to add headers and footers to the `Coffee Shop Inventory` file.

To add headers and footers to the inventory file, follow these steps:

1. Add a header to the Coffee Shop Inventory worksheet that includes your name and the words Coffee Shop and Inventory.

2. Add a footer that displays the current date.

3. Save the file and leave it open for the following exercise.

Previewing and Printing the Document

You are ready to print a hard copy of the Coffee Shop Inventory document, but you want to preview it first.

To preview and print the document, follow these steps:

1. Preview the document to check the alignment and options selected.

2. Center the document between the left and right margins.

3. Increase all the margins to 2 inches.

4. Add gridlines to the file.

5. After you have previewed the document, print 2 copies.

Saving the File as HTML and Close the File

You want to be able to post the file on your company's intranet so that other employees can access the information.

To save the Coffee Shop Inventory file as HTML and close the file, follow these steps:

1. Save the file as HTML.

2. When it has been saved, close the workbook file.

PinPoint Assessment

You have completed the project and the associated lessons, as well as the Checking Your Skills and Applying Your Skills sections. Now use the PinPoint software evaluation mode to assess your comprehension of the specific exam tasks you have just learned. You can also use the PinPoint Trainer Mode and the Show Me tutorials to practice these specific exam tasks.

Project 2

Two

Building a Spreadsheet

Creating an Office Expense Budget

Objectives   **Required Activities**

In this Project, you learn how to

➤ Open an Existing Worksheet ... ... Open Electronic Workbooks

➤ Select Worksheet Items

➤ Use AutoFill

➤ Add and Remove Rows and Columns ... ... Insert, Modify and Delete Rows and Columns

➤ Undo and Redo Actions ... ... Delete Cell Contents

➤ Copy Information

➤ Move Information ... ... Copy and Move Data

➤ Sort Data ... ... Sort Data

Why Would I Do This?

ow that you are familiar with the Excel screen and the basics of entering data and saving files, it's time to work with some of Excel's more powerful editing tools. In Project 1, "Getting Started with Excel," you learned how to create a simple worksheet. In this project, you learn to use Excel to create a budget worksheet that includes office expense information for several months.

Using the sample budget information, you learn how to control the structure of a worksheet by adding and deleting columns and rows. You also learn how to use Excel's editing features to make your work faster and easier.

Lesson 1: Opening an Existing Worksheet

After you create a workbook and save it to your hard disk or floppy disk, you can reopen the workbook and resume working with its data. With Excel, you can open a new workbook file, open an existing workbook file, or work with the default workbook. The default worksheet appears on-screen whenever you start Excel, or when you create a new file using the General Workbook file template.

In this lesson, you open an existing workbook file that contains the worksheet data that you will use throughout this project.

To Open an Existing Worksheet

❶ Start Excel if it is not already running, and click the File menu in the default workbook file.

The File menu opens to display a number of commands.

❷ Choose the Open command.

The Open dialog box appears, as shown in Figure 2.1. The files and folders stored in the default folder, My Documents, are displayed. You can also click the Open File button on the Standard toolbar to get to the Open dialog box.

Figure 2.1
The Open dialog box lists all files in the default folder.

Select a file here——

Default folder——

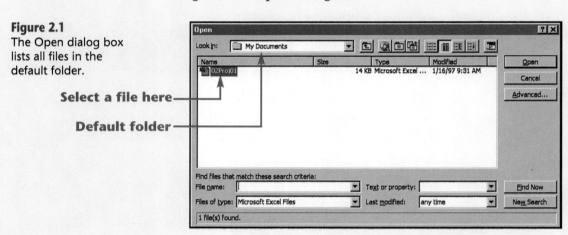

3 **In the Look in list of files and folders, select the Project-02 folder on the CD. Then click the** `Proj0201` **file icon to select it.**

This file may already be selected. If you don't see `Proj0201` in the list, try opening another folder from the Look in drop down list or try looking on another drive. The file may be stored in a different location on your system. If you can't find the file on your computer, ask your instructor for the location of the data files you will use with this book.

If you have problems...

If, when you click the file to select it, the characters in the filename become highlighted instead of the entire file name, it means you changed to Rename mode. In Rename mode, you can change the name of an existing file or folder. To select the file, make sure you click its icon.

4 **Choose Open.**

The office budget sample worksheet (`Proj0201`) appears onscreen, as shown in Figure 2.2. Now use the Save As command to save a copy of this sample file under a more descriptive file name. The original data file will be stored intact.

Figure 2.2
Save the sample file
`Proj0201` as Budget to
use in this project.

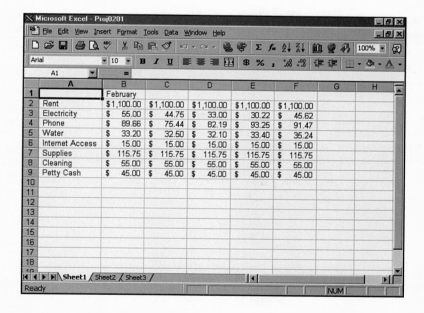

5 **Choose the File menu again and then the Save As command.**

The Save As dialog box appears.

6 **In the File name text box, type** Budget **to replace** Proj0201.

Budget is the workbook file name that is used throughout this project.

continues

To Open an Existing Worksheet (continued)

7 **From the Save in drop-down list, select the appropriate drive and folder for saving the new file.**

If necessary, ask your instructor where you should save the new workbook file.

8 **Choose Save.**

Excel saves the workbook as Budget and automatically closes the original data file. Keep the Budget workbook open to use in the next lesson.

 **Inside Stuff**

To open a file quickly from the Open dialog box, double-click the file's icon in the list of files. If you double-click the file name, however, you may end up in Rename mode.

Lesson 2: Selecting Worksheet Items

Selecting
Designating an item on-screen so you can do something with it. Also called *highlighting*.

In order to build a worksheet, you must learn how to *select* items in the worksheet. When you select an item, you highlight that item so you can make changes to it. You select a cell, for example, so you can copy the cell's content into another cell. You must select a column so that you can change the column's width.

In this lesson, you learn how to select items in the Budget worksheet.

To Select Worksheet Items

1 **Click cell B1 in the Budget worksheet.**

You have selected cell B1 by clicking in it. Once you select a cell, the cell's border is highlighted in bold, the cell's address appears in the name box of the formula bar, and the cell's content appears in the contents area of the formula bar. In addition, the letter heading of the column and the number heading of the row in which the cell is located appear in bold.

2 **Click cell A2, press and hold down the left mouse button and then drag the mouse pointer to cell G2. Release the left mouse button when the mouse pointer is in cell G2.**

Several adjacent cells—called a *range*—are now selected (see Figure 2.3). As you drag the mouse, the name box on the formula bar shows you how many rows and columns you are selecting. Dragging the mouse is an easy way to select a range of cells. After you finish selecting the range, the entire range of selected cells is highlighted, but only the address of the first cell—in this case, A2—appears in the name box, and only the content of the first cell appears in the Formula bar. That's because only the first cell is the active cell.

Range
A cell or a rectangular group of adjacent cells.

Being able to select and specify ranges is very important in Excel because you specify them in formulas, you select them to apply formatting to a block of cells, and you use them in graphing.

Figure 2.3
The first cell in the selected range is active while the rest of the selected cells are highlighted.

Active cell address

Column and row headings are bold

Selected cells

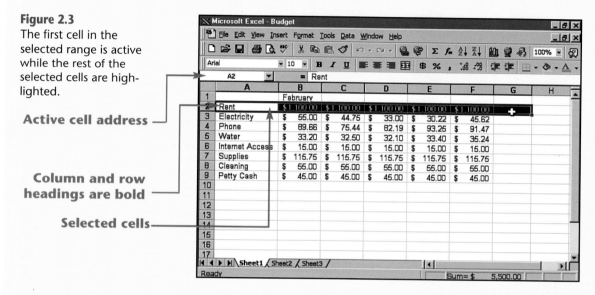

Worksheet frame
The horizontal bar containing the column letters and the vertical bar containing the row numbers, located in the worksheet area.

Now practice selecting an entire column of the worksheet.

③ Click column heading B in the *worksheet frame*.

This selects the entire worksheet column B, as shown in Figure 2.4. Keep the Budget worksheet open to use in the next lesson.

Figure 2.4
You can quickly select a column or row by clicking the column or row heading in the worksheet frame.

Worksheet frame

Click the Select All button to select the entire worksheet

Selected column

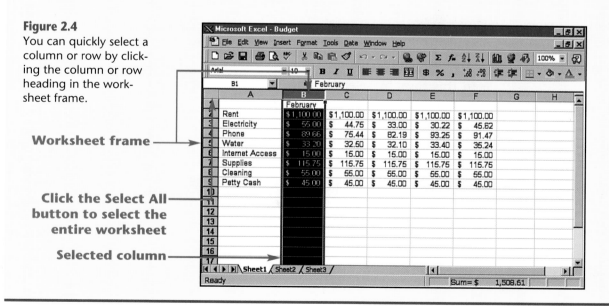

Inside Stuff

You can select two or more rows, columns, or cells by pressing and holding down Ctrl while you click the individual elements. This way, you don't have to select rows, columns, or cells in succession.

To select the entire worksheet, click the Select All button (the gray rectangle) in the top-left corner of the worksheet frame.

To select non-adjacent cells, click the first cell and then press and hold Ctrl and click additional cells. The last cell that you click is the active cell, but the others remain selected.

To select just the content or part of the content of a cell, you can double-click the active cell to display the I-beam mouse pointer and then drag the I-beam across any part of the text or data in the cell or the formula bar to select it.

To select cells with the keyboard, select the first cell in the range, press and hold down ◆Shift and then use the arrow keys to select additional cells.

To select data with the keyboard, position the insertion point where you want to start selecting, press and hold down ◆Shift and then use the arrow keys to move the insertion point to the last item you want to select.

In Excel, the standard notation for identifying ranges is to list the first cell in the range, a colon, and the last cell in the range. For example, if you are referring to the range of cells from A1 to F9, you would type A1:F9.

Lesson 3: Using AutoFill

You have now opened the Budget worksheet and practiced selecting items in the worksheet. The Budget worksheet has information on various expenses over several months, but before the worksheet is complete, a few items need to be changed.

As you can see, row 1 of the Budget worksheet should have column headings for each month of expenses you track. Using the AutoFill command, you can easily select a range of cells to have Excel fill the range with a sequence of information.

In this case, by selecting the cell containing the label February and then selecting a range of cells, you can add a sequence of months (February, March, April, and so on) to the range you select. You can also set up a sequence of numbers, letters, and days of the week by using the AutoFill command.

To Use AutoFill

❶ Click cell B1 in the Budget worksheet.

Cell B1 contains the column heading for the month of February. To build column headings for the rest of the worksheet, you select this cell as the starting value for the fill. This tells Excel the type of series you want to create—in this case, a series of consecutive months.

② Move the mouse pointer to the lower-right corner of cell B1 until the pointer changes to a thin, black plus sign.

When the mouse pointer changes to a black plus sign, also called the fill handle, Excel is ready to select a range of cells to be filled (see Figure 2.5).

Figure 2.5
The fill handle is a thin black plus sign.

Fill handle —

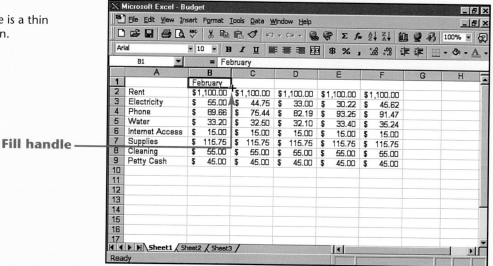

③ Press the left mouse button and drag right to cell F1 and then release the mouse button.

This action selects the range B1 through F1. As you drag, notice that ScreenTips indicate the data that Excel will use to fill each cell. When you release the mouse button, Excel fills the range with months (starting with February and increasing by one month for each cell in the range) and selects it, as shown in Figure 2.6.

Figure 2.6
The AutoFill command is used here to create a series of months.

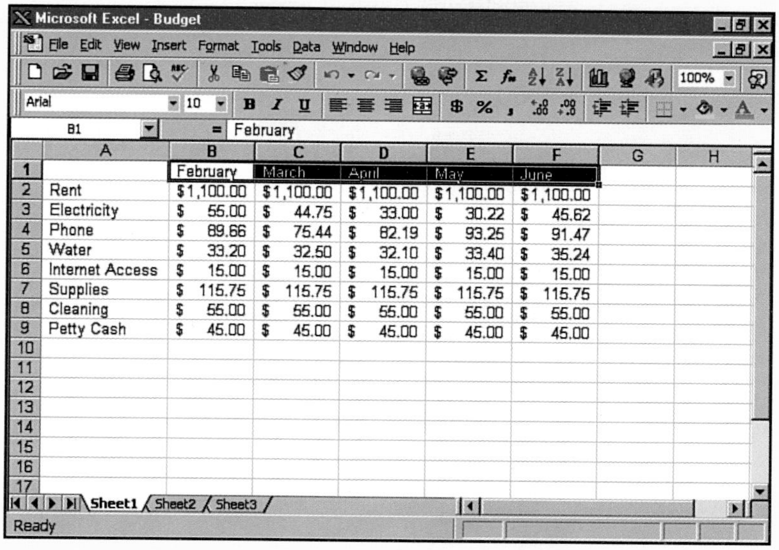

continues

4 **Click any cell.**

This deselects the range. From here, you can take the next step to build your Budget worksheet—adding and deleting columns and rows.

5 **Save your changes and keep the** Budget **worksheet open for the next lesson.**

If you have problems...

When using AutoFill, if you select cells that already contain data, Excel overwrites the data in the cells. You can reverse this action by choosing Edit, Undo before performing any other action.

Inside Stuff

You can fill columns as well as rows. Simply use the fill handle to drag down or up the column the same way you drag left or right to fill a row.

If you want to create a sequence of consecutive increments to fill by example (1, 2, 3, and so on), you enter the first item in the sequence and select that cell. If you want to create a sequence of values in increments other than 1 (5, 10, 15), you enter the data in two cells and select those cells before filling the range.

You may already have noticed that sometimes Excel seems to anticipate what you are going to enter into a cell. For example, you may start typing a column label, and Excel automatically completes the word you have begun—sometimes correctly, sometimes incorrectly. This is a feature called AutoComplete.

With AutoComplete, as you enter new data, Excel considers data you have recently entered to see if they seem to match. If so, Excel automatically enters that same data. For example, if you enter the label *Winter* in a cell and then start typing Wi in another cell, Excel assumes you are entering *Winter* again. If Excel is correct, this saves you some typing. If not, you can edit the entry.

To disable AutoComplete, choose Tools, Options, click the Edit tab and deselect the Enable AutoComplete for Cell Values check box. Then choose OK.

Lesson 4: Adding and Removing Rows and Columns

If you decide to add more information to your worksheet, Excel enables you to add rows and columns. You may, for example, want to add expense information for the month of January to your worksheet. Also, the cost of insurance, a common expense, is not listed in your worksheet. If you no longer want to include certain information, you can also remove columns and rows.

In this lesson, you learn how to add and remove rows and columns in a worksheet.

To Add and Remove Rows and Columns

1 **In the** Budget **worksheet frame, click the row heading for row 8.**

The entire row 8, Cleaning, is highlighted to show that it has been selected.

2 **Choose Insert, Rows.**

The content of row 8 and all rows below it move down one row. A new, blank row is inserted as the new row 8 (see Figure 2.7). Notice that all the rows beneath the new row 8 are automatically renumbered. Excel always inserts the new row *above* the row you select.

Figure 2.7
A new, blank row is inserted into the Budget worksheet.

Inserted row ──

Contents ──
move down

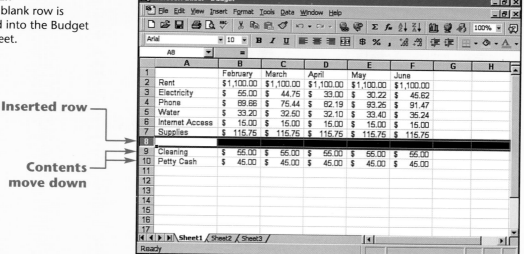

3 **Click cell A8, type** Insurance, **and press** ⏎Enter.

You have inserted and labeled a new row for insurance expenses. Now insert a new column for January's expenses.

4 **In the** Budget **worksheet frame, click the column heading for column B.**

The entire column B, February, is highlighted to show that it has been selected.

5 **Choose Insert, Columns.**

The content of column B and all columns to the right of column B, move to the right and have new letters assigned to them. A new, blank column B is added to the worksheet. Excel always inserts a new column to the *left* of the row you select.

6 **Click cell B1, type** January, **and press** ⏎Enter.

You have inserted and labeled a new column for January expenses. Finally, you decide that you don't want to include Petty Cash expenses in your worksheet. Delete the entire row 10 to remove Petty Cash expenses from your worksheet.

continues

To Add and Remove Rows and Columns   (continued)

7 In the worksheet frame, click the row heading for row 10.

The entire row 10, Petty Cash, is highlighted.

8 Choose Edit, Delete.

Row 10 is now deleted. When you delete a selected column or row, you also delete any content in that column or row. Your worksheet should now look similar to Figure 2.8.

Figure 2.8
Use the Edit, Delete command to remove unwanted columns or rows.

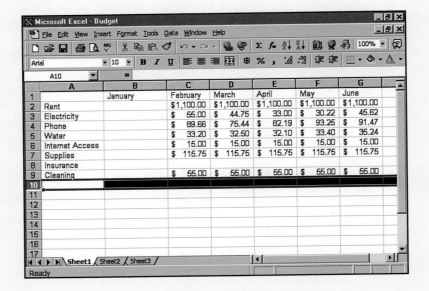

9 Save your changes and leave the Budget worksheet open to use in the next lesson.

If you want to insert more than one row or column at a time, select as many adjacent rows or columns as you need blank rows or columns and then choose Insert, Rows or Insert, Columns. For example, if you want to insert five new rows beginning at row 4, select rows 4 through 8 and then choose Insert, Rows. The same is true for deleting rows and columns. To delete five columns, select the five columns you want to delete and choose Edit, Delete.

You can use shortcut menus to insert or delete columns, rows, and cell contents. Select the item you want to insert or delete, move the mouse pointer to it, and click the right mouse button. Choose the appropriate command from the shortcut menu that appears.

You can also delete only the contents of selected cells. Select the cells and press Del, or choose Edit, Clear, Contents.

If you change your mind about what you added or deleted, choose Edit, Undo. Undo reverses the last action you performed.

If you have problems... If the Delete dialog box appears when you choose <u>E</u>dit, <u>D</u>elete, it means that you didn't select the entire row or column before choosing the command. You can either cancel the dialog box and try selecting the row again or select Entire <u>R</u>ow or Entire <u>C</u>olumn in the dialog box and choose OK to complete the deletion. The same is true for inserting and deleting rows and columns.

Exam Notes To modify a row, you must adjust its height. To modify a column, you must adjust its width.

One way to accomplish these tasks is to point to the separator lines between the column or row headings in the worksheet frame. For a row, drag the top or bottom separator line for that row to increase or decrease its height. For a column, drag the left or right separator line to increase or decrease the width of the column.

Another method is to select a cell in the row or column. Then choose F<u>o</u>rmat, <u>R</u>ow, <u>H</u>eight or F<u>o</u>rmat, <u>C</u>olumn, <u>W</u>idth. Increase or decrease the number in the <u>R</u>ow height or <u>C</u>olumn width text box and choose OK.

For more information and practice in changing the column width, see Project 5, "Improving the Appearance of a Worksheet."

Lesson 5: Undoing and Redoing Actions

By inserting and deleting rows and columns, you have changed the structure of your worksheet. However, when you use insert and delete commands, you can see that it is possible to accidentally make changes you didn't want to make. Luckily, Excel is very forgiving: you can use the Undo command to quickly reverse the last action and the Redo command to quickly reverse the Undo command.

Excel even lets you undo or redo a series of actions; if you don't realize you made a mistake right away, you can still recover the data you need. In this lesson, you practice undoing and redoing actions in your Budget worksheet.

To Undo and Redo Actions

❶ In the worksheet frame, click the heading for row 9 and choose <u>E</u>dit, <u>D</u>elete.

This selects and then deletes row 9.

❷ Choose <u>E</u>dit, <u>U</u>ndo Delete.

Excel reverses the last action you performed, which in this case was the deletion of row 9. The row and all of its contents are put back in the worksheet. Notice that the Undo command includes a description of the last action. The command changes according to the action that will be reversed.

continues

To Undo and Redo Actions   (continued)

3 **Choose Edit, Redo Delete.**

Excel reverses the last action of the Undo command. In this case, Excel deletes row 9 again. Like Undo, the Redo command also includes a description of the last action.

4 **Click in cell A11, type** Miscellaneous, **and press** ↵Enter.

The text is entered in cell A11. At this point, you realize you really need row 9 back in the worksheet. However, the last action you performed was typing text into cell A11. You must use multiple Undo to reverse more than one action.

5 **Click the Undo drop-down arrow on the Standard toolbar.**

A list of the actions that can be reversed is displayed, as shown in Figure 2.9. The most recently performed action is at the top of the list. You can choose to undo as many or as few of these actions as you want.

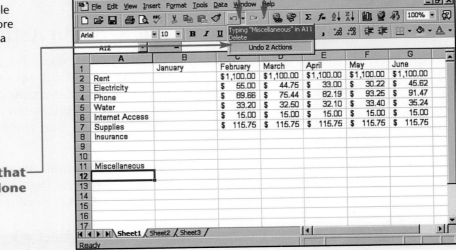

Figure 2.9
You can use multiple undo to reverse more than one action at a time.

List of actions that can be undone

6 **Click the word Delete in the Undo drop-down list.**

Excel reverses the action, as well as any actions above it in the list. The text Miscellaneous is deleted from cell A11, and row 9 is placed back in the worksheet.

7 **Save your changes and leave the** Budget **worksheet open to use in the next lesson.**

You can use multiple level Redo to redo more than one action. Click the Redo drop-down arrow on the Standard toolbar to display the Redo list and then click the last action you want to redo. All of the actions above the selected action are reinstated.

To quickly undo the most recent action, click the Undo button on the Standard toolbar, or press Ctrl+Z.

To quickly redo the most recent action, click the Redo button on the Standard toolbar, or press Ctrl+Y.

If an action cannot be undone, the Undo command and Undo button are dimmed. If an action cannot be redone, the Redo command and Redo button are dimmed.

After you save a file the Undo and Redo buttons are dimmed. You cannot undo or redo actions that occurred before you saved the file.

Lesson 6: Copying Information

By adding and removing columns and rows, you have made some important changes to your Budget worksheet. You still need to insert expense information, however, in the new row for Insurance and the new column for January.

Because you don't have the exact information for your office insurance bills or for your January expenses in this example, assume that you can use information from other parts of your worksheet to estimate these parts of your budget. You might assume, for example, that January expenses are the same as your February expenses. Instead of retyping the February information, you can copy the cells from the February column to the January column.

Copying information from one column to another is much quicker than typing it a second time. You can copy or move text, numbers, and formulas from one cell to another, from one worksheet to another, and from one file to another. Use the Budget worksheet to practice copying and moving data.

To Copy Information

❶ In the Budget worksheet, select cells C2 through C9.

This highlights the expense information that you want to copy from the February column into the January column.

❷ Choose Edit, Copy.

A copy of the selected cells' contents is placed in the Windows **Clipboard**. The Clipboard stores information or formulas that you want to move (copy) to another location. (See the Jargon Watch at the end of this lesson for more about the Clipboard.) A flashing dotted line appears around the copied cells.

continues

To Copy Information   (continued)

❸ Click cell B2.

This selects the location where you want the copied information to appear. You do not have to select a range that is the same size as the range you are copying; Excel automatically fills in the data starting with the one cell you select. (If you do select a range and it's not the same size and shape as the one you copied, you'll get an error message; it's better to click one and let Excel fill in the appropriate range.) Notice that the flashing dotted line still appears around the copied cells, even though the cells are no longer selected. This helps you remember which cells are currently stored on the Clipboard.

❹ Choose Edit, Paste.

The copied cells' content appears in cells B2 through B9, as shown in Figure 2.10. As indicated by the commands you have chosen, this process is called **copying** and **pasting**, and is a very common procedure in Windows applications. The flashing dotted line still appears around cells C2 through C9 because they are still stored on the Clipboard.

Note that the expense information in the January column is exactly the same as the information in the February column. To estimate your office insurance expense, assume for now that your monthly insurance bill is the same as your monthly office rent payment.

Figure 2.10
The January column now contains expense information copied from the February column.

Pasted data ————

Copied data ————

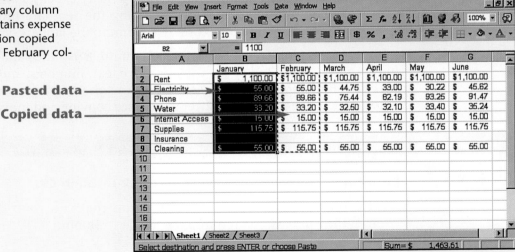

❺ Select cells B2 through G2.

To estimate your insurance expenses, copy the rent expense information that you just selected to the Insurance row.

 ❻ Click the Copy button on the Standard toolbar.

This copies the selected cells the same way as when you use the Edit, Copy command. The cells' contents are stored in the

Clipboard, ready to be pasted. Now the flashing dotted line appears around cells B2 through G2.

7 Click cell B8.

This selects the new location for the copied information.

 8 Click the Paste button on the Standard toolbar.

The contents of the copied cells are pasted into the new location. Again, notice that the Insurance expense information is exactly the same as the Rent information in row 2. In Project 5, "Improving the Appearance of a Worksheet," you use formulas to change the amount you just copied. Save your most recent changes and keep the Budget worksheet open to use in the next lesson.

When you **copy** or **cut** information in Excel, it moves to the Windows **Clipboard**—a part of memory set aside for storing things that you want to move or copy to another location. The cut or copied information stays in the Clipboard until you cut or copy something else. Remember that the Clipboard can hold only one item, although that item can be quite large. Whenever you cut or copy a new piece of information and place it in the Clipboard, it overwrites any information that is already there. Because information that you cut or copy is stored in the Clipboard, you can **paste** the item many times and in many different places.

One thing to keep in mind while you are working in Excel is the difference between the Edit menu commands Cut, Clear, and Delete. Edit, Cut removes an item from the worksheet and moves it to the Clipboard where it is stored for later use. Edit, Clear removes the selected information completely. You can choose Clear, Contents to clear cell contents, Clear, Formats to clear cell formatting, or Clear, All to clear both the formatting and the contents. Edit, Delete removes not only the selected information but the cells containing it as well. If you choose the wrong command by mistake, press Ctrl+z to undo the command, click the Undo button on the Standard toolbar, or choose Edit, Undo.

Lesson 7: Moving Information

Your Budget worksheet now has expense information in every cell, but what if you want to look at a certain type of expense separately? For example, perhaps you want to see how your utility expenses compare to the rest of your expenses.

You can use Excel's Cut and Insert Cells commands to remove cells from one location in a worksheet and place them in another location. You can use these commands to move cells so that you don't have to go to each cell, enter the same information, and then erase the information in the old location.

In this lesson, you move the rows containing utility expenses to another part of the worksheet.

To Move Information

1 Select rows 3 through 5 in the Budget **worksheet frame.**

This highlights the rows of your worksheet that contain utility expenses. These are the rows you will move to another part of the worksheet.

2 Choose Edit, Cut.

The information in rows 3 through 5 moves to the Clipboard (although you can still see it in the worksheet) and a dotted outline appears around the cut text, as shown in Figure 2.11. You can also click the Cut button on the Standard toolbar.

Figure 2.11
Cut cells appear in the worksheet surrounded by a flashing dotted line until you move them to a new location.

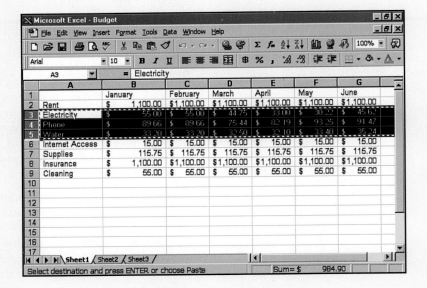

3 Click cell A11 to select it and then choose Insert, Cut Cells.

The rows containing the utility expense information are cut from their original location in the worksheet and are inserted in the new location. The information now appears in rows 8, 9, and 10 (see Figure 2.12).

Table 2.1 shows some shortcuts for the commonly used Cut, Copy, and Paste commands.

You have now completed the changes to the Budget worksheet.

4 Save your changes to the Budget **worksheet and leave it open for the next lesson.**

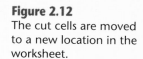

Figure 2.12
The cut cells are moved to a new location in the worksheet.

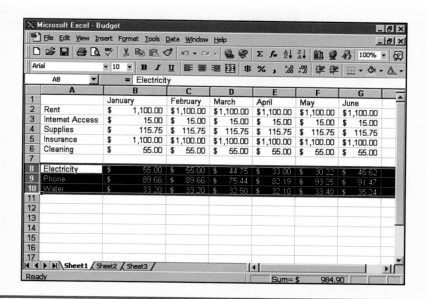

Inside Stuff

You can use Excel's shortcut menus to perform many common commands, including Cut, Copy, Paste, and Insert Cut Cells. To open a shortcut menu, move the mouse pointer to the cell or area you want to affect and then press the right mouse button. To select a command, click its name in the shortcut menu. Make sure that you move the mouse pointer to the correct cell before you click the shortcut menu command. Shortcut menu commands happen at the location of the mouse pointer, not necessarily in the current cell.

You can also use Excel's Cut and Paste commands to remove information from one cell and place it in another cell. Select the cell or cells you want to move and choose Edit, Cut. Select the cell where you want to place the information and choose Edit, Paste. Excel moves the information, but leaves the cells where the information had been intact in the worksheet. You can insert new data or delete the cells.

A handy way of quickly moving one or more cells of data is to select the cells and position the mouse pointer on any border of the cells so that the cell pointer changes to a white arrow. Click and drag the white arrow to the new location. An outline of the cells that you are moving appears as you drag, and a ScreenTip shows you the current active cell where the information will appear if you release the mouse button.

When you release the mouse button, the cells' contents appear in the new location. If the new location already contains information, a dialog box appears asking whether you want to replace the current information. If you still need the data that's currently in the new location, click Cancel. Then insert a new column or row to accommodate the data you want to move without overwriting existing data.

Copying information is also possible by using this drag-and-drop method. The only difference is that you must hold down the Ctrl key as you drag. The cell pointer changes to a white arrow with a small plus sign next to it. When you release the mouse button, a duplicate of the selected range appears in the new location.

Table 2.1—Copying, Cutting, and Pasting		
Command	Tool	Shortcut Key
Edit, Cut	✂	Ctrl+X
Edit, Copy	🗏	Ctrl+C
Edit, Paste	📋	Ctrl+V

Lesson 8: Sorting Data

Your worksheet now has a complete set of data for January through June expenses. Although you've separated the rows for the utilities from the remainder of the expenses, you need to put the first few rows in some sort of order.

In this lesson, you learn to sort the rows in alphabetical order.

To Sort Data

❶ **Click cell A2 in the** Budget **worksheet.**

In a worksheet that has labels in the first column and data in subsequent columns, you only need to select a cell in the list to be able to sort by the information in the rows.

❷ **Choose** Data, Sort **from the Menu bar.**

Excel automatically selects the cells in the list. The selected range stops when Excel encounters a blank row or column. This selected range includes the data that will be sorted.

The Sort dialog box also appears (see Figure 2.13).

Figure 2.13
Select the column on which you want to base the sorting of the rows in the list.

❸ **From the Sort by drop-down list, select Column A.**

Because you want to rearrange the rows so the labels in the first column appear in alphabetical order, you need to select Column A as the column you want to sort by.

_____ 6. The shortcut for the <u>E</u>dit, Cu<u>t</u> command

_____ 7. The shortcut for the <u>E</u>dit, <u>C</u>opy command

_____ 8. The mouse pointer that displays as a black plus sign

_____ 9. This command reverses the last action you performed

_____ 10. A part of the computer's memory that stores information or formulas you want to copy or move to another location

Applying Your Skills

Practice

The following exercises enable you to practice the skills you have learned in this project. Take a few minutes to work through these exercises now.

Rework the Job List Worksheet

In this exercise, follow the steps below to rework the Job List worksheet you created in Project 1. You need to add a job position to the worksheet.

To rework the job list, follow these steps:

1. Open the file Proj0202 from the Project-02 folder on the CD and save it as Job List 2.

2. Insert a new row at row 3 using the <u>I</u>nsert, <u>R</u>ows command.

3. Type Buyer in cell A3.

4. Type 28000 as the salary and Lisa Ford as the Employee.

5. Delete column B using the <u>E</u>dit, <u>D</u>elete command.

6. Save the file.

7. If requested by your instructor, print two copies of the file and then leave it open for the following exercise.

Modifying Rows and Columns in the Job List

In this exercise, follow the steps below to modify the rows and columns in the Job List 2 worksheet.

To modify rows and columns, follow these steps:

1. Increase the height of row 2 of the Job List 2 worksheet to 25.5 by dragging the separator line.

2. Increase the width of columns A and C to 14 by using the F<u>o</u>rmat, <u>C</u>olumn, <u>W</u>idth command.

3. Save the file, and leave it open for the following exercise.

Do all
five

Deleting Cell Contents and Copying and Moving Data ③

Continue reworking the Job List 2 worksheet by deleting cell contents and copying and moving data.

To delete cell contents and copy and move data, follow these steps:

1. Select cell C3, which contains the employee name Lisa Ford.

2. Delete only the contents of this cell.

3. Delete the formula in cell B8.

4. Reorganize the worksheet by moving the Salary column to the right of the Employee Name column. Insert a blank column to the left of the Salary column.

5. Select the data in the Employee Name column. Use the Edit, Cut command to move the information to the Clipboard.

6. Paste the Employee Name information into column B.

7. Delete column D, which is now empty.

8. Delete row 3, which you have decided not to use.

9. Save the Job List 2 workbook and leave it open for the following exercise.

Copying Data in a Worksheet ④

You want a duplicate copy of the Job List 2 data so you can have two versions, sorted two different ways. In this exercise, follow the steps below to copy the data to another section of the worksheet.

To copy data in a worksheet, follow these steps:

1. In the file Job List 2, select all the data from cell A2:E6.

2. Choose Edit, Copy to copy the data to the Clipboard.

3. Move to cell A20.

4. Choose Edit, Paste to paste the data in this section of the worksheet.

5. Press Esc to remove the marquee from the copied data.

6. Save the Job List 2 worksheet, and leave it open for the following exercise.

Sorting Data in a Worksheet ⑤

You decide you would like to display the data in a different order in your worksheet. Use the Sort command in the following exercise to rearrange the data.

To sort data in a worksheet, follow these steps:

1. Click cell A3.

2. Choose Data, Sort.

3. Choose to sort the data by Salary, in Descending order.

4. Move to the second copy of the worksheet data.

5. Sort this data in <u>A</u>scending alphabetical order by Position.

6. Save the worksheet. If requested by your instructor, print two copies and then close it.

The following challenges enable you to use your problem-solving skills. Take time to work through these exercises now.

Challenge

Inserting and Modifying Columns ①

Use the skills you learned in this project to insert and modify columns in the coffee inventory worksheet you created in Project 1.

To insert and modify columns, follow these steps:

Open the Proj0203 from the Project-02 folder on the CD file and save it a `Coffee Shop Inventory 2`. Make the following changes to the file.

1. Insert a column to the left of column A.

2. Type the heading `Item Type` in cell A1.

3. Insert two columns to the left of column C.

4. Type the column heading `Difference` in cell C1.

5. Type the column heading `Order` in cell D1. Enter a value for each item in the list that is the number of units you want to order of each.

6. Change the width of all the columns so that all the text in each column displays.

7. Save the file again and leave it open for the following exercise.

Inserting and Modifying Rows ②

Complete the following exercise to practice inserting and modifying rows in your worksheet.

To insert and modify rows, follow these steps:

Make the following changes to the `Coffee Shop Inventory 2` worksheet:

1. Adjust the height of row 1 so that it is twice as high as the other rows.

2. Insert two rows above row 5. Add data for different type of muffins in each row. You supply the data for each column in the entry.

3. Save the file again and leave it open for the following exercise.

Deleting Items in a Worksheet ③

In this exercise, you practice deleting rows, columns, and the contents of cells in a worksheet.

To delete items in a worksheet, follow these steps:

1. Delete one of the new rows you added to the `Coffee Shop Inventory 2` worksheet in the previous exercise.

2. Delete the column you labeled `Order`.

3. Delete the contents of the column that contains the label `Apple Cinnamon muffins`. Type `Raisin Bran Muffins` into this cell.

4. Save the worksheet and leave it open for the following exercise.

Copying and Moving Data

The following exercise gives you a chance to practice copying and moving data in your worksheet.

To copy and move data in the `Coffee Shop Inventory 2` worksheet, follow these steps:

1. Type the letter `C` in column A next to the first coffee entry.

2. Copy this letter down to all the other rows containing coffee entries.

3. Repeat these steps, using the letter `M` for all the muffin entries.

4. Insert a blank column after the column labeled `Minimum Stock Required`.

5. Move the data in the `Order` column to this column. Delete the extra blank column.

6. Save the worksheet and leave it open for the following exercise.

Sorting Data ⓢ

In the following exercise, you practice sorting data in your worksheet.

To sort data, follow these steps:

1. Sort the `Coffee Shop Inventory 2` worksheet in ascending order by the number in the `Amount In` column.

2. Sort the worksheet in alphabetical order by `Item`.

3. Sort the worksheet by `Item Type`.

4. Save the worksheet and print a copy before closing the file.

PinPoint Assessment

You have completed the project and the associated lessons, as well as the Checking Your Skills and Applying Your Skills sections. Now use the PinPoint software evaluation mode to assess your comprehension of the specific exam tasks you have just learned. You can also use the PinPoint Trainer Mode and the Show Me tutorials to practice these specific exam tasks.

Project 3

Three

Creating Formulas

Expanding the Office Expense Budget Worksheet

Objectives   **Required Activities**

In this Project, you learn how to

➤ Create a Formula

➤ Using Mathematical Operators … … … … … Enter Formulas

➤ Create a Formula by Selecting Cells

➤ Copy Formulas

➤ Use Absolute, Relative, and
   Mixed Cell References   … … … … … … … … Use References (Absolute, Relative and Mixed)

➤ Revise Formulas   … … … … … … … … … Revise Formulas

66 Project 3 Creating Formulas

Why Would I Do This?

Aformula is a calculation that Excel performs on data entered in a worksheet. You can use formulas to add, subtract, multiply, and divide data with basic mathematical operators. You can also use Excel's built-in *functions* to simplify the number of characters required in a formula. Formulas are the most valuable part of spreadsheet software, such as Microsoft Excel. A worksheet full of data would be of little use without built-in ways to perform calculations on the data.

Function
Built-in formulas that automatically perform calculations.

Once you write a formula using cell addresses, you can change the information in one or more of the cells referenced in the formula, and the formula automatically recalculates the result. You can also copy the formula from one location to another in the worksheet, so you do not have to reenter the formula to perform the same calculation on different data.

In this project, you learn how to create basic formulas in your budget worksheet using mathematical operators. You also learn how to use some of Excel's features for automating formulas—including the Formula palette, which enables you to view the result of a formula before you actually enter it in a cell, and the AutoSum button, which quickly finds the total of a row or column of data. Finally, you learn the difference between relative and absolute cell references, how to copy formulas from one location in a worksheet to another, and how to revise formulas.

Lesson 1: Creating Formulas Using Mathematical Operators

You can easily create a basic formula by typing an equation into a cell, just as you did in Project 1, "Getting Started with Excel," to find the total of a list of expenses. To create the formula, type the actual values you want to use in the calculation or the addresses of the cells that contain the values you want to use, separated by the mathematical operators that specify the type of calculation (a plus sign for addition or a minus sign for subtraction, for example). Table 3.1 lists some common mathematical operators.

In this lesson, you open a version of the budget worksheet you created in Project 2, "Building a Spreadsheet," and create some basic formulas.

Table 3.1 Common Mathematical Operators	
Description	Operator
Addition	+ (plus sign)
Subtraction	– (minus sign)
Multiplication	* (asterisk)
Division	/ (forward slash)
Exponents	^ (caret)

To Create Formulas

1 **From the Project-03 folder on the CD, open the file Proj0301 and save it as** Budget2.

This is an expanded version of the office budget worksheet you created in Project 2.

2 **Select cell B5 in the** Budget2 **worksheet.**

Cell B5 is now the current (active) cell, and it is where you want to create your first formula in this example. After looking at the expense worksheet again, you might decide that estimating insurance expenses to be the same as rent is too high. To change the insurance bill estimate, divide the amount of rent in half using a formula.

3 **In cell B5, type the formula** =b2/2.

This formula tells Excel to divide the contents of cell B2 by 2. The equal sign (=) tells Excel that you are about to enter a formula. If you do not type an equal sign, Excel enters the values as text data in the cell. B2 is the cell address of the January rent expense: $1,100. The slash (/) is the operator that tells Excel which mathematical operation you want to perform—in this case, division.

4 **Click the Enter button (the green check mark) on the formula bar.**

This tells Excel to enter the formula in the cell and calculate the formula. The result of the formula appears in cell B5, as shown in Figure 3.1. Notice that the formula =B2/2 appears in the formula bar. The formula is entered in cell B5, but Excel displays the result of the formula—not the formula itself. Now try using the Formula palette to create a formula for the February insurance bill.

Figure 3.1
The result of the formula appears in the cell; the formula itself appears in the formula bar when you select the cell containing the formula.

Formula

Result

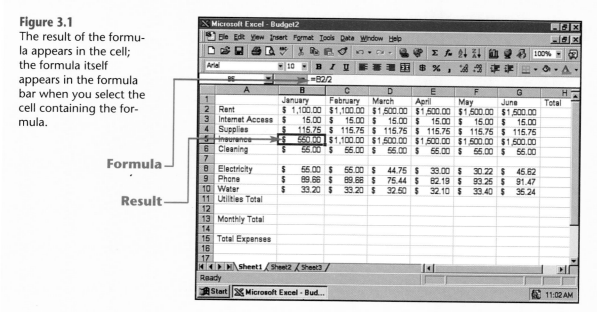

continues

To Create Formulas (continued)

If you have problems...

If your formula results in #NAME? instead of a value, it means you made a mistake entering the formula. You may have typed a cell address that doesn't exist, one of the cells in the formula may have an error, the operator you are using may be incorrect—for example, back slash (\) instead of slash (/)—or you may be trying to perform an impossible calculation. Check your formula carefully, correct any mistakes, and try again.

⑤ Select cell C5 and press Del.

This deletes the contents of cell C5. To enter a new formula with the Formula palette, the active cell must be empty.

⑥ Click the Edit Formula button on the formula bar.

Excel inserts an equal sign into the formula bar and opens the Formula palette (see Figure 3.2). With the Formula palette, you can see the result of the formula as you create it. You can also select functions to include in the formula, as you will learn in Project 4, "Calculating with Functions."

⑦ Type c2.

The cell address appears in the formula bar and in the active cell. In the Formula palette, you can see the result of the formula so far, which is simply the value of cell C2, $1,100 (see Figure 3.2).

Figure 3.2
Using the Formula palette, you can see the result of a formula as you create it.

Functions button

Formula palette

Edit Formula button

Formula result

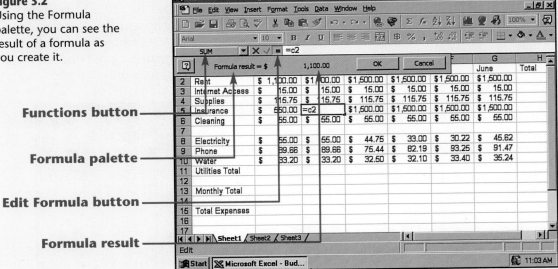

⑧ Type *.5.

This completes the formula for multiplying the value of cell C2 by one-half (0.5). The asterisk is the operator for multiplication. (Press +Shift+8 to enter the asterisk.) Notice that Excel updates the result of the formula in the Formula palette.

❾ Click OK in the Formula palette.

Excel closes the palette, enters the formula in cell C5, and displays the result. You can click the Enter button or press ⏎Enter instead of clicking OK.

❿ Save the changes you have made to the Budget2 **worksheet and keep it open.**

In the next lesson, you learn how to create formulas by selecting cells.

The parentheses in a formula tell Excel which order to use when performing calculations. For example, if you want to add two numbers and then divide them by 2, use the formula =(A12+B12)/2. The part of the formula in parentheses takes precedence over the other parts of the formula.

If you don't use parentheses in a formula, Excel sets precedence in the following way: exponential calculations first, multiplication and division second, and addition and subtraction third. Therefore, with a formula such as =B12+C12/A10, Excel first divides C12 by A10 and then adds the resulting number to B12. If you want to add the first two cells and then divide, use the formula =(B12+C12)/A10.

You can use Excel's AutoCalculate feature to find out the result of a calculation without actually entering a formula. Simply select the cell or range of cells you want to total and look at the AutoCalculate button on the Status bar. By default, Excel uses the SUM function. To select a different function, right-click the AutoCalculate button and choose the function you want to use.

Lesson 2: Creating Formulas by Selecting Cells

You can also enter cell addresses into formulas by selecting the cell or range of cells in the worksheet. This simplifies the process of creating a formula and also helps to ensure that you enter the correct cell address that you want to use.

In this lesson, you create a formula for totaling the monthly utility expenses by selecting the cells you want to include. You then create a formula that includes a function and a selected range of cells.

To Create Formulas by Selecting Cells

❶ In the Budget2 **worksheet, select cell B11 and click the Edit Formula button.**

You want the result of the formula displayed in cell B11. To calculate the total, add the values in cells B8, B9, and B10.

continues

To Create Formulas by Selecting Cells   (continued)

2 Click cell B8.

Excel enters B8 into the formula. A flashing dotted line appears around the cell to remind you that it is the cell you selected for the formula. Also, the value of cell B8 appears in the Formula palette.

3 Type +, click cell B9, and then type + again and click cell B10.

The formula appears in the formula bar and in cell B11. You can see the result of the formula in the Formula palette (see Figure 3.3).

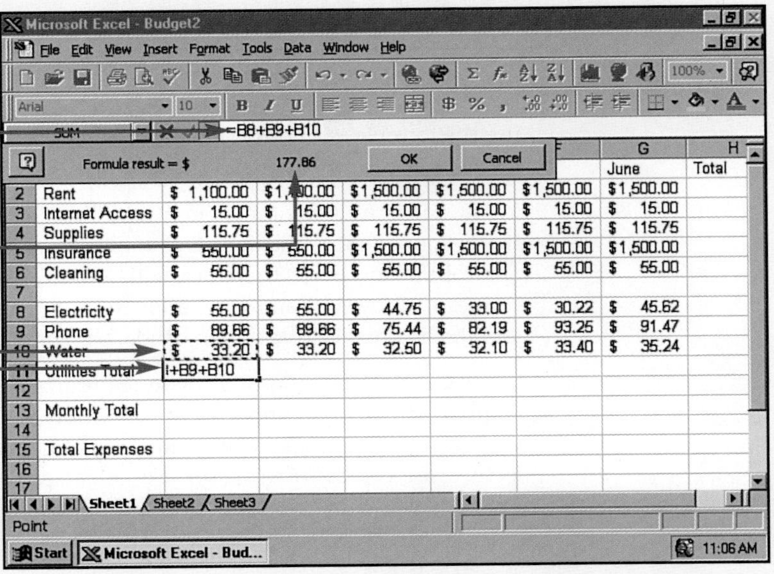

Figure 3.3
Click a cell to enter its address into the current formula.

4 Click OK in the Formula palette.

Excel enters the formula in cell B11 and displays the results in that cell. Now, try creating a formula to calculate the total of January's expenses by clicking the AutoSum button and selecting a range of cells.

5 Select cell B13 and click the AutoSum button on the Standard toolbar.

Clicking the AutoSum button automatically enters a formula that uses the SUM function to calculate the total of the cells above or to the left of the active cell. In this case, the formula =SUM(B8:B12) appears in cell B13 and in the formula bar. SUM is the function; the address of the range to be added appears selected within the parentheses (see Figure 3.4). However, to correctly calculate January's expenses, you must add the values in cells B2:B10. Before you enter the formula into the active cell, change the range in the formula so that it includes cells B2:B10.

6 Click cell B2, drag down to cell B10, and then release the mouse button.

Dragging across the cells selects them; they replace the range previously entered in the formula.

Figure 3.4
Use the AutoSum button to quickly create a formula for adding values in the cells above or to the left of the selected cell.

Formula ——
Currently selected range ——
AutoSum button ——

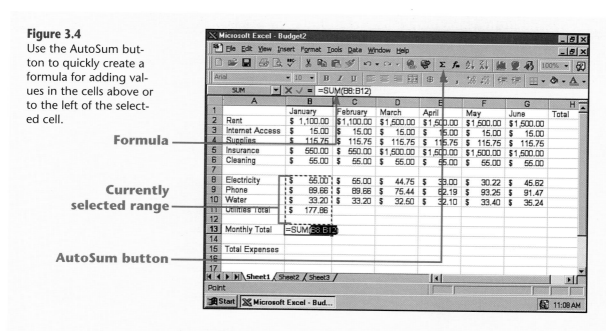

✅ **❼ Click the Enter button on the Formula bar.**

The values in cells B2 to B10 are totaled, and the result, $2,013.61, appears in cell B13 (see Figure 3.5). Now use AutoSum to enter a formula totaling all the rent expenses in the worksheet.

Figure 3.5
You can quickly build a formula by selecting a range of cells.

Formula ——
Result ——

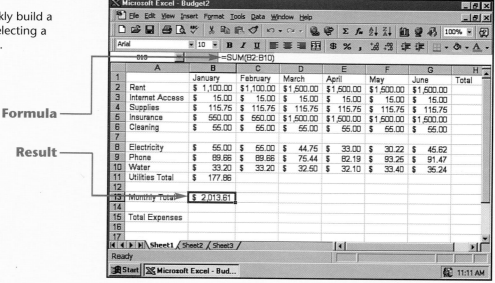

Σ **❽ Select cell H2 and click the AutoSum button on the Standard toolbar.**

This time, clicking the AutoSum button totals the cells to the left of the cell you selected. The formula =SUM(B2:G2) appears in the formula bar. This formula is correct for totaling all rent expenses.

continues

To Create Formulas by Selecting Cells   (continued)

⑨ Click the Enter button on the formula bar.

Excel enters the formula and displays the result, $8,200, in cell H2, as shown in Figure 3.6.

⑩ Save your changes and leave the Budget2 **worksheet open.**

You learn to copy formulas in the next lesson.

Figure 3.6
The result of the formula in the formula bar appears in cell H2.

Formula ——

Result ——

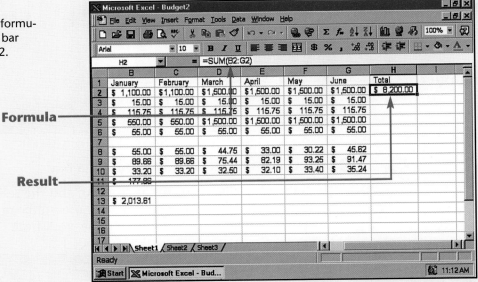

Range Finder
A feature of Excel that helps you locate cells referenced in a formula by color coding them. The range in the formula is highlighted in the same color as the range in the worksheet.

You can revise formulas by changing the cell addresses in a few different ways. You can simply click in the formula bar to position the insertion point where you want to make a change and then delete the incorrect characters and type the correct ones.

When you click in the formula bar to edit a formula, Excel starts the *Range Finder*. You can use the Range Finder to replace cell addresses in the formula. When the Range Finder is active, Excel displays each cell address or range in the formula in a different color and highlights the actual cells in the worksheet in corresponding colors.

To change an address in the formula, drag the corresponding colored cell border to the correct address in the worksheet. To add or remove cells from a range, drag the handle on the lower-right corner of the colored border to include more or fewer cells. When you finish making changes, click the Enter button on the Formula Bar. You can also start the Range Finder by double-clicking the cell that contains the formula you want to change.

You will find more information on editing formulas in Lesson 5, "Revising Formulas."

Lesson 3: Copying Formulas

After you create a formula, you can copy it to other cells or worksheets to help speed up your work. You copy formulas in Excel using the same techniques you used in Project 2 to copy cells and data.

When you copy a formula from one cell to another, Excel automatically changes the formula so that it is *relative* to its new location. That means that it changes the cell addresses in the formula, thus making it correct in the new location. For example, if you copy a formula that adds the contents of cells A1:A9 from cell A10 to cell B10, Excel automatically changes the formula to add the contents of cells B1:B9.

Now copy formulas in the Budget2 worksheet.

To Copy Formulas

1 Select cell C5 in the Budget2 worksheet.

Cell C5 contains the formula =C2*0.5, which is the formula you want to copy to the rest of the cells in the Insurance row.

2 With the mouse pointer in cell C5, click the right mouse button.

A shortcut menu appears, which you can use to copy the formula.

3 Click the Copy command on the shortcut menu.

The shortcut menu disappears and the formula is copied to the Clipboard. Remember, you are copying the formula, not the value in the cell.

4 Select cells D5 through G5.

This is the range where you want to paste the copied formula.

5 Move the mouse pointer to the active cell (D5), right-click to open the shortcut menu, and then choose the Paste command.

Excel pastes the copied formula into the selected cells, as shown in Figure 3.7. Again, make sure that you move the mouse pointer to the active cell before you issue the Paste command. Notice that the formulas copied into each cell are *relative* to the new cells. For example, the formula in D5, =D2*0.5, refers to rent information for the month of March rather than the month of February. Because there was an increase in rent in March, there is also an increase in the insurance expense for March. The results of the new formulas are displayed in each cell.

Now copy the formula for the Utilities total for the rest of the months using buttons on the Standard toolbar.

continues

To Copy Formulas   (continued)

Figure 3.7
The formula calculates the Insurance amount and enters the result in the correct cells.

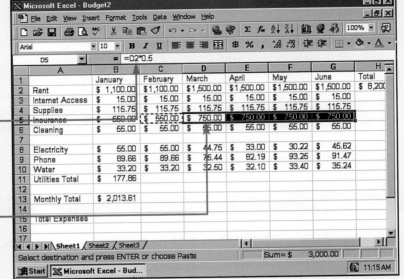

Pasted formula becomes relative to the new location

Active cell

If you have problems...

The flashing dotted line remains around the cell you copied to the Clipboard until you copy or cut another selection. You can continue working as usual, but if you find the flashing dotted line distracting, simply press Esc to cancel it.

 6 **Select cell B11 and click the Copy button on the Standard toolbar.**

You can use the toolbar buttons or menu commands to copy and paste formulas the same way you copy text or numbers.

7 **Select cells C11 through G11.**

You want to paste the formula into these cells.

 8 **Click the Paste button on the toolbar.**

Excel copies the formula to add the Utilities total in each month to the cells you selected. Again, notice that the cell references in the formulas refer to the appropriate month in each case.

Now use the fill handle to copy the formula calculating the totals for each expense category.

9 **Select cell H2 and move the mouse pointer to the lower-right corner of the cell so that the pointer changes to a thin black plus sign.**

You can use the fill handle to copy the contents of a cell to other cells, just as you used it to fill a range with a series of data in Project 2. You may have to scroll the worksheet to see all of column H.

10 **Click the left mouse button and drag down to select cells H3 to H11.**

This selects the range you want to fill. When you release the mouse button in cell H11, Excel fills the range with the formula and displays the results of the formula in each cell. Again, the formulas are relative to their locations. Finally, copy and paste the formula to calculate the monthly totals.

⓫ Select cell B13 and drag the fill handle right to cell H13.

Excel copies the formula from cell B13 to the other cells in the row. The results appear, as shown in Figure 3.8. Since you don't need the formula in cell H7, delete it now.

⓬ Click cell H7 to make it active, press Del, and press ↵Enter.

Excel deletes the contents of the cell.

⓭ Save your changes to the Budget worksheet.

In the next lesson, you learn how to use absolute cell references in a formula.

Figure 3.8
You can quickly fill in a worksheet by copying formulas.

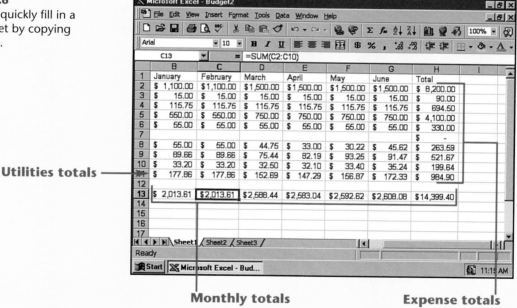

Utilities totals

Monthly totals   Expense totals

Lesson 4: Using Absolute Cell References

As you learned in Lesson 3, when you copy a formula, Excel assumes that the formula is relative. If, for example, you copy the formula =SUM(A2:A9) from cell A10 to cell B10, the formula automatically changes to =SUM(B2:B9). No matter where you copy the formula, it updates to reflect the cells that are relative to it.

However, if you want to copy a formula to another cell and have it return exactly the same result as in the original location, you must specify *absolute* cell references. To do so, add a dollar sign ($) before the values specifying the cell address. In other words, you insert a dollar sign before each column and row indicator in the formula. For example, to copy =SUM(A2:A9) and make sure that the resulting value is the same no matter where in the worksheet the formula is pasted, change the formula to =SUM($A$2:$A$9).

In this lesson, you create a formula that uses absolute cell references so you can copy the formula to a different location in the worksheet and obtain the same result.

To Use Absolute Cell References

❶ In the Budget2 **worksheet, click cell H13 and then the Copy button on the Standard toolbar.**

This copies the formula in H13 to the Clipboard. This formula calculates the total expenses for the six month period included in the worksheet by adding each expense total. You would like to display this total in cell B15 as well. First, see what happens when you copy and paste the relative formula.

❷ Click cell B15 and then the Paste button on the Standard toolbar.

Excel pastes the formula into cell B15 and displays the results, as shown in Figure 3.9. Notice that the result is not the same as in cell H13 because Excel has automatically changed the cell references in the formula so they are relative to the new location.

Figure 3.9.
When you copy and paste a relative formula, the result may not be the value you want.

Copied formula ——
Original result ——
Active cell ——

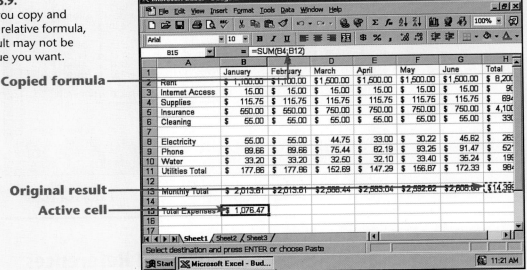

❸ Press Del **to delete the formula from cell B15 and select cell H13 again.**

To be sure that Excel returns the actual total of all expenses, you must make the cell references in the formula absolute.

❹ Click in the Formula bar and position the insertion point between the open parentheses and the first column letter H.

This places the insertion point in the formula where you want to make a change. You want to insert a $ in front of each column and row reference in the formula (see the following Exam Note for information on Relative Cell References). When you click in the formula bar, Excel assumes you want to change the cell addresses in the formula, so it activates the Range Finder. You can ignore the Range Finder; Excel will close it automatically.

Figure 3.10
Dollar signs in a formula tell Excel to use absolute cell references.

Formula with absolute cell references

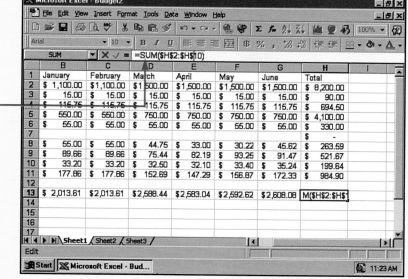

❺ Type $ and press →; type $ and press → twice; type $ and press →; type $.

You should now have a dollar sign in front of each column and row reference in the formula, as shown in Figure 3.10.

 ❻ Click the Enter button on the formula bar.

Excel enters the new formula in cell H13. The result of the formula is the same. Now see what happens when you copy and paste the formula with absolute cell references.

  ❼ With cell H13 still selected, click the Copy button on the Standard toolbar, select cell B15, and then click the Paste button on the Standard toolbar.

Excel copies the formula exactly as it appears in cell H13 into cell B15 and displays the result, as shown in Figure 3.11.

❽ Save your changes to the Budget worksheet.

In the next lesson, you learn how to revise formulas.

continues

To Use Absolute Cell References   (continued)

Figure 3.11
Formulas with absolute cell references return the same results regardless of their location in a worksheet.

Formula ———

Result ———

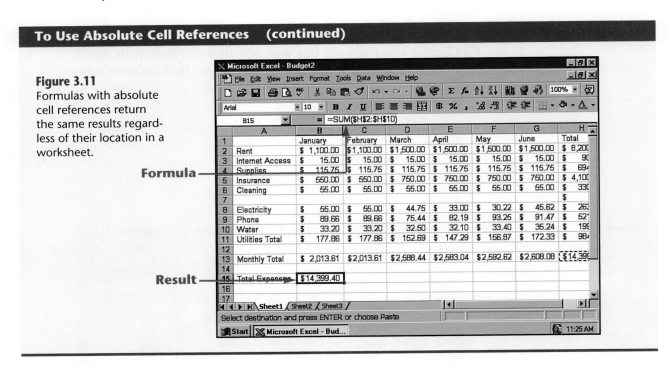

The placement of the dollar signs determines which references stay constant, or absolute, and which references do not. A mixed reference is only partially absolute, such as A\$2 or \$A2. When a formula that uses a mixed reference is copied to another cell, part of the cell reference (the relative part) is adjusted. For example, if a formula in B3 is \$B1*5 and you copy it to C5, the new formula will be \$B3*5. Because the dollar sign precedes the column letter, that letter is absolute and stays constant when the formula is copied. But the row does not have a dollar sign before it, so it is relative and changes when it's copied to another row.

Lesson 5: Revising Formulas

You must be careful when writing formulas to include the correct cell references, have your parentheses in the correct place (and paired), and use the correct mathematical operators. If your formula doesn't work, you must correct it. Revising a formula is similar to editing text and numbers in your worksheet.

In this exercise, you insert a column for the month of July, which means you must adjust the formulas for the expense totals.

To Revise a Formula

1 Click H1 in the Budget **worksheet and choose** **I**nsert, **C**olumns.

A new column appears between the column for June and the Total column. This new column is for the July expenses.

2 Type July **in H1 and press** ↵Enter.

For the purposes of this exercise, you can assume that the expenses for July are the same as those for June. You need to copy the data for June into the July column. You should also copy the formula that totals the column.

3 Select the range G2:G13, click the Copy button on the Standard toolbar, click H2, and then click the Paste button.

The totals in column I don't change even when you put the new data in the July column. When you click I2, you'll see that the formula still reads =SUM(B2:G2). To be correct, the formula needs to be changed to =SUM(B2:H2).

4 Double-click I2.

Double-clicking the cell where the formula is puts the cell in edit mode (you could also have clicked in I2 and then pressed F2 or clicked in the formula bar). The formula appears in the cell, as does an insertion point, and the range cited in the formula is marked by a special outline (see Figure 3.12).

Figure 3.12
The range cited in the formula is marked with a special outline.

Marked range ——

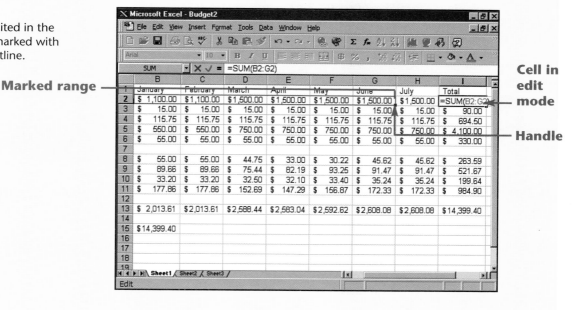

Cell in edit mode

Handle

5 Point at the small box (handle) at the lower-right corner of the marked range.

When you point at the handle, the cell pointer changes to a thin plus sign.

continues

To Revise a Formula (continued)

6 Drag the handle to the right until the range includes H2.

As you drag, the range increases to include H2. After you release the mouse button, the formula in I2 reads `=SUM(B2:H2)`.

Instead of dragging to establish a new range, you could delete or enter new formula information in the cell or the formula bar.

7 Press ⏎Enter or click the Enter button.

Excel accepts the modified formula. Now you need to copy that formula to cells I3 through I11. You don't need to change the formula in I13 because it totals I2 through I10 instead of totaling across (you might note, however, that when you added a column, the absolute addresses changed to move over one column).

8 Click I2, drag the handle on the lower-right corner down to include I11, and then release the mouse button.

After you release the mouse button, the formulas in cells I3 through I11 include the data in the July column.

9 Save the worksheet.

You have now completed the lessons on creating basic formulas. Save the changes you have made to the Budget2 worksheet. If requested by your instructor, print two copies and close the `Budget2` file. If you have completed your session on the computer, exit Excel and Windows 95. Otherwise, continue with the "Checking Your Skills" and "Applying Your Skills" section at the end of this project.

Project Summary

To	Do This
Enter a formula.	Type an equal sign (=) and then the formula.
Open the Formula palette.	Click the Edit Formula button on the Formula palette.
Automatically total a row or column of cells.	Click the AutoSum button on the Standard toolbar.
Copy a formula.	Select the cell containing the formula, click the Copy button, select the cell where you want to paste the formula, and click the Paste button.
Use absolute cell reference.	Type a dollar sign in front of the row number and column letter in the cell address in the formula.

To	Do This
Edit a formula.	Double-click the cell that contains the formula and then make any necessary changes.

Checking Your Skills

True or False

For each of the following, check *T* or *F* to indicate whether the statement is true or false.

__T __F **1.** Excel can only use mathematical operators for addition and subtraction.

__T __F **2.** Excel automatically updates the result of a formula when you change a value referenced in the formula.

__T __F **3.** To make a cell address absolute, you must type a dollar sign before each row and column reference in the formula.

__T __F **4.** You can use the fill handle to copy a formula from one cell to an adjacent cell.

__T __F **5.** You can only reference one cell address in each formula.

__T __F **6.** A mixed cell reference is a reference that is only partially absolute.

__T __F **7.** By default, when you copy a formula, it is relative to its new location.

__T __F **8.** If a formula is relative to its new location, this means that the cell address does not change when you copy it to a new location.

__T __F **9.** An advantage to using the Formula palette is that you can see the result of the formula as you create it.

__T __F **10.** When you click in the formula bar to edit a formula, Excel starts the Range Finder.

Multiple Choice

Circle the letter of the correct answer for each of the following questions.

1. Which of the following is a valid formula?

    a. B3+B4+B5

    b. (B3+B4+B5)

    c. =B3+B4+B5

    d. $B$3+$B$4+$B$5

2. Which of the following cannot be used to copy a formula?

    a. the Copy button on the Standard toolbar

    b. the Edit, Copy command

    c. the fill handle

    d. the Range Finder

3. Which of the following is a valid mathematical operator?

    a. ^ (caret)

    b. @ (at sign)

    c. $ (dollar sign)

    d. ? (question mark)

4. What appears in the active cell where you enter a formula?

    a. the formula

    b. the result of the formula

    c. the cell address

    d. an equal sign

5. What function is used to add the values in a range of cells?

    a. ADD

    b. PLUS

    c. SUM

    d. TOTAL

6. Which of the following actions *does not* put the cell in Edit mode so you can revise a formula?

    a. right-clicking the cell

    b. pressing

    c. double-clicking the cell

    d. clicking the formula bar

7. If you do not use parentheses in a formula, which type of calculation takes precedence?

    a. exponential calculations

    b. multiplication

    c. division

    d. addition

8. What is the operator for multiplication?

    a. caret

    b. asterisk

    c. forward slash

    d. backward slash

9. What is the resulting function when you copy the function =SUM(C2:C10) from cell C12 to cell E12?

    a. =SUM(C2:C10)

    b. =SUM(D2:D10)

    c. =SUM(E2:E10)

    d. =SUM(D4:E12)

10. When you copy the formula =$C$2+$C3 from cell C4 to cell D5, what is the resulting formula?

    a. =$D$1+$D$2

    b. =$D$2+$D$3

    c. =$C$1+$C2

    d. =$C$2+$C4

Completion

In the blank provided, write the correct answer for each of the following statements.

1. Type a dollar sign in front of a cell address to make the reference _____.

2. Click the Edit Formula button on the Formula bar to open the _____ _____.

3. Every formula must start with an _____ sign.

4. To quickly create a formula to total a row or column of numbers, click the _____ button.

5. To make sure Excel performs one calculation before another in a formula, enclose the first calculation in _____.

6. To find out the result of a calculation without actually entering a formula, use the _____ feature.

7. Clicking the _____ button automatically enters a formula that uses the SUM function to calculate the total of the cells above or to the left of the active cell.

8. To remove the flashing dotted line around the cell you copied to the Clipboard, press _____.

9. When you click the Edit Formula button, Excel inserts a _____ into the formula bar and opens the Formula palette.

10. A cell address that contains both an absolute reference and a relative reference (such as $C2) is called a _____ reference.

Matching

In the blank next to each of the following terms or phrases, write the letter of the corresponding term or phrase.

a. relative

b. Range Finder

c. addition and subtraction

d. absolute

e. formula

f. multiplication and division

g. ^ (caret)

h. exponential calculations

i. function

j. / (forward slash)

_____ 1. A built-in formula that automatically performs calculations

_____ 2. A calculation to Excel performs on data entered in a worksheet

_____ 3. The mathematical operator for division

_____ 4. The mathematical operator for exponents

_____ 5. Helps you locate cells referenced in a formula by color coding them

_____ 6. A formula that is updated to reflect its new location

_____ 7. A formula that remains exactly the same, no matter where it is copied in the worksheet

_____ 8. The first calculation performed in a formula

_____ 9. The second calculation performed in a formula

_____ 10. The third calculation performed in a formula

Applying Your Skills

Practice

The following exercises enable you to practice the skills you have learned in this project. Take a few minutes to work through these exercises now.

Calculating Weekly Salaries

You want to enter a formula to calculate the weekly salaries in the Job List worksheet.

To calculate weekly salaries, follow these steps:

1. Open the file Proj0302 from the Project-03 folder on the CD and save it as Job List 3.

2. Insert a blank column to the left of column D.

3. Label the column Weekly Rate.

4. Enter a formula into cell D3 to calculate the weekly rate Gary Edwards earns by dividing his salary by 52.

5. Copy the formula in cell D3 to D4:D6.

6. Use the AutoSum button to total the Salary and Weekly Rate columns.

7. Save the worksheet, and leave it open for the following exercise.

Revising the Weekly Rate Formula

Instead of displaying the employees' weekly rates, you decide the monthly rate would be more useful. Revise the formula to display the monthly rate.

To revise the weekly rate formula, follow these steps:

1. Select cell D3 in the Job List 3 worksheet.

2. Double-click in the cell to change to Edit mode.

3. Change the formula to divide by 12 instead of 52.

4. Copy the revised formula in D3 to cells D4:D6.

5. Change the heading in column D to Monthly Rate.

6. Save the worksheet and leave it open for the following exercise.

Calculating Health Insurance Expenses

Health insurance costs are billed to each employee as a percentage of their salary. Because the percentage can change depending on insurance costs for that year, you want to enter the percentage into a cell and then reference this cell when you enter the formula.

To calculate health insurance expenses, follow these steps:

1. Insert a column to the left of column E in the Job List 3 worksheet.

2. Type the heading Monthly Insurance Premium.

3. In cell A13, type Insurance Percentage.

4. In cell B13, enter .025.

5. Select cell E3 and then type a formula to calculate the insurance costs. It should be the monthly rate multiplied by the insurance percentage costs. Use an absolute cell address when multiplying the insurance percentage.

6. Copy this formula down to E4:E6. If the formula was entered correctly, the reference to cell B13 should not change when the formula is copied.

7. Enter the SUM function into cell E7 to calculate the total insurance premiums.

8. Save the file. If requested by your instructor, print two copies of the worksheet and then close it.

Estimating Attendance

Now that you are familiar with Excel formulas, you can make use of them to estimate how many people will attend the monthly coffee tasting you hold at the shop.

To estimate attendance, follow these steps:

1. Open the file Proj0303 from the Project-03 folder on the CD and save it as Attendance.

2. Assuming that 3/4 of the number of invitees will actually attend a tasting, enter a formula in cell D3 to calculate the estimated number of attendees.

3. Copy the formula from cell D3 to cells D4:D8.

4. Use AutoSum to enter a formula calculating the total number of invitees and the total number of attendees.

5. Change the number of guests invited in October to 15 and in November to 20.

6. Save the changes to the worksheet. If requested by your instructor, print two copies of the worksheet, and leave it open for the following exercise.

Changing the Estimate Formula

You realize now that your 75 percent estimate for people attending the coffee tasting was unrealistic. A better estimate would be 60 percent. Edit the formula in the following exercise.

To change the estimate formula, follow these steps:

1. In the Attendance worksheet, change the formula in cell D3 to calculate 60% of the people invited in cell C3.

2. Copy this new formula from cell D3 to cells D4:D8.

3. Save the changes to the worksheet. If requested by your instructor, print two copies of the worksheet and then close it.

Challenge

The following challenges enable you to use your problem-solving skills. Take time to work through these exercises now.

Calculating Costs

Calculate the costs of ordering inventory for your coffee shop.

To calculate costs, follow these steps:

1. Open the file Proj0304 from the Project-03 folder on the CD and save it as March Orders.

2. In cell B7, create a formula that calculates the cost of ordering Arabica in March by multiplying the price per pound by the amount ordered.

3. Copy the formula to cells C7 and D7 to find the cost of ordering French Roast and Kona, respectively.

4. In cell B8, create a formula that calculates the total cost of ordering coffee in March.

5. Save your work. If requested by your instructor, print two copies. Close the March Orders file.

Calculating Salaries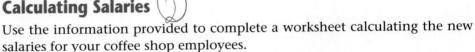

Use the information provided to complete a worksheet calculating the new salaries for your coffee shop employees.

To calculate salaries, follow these steps:

1. Open the file Proj0305 from the Project-03 folder on the CD and save it as Salary.

2. In cell D4, enter a formula that calculates the new salary for the buyer by multiplying the old salary by the percent of increase and then adding that total to the old salary.

3. Copy the formula from cell D4 to cells D5:D8.

4. In cell B10, use AutoSum to enter a formula to calculate the total of the old salaries.

5. Copy the formula from cell B10 into cell B11 and then edit the range in the formula so it calculates the total of the new salaries. (*Hint:* You can type the new range, select the new range, or use the Range Finder to change the range.)

6. In cell B13, enter a formula to calculate the increase in salary.

7. Save the changes to the worksheet. If requested by your instructor, print two copies of the worksheet. Then close it.

Calculating Advertising Costs

Use the worksheet provided to calculate the costs of advertising your coffee shop and to determine which type of advertisement generates the most effect in terms of revenue and which generates the most profit.

To calculate advertising costs, follow these steps:

1. Open the file Proj0306 from the Project-03 folder on the CD and save it as Ad Costs.

2. In cell F3, enter a formula to calculate the profit generated by the print ad by subtracting the cost from the effect.

3. Copy the formula from cell F3 to cells F4 and F5.

4. In cell B7, create a formula for totaling the cost of the three ads.

5. In cell B8, create a formula for totaling the effect of the three ads.

6. In cell B9, create a formula for totaling the profits generated by the three ads.

7. In cell G3, create a formula to calculate the print ad's percentage of the total effect.

8. Copy the formula from cell G3 to cells G4 and G5. Make sure that the copied formula references the correct cells.

9. In cell H3, create a formula to calculate the print ad's percentage of the total profit, using an absolute cell reference for cell B9, and then copy the formula from cell H3 to cells H4 and H5.

10. Save the changes to the worksheet. If requested by your instructor, print two copies of the worksheet and then close it.

Using a Formula to Calculate Sales Commission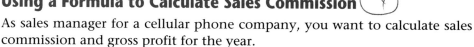

As sales manager for a cellular phone company, you want to calculate sales commission and gross profit for the year.

To use a formula to calculate sales commission, follow these steps:

1. Open the file Proj0307 from the Project-03 folder on the CD and save it as Profit Loss Statement.

2. In cell B7, enter the formula =B5*.025 to calculate sales commissions of 2.5% of the total sales.

3. Copy this formula to cells C7:D7.

4. Enter the formula =B5-B6-B7 into cell B9 to calculate the gross profit (sales minus expenses minus sales commission).

5. Copy this formula to cells C9:D9.

6. Save the workbook and leave it open for the following exercise.

Using an Absolute Cell Reference

You now need to calculate taxes due for the year by multiplying the tax rate by the gross profit.

To use an absolute cell reference, follow these steps:

1. In cell B11 of the Profit Loss Statement Worksheet, enter the formula =B9*$B$17. The address for B17 is absolute because the formula should always refer to this cell.

2. Copy this formula to C11:D11.

3. In cell B13, enter a formula to calculate the net profit. This formula should then be copied to cells C13:D13.

4. Save the changes to the worksheet. If requested by your instructor, print two copies of the worksheet and then close it.

PinPoint Assessment

You have completed the project and the associated lessons, as well as the Checking Your Skills and Applying Your Skills sections. Now use the PinPoint software evaluation mode to assess your comprehension of the specific exam tasks you have just learned. You can also use the PinPoint Trainer Mode and the Show Me tutorials to practice these specific exam tasks.

Project 4

Four

Calculating with Functions

Projecting Office Expenses

Objectives   **Required Activities**

In this Project, you learn how to

➤ Name Ranges   ... ...   Create and Name Ranges

➤ Use Named Ranges

➤ Print Ranges ... ...   Print the Screen and Ranges

➤ Clear and Format Ranges   ... ...   Clear and Format Ranges

➤ Copy and Move Ranges ... ...   Copy and Move Ranges

➤ Use Functions   ... ...   Use Worksheet Functions

➤ Build Formulas with Functions   ... ...   Use the AVERAGE, MIN, and MAX Functions

➤ Use Conditional Statements

Why Would I Do This?

I n Project 3, "Creating Formulas," you learned to devise formulas to calculate values in your worksheet and use cell addresses to refer to specific cells. You also learned how to use simple functions to help speed up your work with formulas. In this project, you expand your knowledge of formulas and functions so that you can easily perform more complex calculations. You learn to automate data input using such functions as TODAY (which inserts the current date in a worksheet). You also learn how to use conditional functions, such as IF, to provide different answers depending on the results of your calculations.

Another useful feature of Excel that can help you simplify the process of creating formulas is the range name. You can assign a descriptive name to a value or a formula in a single cell or a range of cells and then use the assigned name rather than the cell addresses when specifying cells that you want to use. You also learn how to print, clear, format, copy, and move ranges.

In this project, you use range names and functions to project the costs of rent, paper, and other supplies for your office for the coming months.

Lesson 1: Naming Ranges

When you create a worksheet and plan to use a cell or range of cells many times, you may want to name the range. For example, you can name the range containing the total income to make the income range easy to use in formulas. Rather than look up the address of the range, simply name the range income and use the range name in the formula in place of the range address. You can also use range names in other Excel commands and to move around the worksheet.

Range names can be up to 255 characters long, but you should keep them short so that you can easily remember them and have more room to enter the formula. Range names of up to 15 characters can be displayed in most scrolling list boxes. Additionally, observe the following rules when naming ranges:

- Both uppercase and lowercase letters can be used.

- Range names cannot contain spaces.

- Range names must begin with a letter or underscore.

- Any characters except math operators and hyphens can be used.

- Range names can contain numbers, but cannot start with a number.

Avoid combinations of letters and numbers that look like a cell address (such as a34) because that can be confusing. Choose names that describe the contents or the use of the range, such as expenses, income, and average.

Try naming ranges using the sample office expenses worksheet supplied for this project.

To Name Ranges

❶ From the Project-04 folder on the CD, open the file Proj0401. Save the file as Office.

❷ Click cell B3 and drag to cell C4 to select the range B3:C4.

This is the first range you want to name. (You learned the different methods for selecting cells and ranges in Project 2, "Building a Spreadsheet.")

❸ Open the Insert menu, move the mouse pointer to the Name command, and then choose Define from the submenu that appears.

The Define Name dialog box appears (see Figure 4.1). By default, Excel assumes that the label text from the row in which the active cell is located will be the range name and enters it in the Names in Workbook text box. The selected range address is entered in the Refers To text box, including the current worksheet name, Sheet1, and absolute references.

Figure 4.1
Use the Define Name dialog box to name ranges.

The range name appears here

You can enter a range address here

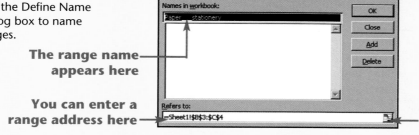

Click here to collapse dialog box

❹ Replace the default name Paper_stationery **(in the Names in Workbook text box) with** paper97.

This name describes the cells in the range, which includes all your paper expenses for 1997.

❺ Click OK.

The dialog box closes, and the selected range is now named paper97. Notice that the range name appears in the Name Box in the Formula bar because the range is still selected. Now name another range.

❻ Select cells F3 through G4 in the worksheet.

This selects the next range you want to name.

❼ Open the Insert menu, move the mouse pointer to the Name command, and then choose Define from the submenu that appears.

This opens the Define Name dialog box again. Notice that the paper97 range name now appears in the Names in Workbook list.

continues

To Name Ranges   (continued)

8 **In the Names in <u>W</u>orkbook text box, type** paper98 **and click the <u>A</u>dd button.**

The new range name appears in the Names in Workbook list. Now try naming a range without closing the Define Names dialog box.

9 **In the Define Name dialog box, click the Collapse button at the right end of the <u>R</u>efers To text box (refer to Figure 4.1).**

This collapses the dialog box so that you can select the range you want to name in the worksheet. Only the <u>R</u>efers To text box is still visible on the screen with the absolute reference to the current range entered: $F$3:$G$4. Now, select the new range you want to name.

10 **Select cells B5 through C6 in the worksheet.**

A flashing dotted line appears around the selected cells, and the <u>R</u>efers To text box displays the new range address, as shown in Figure 4.2. The flashing dotted line indicates the cells that you have selected to include in the named range. Cells F3:G4 are still selected and highlighted in the worksheet, and cell F3 is still the active cell.

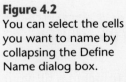
If you have problems...

If the collapsed dialog box covers the cells you want to select, simply drag it out of the way. To drag it, point at the title bar, press and hold the left mouse button, and drag. Release the mouse button when the box is where you want it.

Figure 4.2
You can select the cells you want to name by collapsing the Define Name dialog box.

New range address ⎯

Current cell ⎯

Selected cells for ⎯
the new range

Click here to expand ⎯
the dialog box

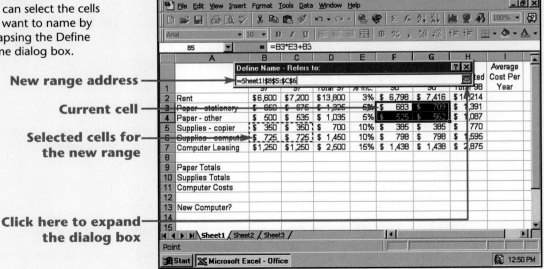

⑪ Click the expand button at the right end of the Refers To text box.

Excel expands the Define Name dialog box. The new range now appears in the Refers To text box, but you must still enter a name for the new range.

⑫ In the Names in Workbook text box, replace paper98 **with** supplies97, **and click Add.**

The supplies97 range includes all your expenses for supplies for 1997. Now name one more range.

⑬ Click the button to collapse the Define Name dialog box and select cells F5 through G6 in the worksheet.

⑭ Click the button to expand the Define Name dialog box, name the new range supplies98, **and click Add.**

You have now named four ranges that you can use later to build formulas and move around the worksheet. All four are listed in the Define Name dialog box.

⑮ Click OK to close the dialog box.

Click anywhere outside the selected cells to better see your worksheet.

⑯ Save your work and keep the Office worksheet open to use in the next lesson.

Exam Notes

To quickly name a range, select the range, type the name in the Name Box on the formula bar, and press ↵Enter. If you add or delete cells, rows, or columns to a named range, you may have to redefine the range to be sure it includes all of the cells you want.

You can delete the name of a range by choosing Insert, Name, Define to open the Define Name dialog box. Select the name in the Names in Workbook list, and click Delete. Click OK to close the dialog box. If you delete the definition of a named range in a cell with a formula that uses it, #NAME? appears in the cell. You must edit the formula to include the correct range, cell, or value so that the formula can compute the result. Alternatively, delete the formula.

Lesson 2: Using Named Ranges

You can use a named range in any formula to quickly and easily refer to a specific cell or range of cells. You can also use the Name Box in the formula bar to quickly move to and select a named range. Now practice using named ranges to move around the Office worksheet.

To Use Named Ranges

1 In the Office **worksheet, click the drop-down arrow to the right of the Name Box in the formula bar (see Figure 4.3).**

This displays a list of the named ranges that you created for this worksheet, as shown in Figure 4.3.

Figure 4.3
The Name Box lists the named ranges.

Name box ——▶

List of named ranges ——▶

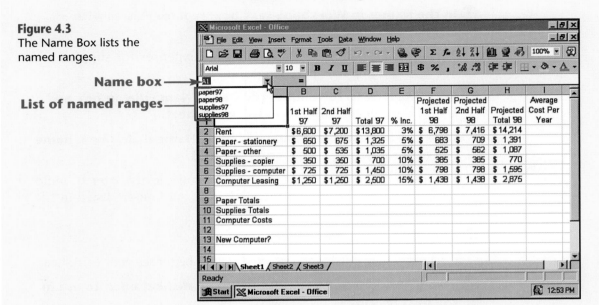

2 From the Name Box drop-down list, select paper98**.**

This selects the range paper98, as shown in Figure 4.4. You can now edit, copy, move, or otherwise modify the named range. This short-cut for moving to named ranges is especially useful when you create workbooks that contain multiple worksheets. Now try moving to another named range.

Figure 4.4
Selecting the name of the range in the Name Box list selects the entire range of cells.

Range name ——▶

Selected range ——▶

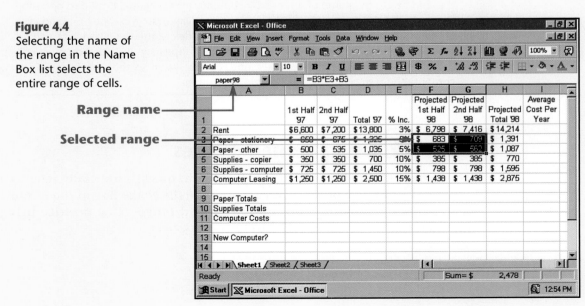

3 Click the Name Box drop-down arrow and select `supplies97`.

The `supplies97` range is now selected in the worksheet. Notice that the name of the range appears in the Name Box. You can also move to a named range by pressing F5 (Go To), selecting the range name, and then choosing OK.

Save your work and keep the Office worksheet open where you learn to print ranges.

To use a range in a formula, simply type the name in the formula in place of the range address. You learn more about using range names in formulas in Lesson 7.

Inside Stuff

In Excel, you can also name your worksheets and reference them in formulas. (As you learned in Project 1, "Getting Started with Excel," each Excel file is called a workbook, and each workbook is made up of one or more worksheets.) At the bottom of each worksheet is a sheet tab with the default sheet name on it. The first sheet is called `Sheet1`, the second sheet is called `Sheet2`, and so on. To view a different sheet, click its tab. To change a sheet name, double-click the sheet tab, type the new name, and press ↵Enter.

To reference a worksheet, type the worksheet name followed by an exclamation point and the cell address, range address, or range name. For example, if you have a workbook for a five-year forecast with each year's data on a different worksheet, you can reference the different worksheets to create formulas to total, average, or in other ways work with the data from each worksheet. You saw an example of this in the Refers To text box in the Define Name dialog box while you were naming ranges in Lesson 1.

If you have problems...

If you use a range name in a formula before you assign the name, Excel returns the error message #NAME?. Name the range first, and then you can use it in a formula.

If you receive an error message dialog box when using the named range in a formula, check for spaces, math operators, or numbers at the beginning of the name. If the name contains any of these, remove the offending characters and try your formula again. Before you can make changes, you must first respond to the dialog box; click OK to make changes to your name or choose Help to get online help from Excel.

Lesson 3: Printing Ranges

In Project 1, you learned how to print an entire worksheet. However, there are times when you only want to print a portion of the worksheet. There are two ways to do this—set a print area (or range) or name a range and select it before you print.

To Print a Range

① **Select the range of cells from A1 through I13.**

Selecting the range indicates the portion of the worksheet you want to print.

② **Choose File, Print Area and then select Set Print Area.**

When you click outside the selected range to turn the selection off, you see a dashed line border around the range you selected as your print range (see Figure 4.5).

Figure 4.5
After you set a print area, a dotted line border appears on the worksheet indicating the range.

Print area border

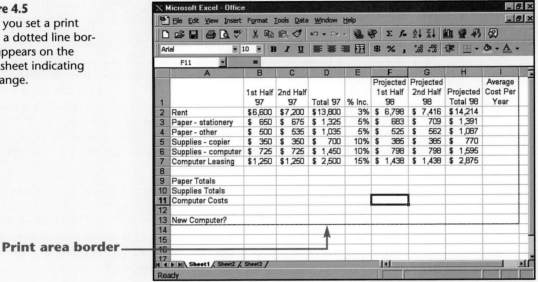

③ **Choose File, Page Setup and then click the Sheet tab.**

The print range you set automatically appears in the Print area box when you open the Page Setup dialog box (see Figure 4.6). You adjust the print area for a specific printing job by changing the range in that box.

Figure 4.6
The print area you set appears in the Print area box of the Page Setup dialog box.

Print area

Collapse Dialog button

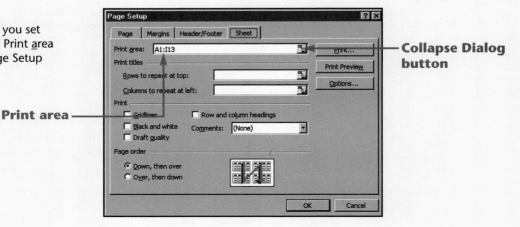

4 **Click the Collapse Dialog button at the right of the Print area box.**

The dialog box shrinks to only the title box and the Print area box. If the box blocks your view of the worksheet, drag it by its title bar to another location on the screen.

5 **Select the range A1:H7.**

The newly selected range has a flashing dotted line around it, and the Print area box text has changed to read $A$1:$H$7.

6 **Click the Expand Dialog button at the right of the Print area box.**

The entire Page Setup dialog box is now visible.

7 **Choose Print Preview to see how Excel would print the designated range.**

8 **Click Close.**

Now the new range is marked by the dashed line border.

9 **Choose File, Print Area, Clear Print Area.**

The dashed line border disappears.

10 **Select the range A2:H7 and choose Insert, Name, Define. Type print in the Names in workbook box and choose OK.**

By naming a range, you avoid having to select or set a print range. Then you can select the range and print the selection.

11 **Select print from the Name Box on the formula bar.**

The range is highlighted on the screen.

12 **Choose File, Print. Select Selection under Print what and then choose OK.**

Excel prints only the range you have selected.

13 **Save your file and leave it open for the next lesson.**

If you just want to print a range one time, you don't have to name the range. All you have to do is select the range of cells and choose File, Print. In the Print what area, click Selection. Then choose OK.

Lesson 4: Clear and Format Ranges

Once you're able to work with ranges, you can expand what you learned about a cell to a group of cells. For example, to delete the contents of a cell, you simply press Del. To delete the contents of a range, select the range and then press Del. Table 4.1 lists different ways to clear ranges or delete range contents.

Table 4.1 Clearing Ranges	
To	Do This
Delete the data from a range.	Select the range and press Del, or choose Edit, Clear, Contents.
Remove the range and all the data.	Select the range and choose Edit, Delete.
Clear the formatting from a range.	Select the range and choose Edit, Clear, Formats.
Clear cell contents, formatting, and comments from a range.	Select the range and choose Edit, Clear, All.

In this lesson, you learn some simple range formatting and then how to clear that formatting from the range.

To Format and Clear Ranges

❶ Select the range B1:I1.

❷ Click the Bold button on the Formatting toolbar.

The titles in that row all become boldface.

❸ Choose Edit, Clear, Formats.

This command removes any formatting applied to the range without deleting the data.

❹ Click A15 and type EXAMPLE. **Press** ↵Enter.

❺ Click A15 and click the Italic button on the Formatting toolbar.

The text in cell A15 becomes italic.

❻ Press Del.

The text in that cell disappears completely. You eliminated the contents, but if you had any formatting in that cell it would have remained. Check the Formatting toolbar and notice that the Italic button still looks depressed when A15 is active.

❼ Click A15 and type SAMPLE. **Press** ↵Enter.

SAMPLE appears in italic. The previous formatting applied to the cell remains.

❽ Click A15 and choose Edit, Clear, All.

The cell contents disappear, as does the formatting. The next character you enter in that cell will not appear in italic. When you check the Formatting toolbar, the Italic button is no longer depressed.

You learn more about formatting your worksheet in Project 5, "Improving the Appearance of a Worksheet."

❾ Save the file, but leave it open for the following lesson.

Lesson 5: Copy and Move Ranges

Copying and moving ranges is similar to working with a single cell. When you copy the range, the original stays in place and a duplicate is stored in the Clipboard. Cutting the range, on the other hand, removes it from the worksheet and places it in the Clipboard. Pasting places the item stored in the Clipboard back into the worksheet beginning at the active cell.

In this lesson, you practice copying and moving ranges within the worksheet.

To Copy and Move Ranges

1 **From the Name Box on the formula bar, select the** `print` **range.**

The `print` range is selected in the worksheet. You are going to copy that range to another location further down in the worksheet where you can manipulate the data without disturbing the original range.

2 **Click the Copy button on the Standard toolbar.**

This action stores a duplicate of the range in the Clipboard.

3 **Click A20 and then click the Paste button on the Standard toolbar.**

The contents of the Clipboard appear in the worksheet with the upper-left cell of the range displayed in the active cell A20.

4 **Select the range F20:G25 and press** `Del`.

The contents of the cells in the F20:G25 are removed. In this portion of the worksheet, the projects are for the total year of 1998, so first and second half projections aren't necessary.

5 **Select the range H20:I25, point to the border, and drag the range over to the vacant range of cells from F20 to G25.**

Because the cell references in the formulas in this range refer to data you deleted, you see `#REF` instead of a number in the F column.

6 **Click F20 and enter the formula** `=D20*E20+D20`.

This formula multiplies the 1997 total by the percentage increase and then adds that result to the 1997 total. That formula needs to be copied to the rest of the cells in the `Projected` column.

7 **Point to the handle on the lower-right corner of the active cell (F20) and drag down. Release the mouse button after you reach F25.**

If you have problems...

If you see ##### in the a cell instead of a number, the column isn't wide enough to hold the numbers. Choose Format, Column, AutoFit Selection to have the column automatically widen to accommodate the number.

continues

To Copy and Move Ranges (continued)

The formula has been copied to each of the cells. Because you no longer need this portion of the worksheet, delete the range from A20 to G26.

8 Select **A20:G25** and choose **E**dit, Cl**e**ar, **A**ll.

9 Save the file but leave it open for the next lesson.

Lesson 6: Using Functions

As you learned in Project 3, **functions** are shortened formulas that perform specific operations on a group of values. You have already used the SUM function to total columns and rows of numbers, so you know that SUM is the function to automatically add entries in a range. Excel provides hundreds of functions that fit into 10 categories to help you with tasks, such as determining loan payments and calculating interest on your savings. Table 4.2 describes some common functions used in Excel.

Table 4.2	Common Functions	
Function	Category	Description
AVERAGE	Statistical	Displays the average of a list of values.
AVERAGEA	Statistical	Displays the average of a list of arguments, including numbers, text, and logical values.
CELL	Information	Returns information about a cell or its contents.
DATE	Date & Time	Lists the date according to the computer's clock.
ERROR.TYPE	Information	Displays a number corresponding to one of Excel's error values. Used to debug macros and worksheets.
EVEN	Math & Trig	Rounds a value up to the nearest even integer.
MAX	Statistical	Finds the largest value in a list of numbers.
MAXA	Statistical	Finds the largest value in a list of arguments, including text, numbers, and logical values.
MIN	Statistical	Finds the smallest value in a list of numbers.
MINA	Statistical	Finds the smallest value in a list of arguments, including text, numbers, and logical values.
NOW	Date & Time	Calculates the current date and time on the computer's clock.

Function	Category	Description
ODD	Math & Trig	Rounds a value up to the nearest odd integer.
PMT	Financial	Calculates the periodic payment amount needed to repay a loan.
PRODUCT	Math & Trig	Calculates the product of a list of values by multiplying each value in turn.
ROUND	Math & Trig	Rounds a value to a specific number of decimal places.
SUM	Math & Trig	Adds a list of values.
TIME	Date & Time	Lists the time according to the computer's clock.
TODAY	Date & Time	Calculates the serial number for the current date and displays it in date format. It is used for date and time calculations.

You can enter functions into Excel formulas in many ways. If you know the name of the function you want to use, you can type it into the cell where you want the result to appear, or you can type it into the formula bar. You can also use the Formula palette or the Paste Function dialog box to select from a list of functions.

In this lesson, you learn to include functions in formulas using the different methods described above. You also learn how to include range names in formulas and how to use the TODAY function, which displays the current system date. Try using functions to build the Office worksheet now.

To Use Functions

❶ Click cell D2 in the Office worksheet.

Cell D2 already contains a formula that uses the SUM function to calculate the total rent for 1997. You can see the formula in the formula bar and the result of the formula in cell D2. Now, try using the TODAY function to enter today's date in a cell in the worksheet.

❷ Select cell A1 in the Office worksheet.

This is where you want the result of the formula—today's date—to appear. To create a formula using a function, you can type the formula in the cell or the formula bar.

❸ Type =today() **and click the Enter button (the green check mark) on the formula bar.**

This is the formula that uses the TODAY function to calculate today's date. Excel enters the system date in cell A1. Like all formulas, functions begin with an equal sign. You then type the function name in uppercase or lowercase letters without leaving any spaces. The

continues

To Use Functions   (continued)

Arguments
The values on which the function performs its calculations. An argument can be a single cell, a range of cells, or any value you enter.

function name is followed by the function *arguments*, which are enclosed in parentheses and separated by commas. With the TODAY function, you do not need to include any arguments. Now use the Formula palette to enter a function to find the total amount you will spend on paper in 1997.

❹ **Select cell D9 and click the Edit Formula button on the formula bar.**

Excel opens the Formula palette. With the Formula palette, you can select a function and enter the arguments you want to use.

❺ **Click the drop-down arrow to the right of the Function button.**

A list of functions appears, as shown in Figure 4.7. The most recently used functions appear at the top of the list. You can click More Functions to open the Paste Function dialog box and display additional functions.

Figure 4.7
In the Formula palette, you can select a function from the Function drop-down list.

Function button

Function list

Click here to display additional functions

Edit Formula button

Formula palette

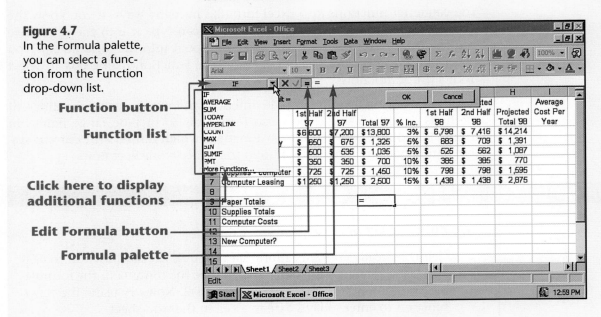

❻ **Select** SUM.

Excel inserts the SUM function into the formula and expands the Formula palette, as shown in Figure 4.8. In the expanded palette, you can enter arguments, read a description of the function, and preview the result of the formula. Excel guesses which cells you want to total and displays the range address in the Number 1 text box. In this case, however, it guesses wrong. To correct the formula, you must enter the correct arguments or range of cells that you want to total.

If you have problems...

If the SUM function does not appear in the drop-down list of functions, select More Functions to open the Paste Function dialog box. In the Function Category list, select All and then scroll down in the Function Name list and select SUM. Choose OK to enter the SUM function in the formula.

Figure 4.8
The Formula palette expands for the SUM function.

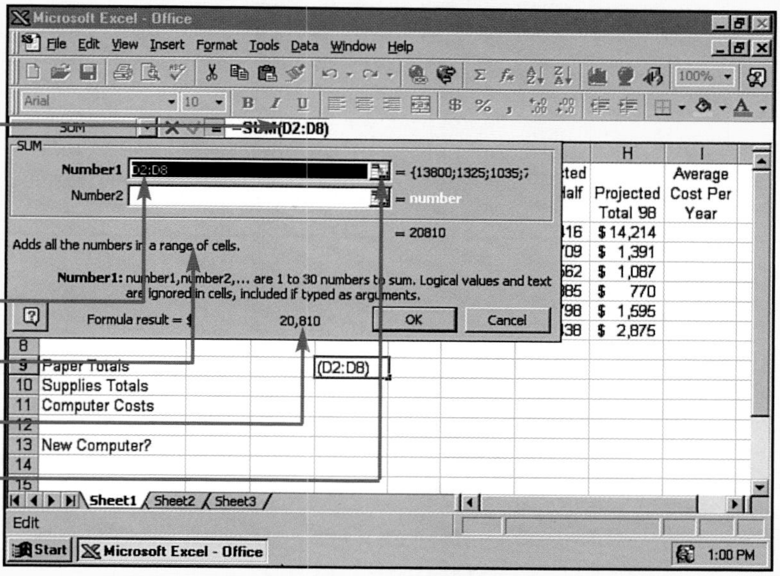

Arguments also appear within parentheses in the formula

Arguments appear here

Function description

Formula result

Click here to collapse the Formula palette

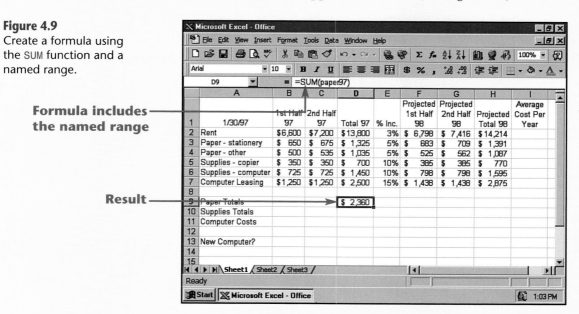

❼ In the Number 1 text box, type paper97 **and click OK.**

This enters the named range paper97 into the formula as the argument and tells Excel to calculate the total. The amount spent for paper in 1997 now appears in cell D9 (see Figure 4.9).

Figure 4.9
Create a formula using the SUM function and a named range.

Formula includes the named range

Result

continues

To Use Functions   (continued)

If you have problems...

If you enter a function with a mistake in it, Excel displays an error message in the cell, such as #NAME? or #VALUE?. If Excel thinks it knows the problem, it displays a message box asking if it is okay to go ahead and correct it. Choose <u>Y</u>es to have Excel automatically correct the formula, or <u>N</u>o to try to fix it on your own.

When troubleshooting formulas, first make sure that you used an existing named range and then check for typos in the range name. Study the formula and check the range name for invalid characters, such as punctuation marks and mathematical operators. The error message #NAME? appears if your range name contains any of these symbols. Remove the offending symbol or number and try again.

Now enter functions to total the rest of your paper and supply expenses for 1997 and 1998.

8 In cell D10, type =sum(supplies97) **and then press** Enter.

The sum showing the total spent for supplies in 1997 appears in the cell. You could also click the Enter button on the formula bar instead of pressing Enter.

Σ

9 Select cell H9 and then click the AutoSum button on the Standard toolbar.

The SUM function with the incorrect range as the argument appears in cell H9.

✓

10 In the worksheet, select cells F3:G4 and then click the Enter button on the formula bar.

This replaces the incorrect range in the formula with the correct range—paper98—and enters the formula. The projected total paper expenses for 1998 appears in cell H9. As you can see, there are many ways to enter functions and arguments into formulas in Excel. You can decide for yourself which is the easiest method or which is the most appropriate. Enter one more formula for totaling the expenses for supplies for 1998.

11 Select cell H10, click the Edit Formula button and then choose SUM **from the Function drop-down list.**

Excel opens the Formula palette with the wrong range entered as the argument. Try selecting the correct range to insert it into the formula.

12 Click the collapse button at the right end of the Number 1 text box (refer to Figure 4.8).

Excel collapses the Formula palette so you can select the cells you want to use in the worksheet. Only the Number 1 text box appears on the screen.

⑬ Select cells F5:G6 to enter the `supplies98` **range and then click the expand button at the right end of the Number 1 text box.**

Excel expands the Formula palette with the correct range entered in the formula.

If you have problems...

If the collapsed palette covers the column or row labels, you should still be able to select the correct range by counting the rows and columns or by referring to the numbers and letters that are visible. If the palette covers the range that you want to select, you must move it out of the way while it is full-size. To move or expand it, point anywhere within the palette area and click and drag to move it out of the way. When it is out of the way, try collapsing it and selecting the cells again.

---

⑭ Click OK in the Formula palette.

The projected total expense for supplies in 1998 appears in cell H10. Your worksheet should now look similar to the one shown in Figure 4.10.

⑮ Save your work and keep the Office worksheet open for the next lesson in which you create more complex formulas with functions.

Figure 4.10
Use functions to project the costs of paper and supplies for 1998.

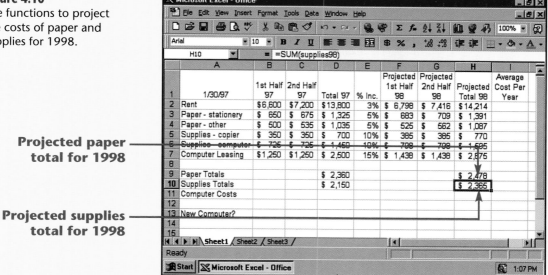

Projected paper total for 1998

Projected supplies total for 1998

If you have problems...

If you think a function that uses a range is not returning the correct answer, make sure that the range is entered correctly. Ensure that all cells you need are included and that no extra cells containing data are included.

Several differences exist between regular formulas and **functions**. One difference is that you can customize regular formulas more to your liking. You use functions as shortcuts to tell Excel how to calculate values.

As demonstrated in Project 3, entering a function, such as =SUM(B2:B9), is quicker and easier than entering its corresponding formula: =B2+B3+B4+B5+B6+B7+B8+B9. In a regular formula, you must specify every operation to be performed. That's why there are so many plus signs in the preceding formula. In a function, however-er, the operations are programmed in, so you need only supply the necessary information in the form of arguments. In the function =SUM(B2:B9), B2:B9 is the argument. Functions can include multiple arguments, as you learned in Lesson 4.

When you add arguments to a function, you must use the proper syntax, which is simply the exact and correct way to type commands and functions. In general, computer programs are inflexible about even one wrong keystroke, such as a missing comma.

If your formula returns an error message, use the Excel Help feature to find out more about the syntax for the specific function you are trying to use.

You can also use the Paste Function dialog box to select a function. Click the Paste Function button on the Standard toolbar to open the dialog box. It displays a list of functions grouped by category. Select the category and the function you want to use and then click OK. Excel inserts the function into the formula and opens the Formula palette, so you can enter the arguments you want to use.

Instead of typing a range into a function, you can use the mouse to select the range. For example, you can type =SUM(and then drag the mouse to select the range. Excel enters the range in the formula bar as you drag, as well as the closing parenthesis. End the function by pressing ↵Enter to calculate the formula.

Another way to enter the name of a range in a function or formula is to use the Paste Name dialog box. When you reach the place in the formula where you want to insert the named range, press F3. The Paste Name dialog box appears with a list of named ranges. Choose the name of the range from the Paste Name list box. Click OK to close the dialog box and then continue creating the formula.

Also, don't forget that you can quickly check the result of a calculation without actually entering the formula by using the AutoCalculate button on the status bar.

Lesson 7: Building Formulas with Functions

Functions are easy to use in building complex formulas. For example, you can add two SUM functions together (as you do in this lesson using the Office worksheet). You can also *nest* functions by using them as arguments for other functions.

Nest
To place one function within another.

This lesson shows you how to create complex formulas by combining and nesting functions.

To Build Formulas with Functions

1 In cell I2 of the Office worksheet, enter the formula `=average(b2+c2,f2+g2).`

This enters the formula and calculates the average cost of rent per year. When you use two arguments in a function, you separate them with a comma. Don't forget to click the Enter button on the formula bar.

Note that you can get the same result from the simple formula `=average(d2,h2).` In general, it's best to use the simplest formula possible in your worksheets. You are asked to build more complex formulas in this lesson to learn how functions can be used together. See the following Exam Note for other important functions.

If you have problems...

If the average doesn't appear to be correct, make sure that the ranges you used don't include any extra cells with values or labels. When using the AVERAGE function, be sure to use only the specific cells with the contents you want to average.

2 Select cell I2 again, click the right mouse button to open the shortcut menu and choose Copy.

This copies the formula in cell I2 to the Windows Clipboard.

3 Select cells I3 through I7, open the shortcut menu, and then choose Paste.

This copies the formula to cells I3 through I7 where the results are displayed, as shown in Figure 4.11. Because no decimal places are displayed, Excel rounds the totals to the nearest whole number; however, the actual value is used in all calculations. The formulas in the cells are relative. In Project 3, you learned that *relative* means that the formula conforms to its current address, no matter where it was first entered. In this example, the formula is always relative to the numbers in the cells to the left of the formula's current cell address.

4 In cell D11, enter the formula `=sum(b6:c6)+sum(b7:c7).`

This calculates the total computer costs for 1997 by adding the total costs of computer supplies and the total costs of computer leasing. You built the formula by combining two functions with the plus sign operator.

Once again, you are using more complex formulas than are necessary, so you can learn the different methods of entering functions. You can get the same result with the simple formula `=D6+D7,` which adds the total computer supplies and computer leasing expenses for the year.

Now use the Formula palette to enter a formula to calculate the total computer costs for 1998.

continues

To Build Formulas with Functions   (continued)

Figure 4.11
The function averages the values relative to its current cell address.

Formula ——
Result ——

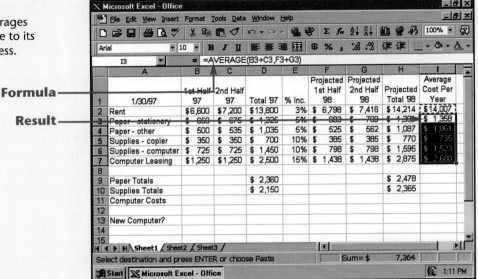

5 **Select cell H11, click the Edit Formula button, and choose the** SUM **function.**

Instead of combining two SUM functions to complete the formula, try using two arguments within one function.

6 **In the Number 1 text box, type the range** f6:g6 **and press** Tab⁺⁴**. Then, in the Number 2 text box, type the range** f7:g7 **and click OK.**

Excel sets up the formula by enclosing the arguments in parentheses and separating them with a comma. The projected total computer cost for 1998 appears in cell H11, as shown in Figure 4.12.

Figure 4.12
When you enter functions using the Formula palette, Excel automatically uses the correct syntax.

Formula ——
Result ——

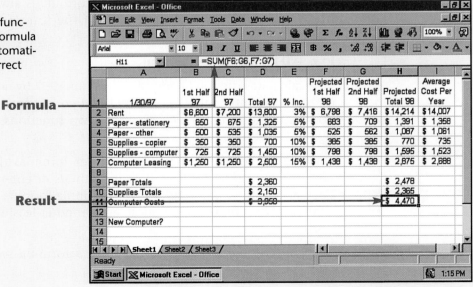

Now create a complex formula to calculate the average total computer cost per year. Use your choice of methods to enter the formula.

7 In cell I11, enter the formula =average(sum(b6:c7),sum(f6:g7)).

In this formula, the SUM functions are nested as arguments for the AVERAGE function. Excel calculates the sum of B6:C7 and the sum of F6:G7 and then finds the average of the two resulting values. By combining several functions, you have created a formula that calculates the average total computer cost per year, as shown in Figure 4.13. Note the placement of the parentheses, which specify the arguments that are used for each function.

Again, note that you can also achieve the same result with the simpler formula =AVERAGE(D11,H11), which adds the total costs for 1997 and 1998 and then finds the average of the two. Note also that D11 equals SUM(D6:D7) and that H11 equals SUM(H6:H7). In creating the more complex formula, you have simply replaced the SUM functions for cells D11 and H11.

Figure 4.13
You can nest formulas to perform several calculations at once.

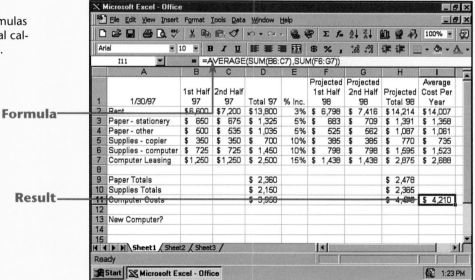

You have now created formulas to calculate all the information you need to track your office expenses.

8 Save your work and keep the Office worksheet open for the next lesson, where you use a function to tell you whether you would save money by purchasing a personal computer instead of leasing it.

Exam Notes

In addition to the AVERAGE function, there are two commonly used but important functions that determine the largest or smallest value in a set of values.

The **MIN** function returns the smallest value in a set of values. It is written as =MIN(number1,number2,…). For example, the formula =MIN(A1:A12) would return the smallest value in the cells A1 through A12.

The **MAX** function returns the largest value in a set of values. It is written as `=MAX(number1,number2,…)`. For example, the formula =MAX(B4:G4) returns the largest value in the cells B4 through G4.

If you have problems...

A common mistake in complex functions involves parentheses. Be sure that for every open parenthesis, there is a corresponding close parenthesis. All parentheses must be placed in the correct location to avoid a syntax error.

Another fairly common mistake is substituting a plus sign for the colon in a SUM formula. The formula `=SUM(D10:I10)` is much different than `=SUM(D10+I10)`. In the latter formula, only the first and last cells are added, whereas in the first formula, all cells from D10 to I10, including D10 and I10, are added.

If Excel responds with the error message. `#NAME?`, don't worry. Simply check your formula carefully to make sure that all parentheses are present and all addresses are correct. If you still can't find the problem, check the values and formulas in the referenced cells for typos. One typographical error can affect formulas in many parts of the worksheet if the formulas refer to the cell containing the error.

Inside Stuff

A colon between the cell addresses in a range argument (such as `F6:G7`) is simply the standard method that Excel uses to show the range. A comma is used to separate arguments in a function.

To nest one function within another using the Formula palette, simply make sure the insertion point is in the location where you want the nested function to appear in the formula and then select the function from the Function drop-down list. The insertion point can be in an argument text box in the Formula palette or in the formula bar. Excel will open the Formula palette for the nested function. When you have entered all of the arguments for the nested function, click in the formula bar to display the Formula palette for the original function.

Remember, when you paste a formula from one cell into another, each cell reference in the original formula is converted to a relative reference.

Lesson 8: Using Conditional Statements

Your Office worksheet now contains information and formulas that you need to track the cost of running an office over two years. Now look at how you can have the worksheet calculate whether you should purchase computer equipment instead of continuing to lease it.

Conditional statement
A function that returns different results depending on whether a specified condition is true or false.

Using *conditional statements,* you can implement different actions depending on whether a condition is true or false. The simplest conditional function in Excel is the IF function: if the condition is true, Excel displays one result; if the condition is false, Excel displays a different result.

Try using the IF function to see whether your computer costs are sufficiently high to warrant purchasing a personal computer.

To Use Conditional Statements

① Select cell B13 of the Office worksheet.

② Click the Paste Function button on the Standard toolbar.

The Paste Function dialog box opens.

③ Choose Logical in the Function Category list and then choose IF in the Function Name list.

Excel displays the function syntax—=IF(logical_test,value_if_true, value_if_false)—at the bottom of the dialog box, along with a description of the function (see Figure 4.14).

Figure 4.14
You can use the Paste Function dialog box to select a function to insert into a formula.

Selected function

Function syntax

Function description

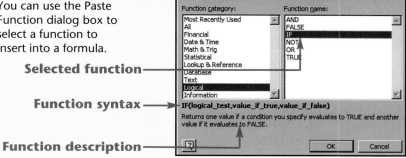

For this example, the logical test is whether or not your yearly computer costs are greater than $4,000. If they are, then it makes sense to purchase a computer. If they are not, then it makes sense to continue leasing.

④ Click OK.

Excel pastes the selected function into the formula and opens the Formula palette, so you can enter the arguments (see Figure 4.15).

⑤ In the Logical_Test text box, type I11>4000 and press Tab⇆.

This enters the logical test argument and moves the insertion point to the next text box. I11 refers to the cell where the average total computer costs are calculated, the > sign is the mathematical operator that means greater than, and 4000 is the value you want to use for comparison.

⑥ In the Value_if_true text box, type YES!, including the exclamation mark, and press Tab⇆.

This enters the value_if_true argument of the function. It tells Excel what value to display in the cell if the condition is true. In other words, if the total average cost per year is greater than $4,000, Excel will enter YES! in the current cell.

continues

To Use Conditional Statements   (continued)

Figure 4.15
The Formula palette can be used for creating a conditional formula with the IF function.

Logical test argument

Value if true argument

Value if false argument

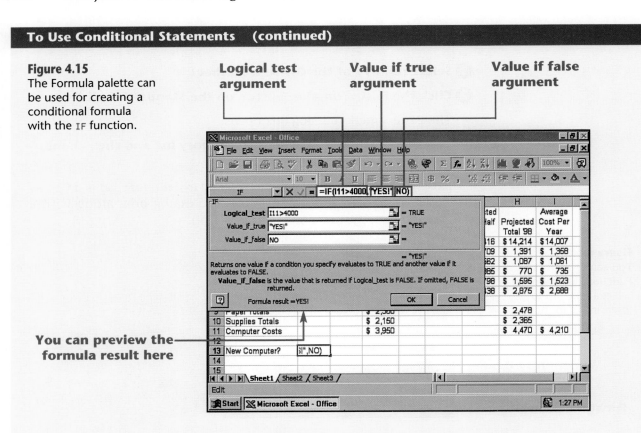

You can preview the formula result here

7 In the Value_if_false box, type NO.

This enters the `value_if_false` argument. It tells Excel the value to display if the condition is false—that is, if the value in cell I11 is less than $4,000. The Formula palette should now look like the one in Figure 4.15.

8 Click OK.

Excel performs the calculation, and the word YES! should now appear in cell B13, as shown in Figure 4.16. When you use the IF function, Excel tells you that you should purchase the computer based on the information currently in the worksheet. If the projected expenses were to decrease so that the average total was less than $4,000, Excel would return NO as the response.

Save your work. If requested by your instructor, print two copies and close the worksheet. If you have completed your session on the computer, exit Excel and Windows 95 before turning off the computer. Otherwise, continue with the "Applying Your Skills" section at the end of this project.

Figure 4.16
The result of the conditional statement is Yes!

Conditional statement formula

Result

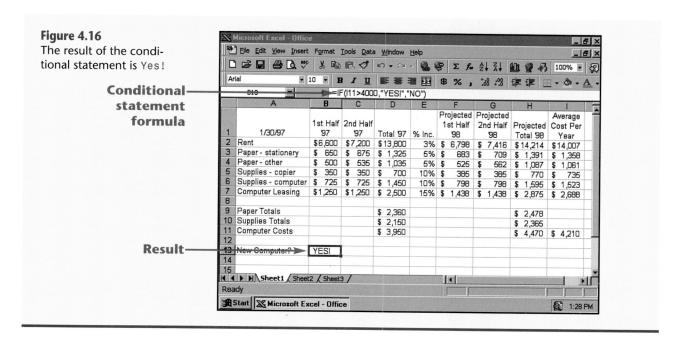

Conditional statements use many mathematical terms that can be confusing. In most cases, however, a conditional statement takes the form of a simple if/then sentence: if this happens, then that happens.

Conditional statements or arguments, such as the one in this lesson, typically use a **logical operator**. Logical operators include the following:

Operator	Meaning
=	Equal
<	Less than
>	Greater than
<=	Less than or equal to
>=	Greater than or equal to

Think of these operators simply as replacements for the words in the "Meaning" column above.

Project Summary

To	Do This
Name a range.	Select the range, choose Insert, Name, Define, type a name in the Names in Workbook text box, and click OK.

continues

To	Do This
Select a named range.	Click the drop-down arrow in the Name Box in the formula bar and choose the range name.
Print a range.	Select a range and choose File, Print Area, Set Print Area. Then print the worksheet as normal.
Clear a range.	Select the range and choose Edit, Clear. Choose Formats to clear just the formatting, Contents to clear just the contents, or All to clear the contents and formatting.
Copy a range.	Select the range and choose Edit, Copy. Click the cell where you want the duplicate range to go and choose Edit, Paste.
Move a range.	Select the range and choose Edit, Cut. Click the cell where you want the range to go and choose Edit, Paste.
Enter a function in a formula.	Type an equal sign followed by the function name and the arguments enclosed in parentheses (separated by commas). Or click the Paste Function button on the Standard toolbar, select the function, and then click OK. Or, open the Formula palette and select the function from the Function drop-down list. Complete the formula and then click OK.
Perform *what-if* analysis on data.	Use the logical IF function.

Checking Your Skills

True or False

For each of the following, check *T* or *F* to indicate whether the statement is true or false.

__T __F **1.** You can name a range, but not an individual cell.

__T __F **2.** Range names can consist of up to 255 characters.

__T __F **3.** If Excel displays the error message #NAME? when using a named range in a formula, check to make sure you have the equal sign in the name.

__T __F **4.** An IF function includes a condition and two arguments.

__T __F **5.** Use the CALENDAR function to display the current system date.

__T __F **6.** To print a certain area of a worksheet, use the Set Print Area option.

__T __F **7.** You can use both upper- and lowercase letters in a range name.

_T _F **8.** Range names must begin with a letter, underscore, or number.

_T _F **9.** You cannot use spaces in a function name.

_T _F **10.** You cannot delete the name of a defined range.

Multiple Choice

Circle the letter of the correct answer for each of the following.

1. _____ is a collection of cells that you can use in a formula.

    a. `B2...B2`

    b. `B2:G2`

    c. `B2:G2,B6`

    d. `B4+C4,C6`

2. Which of the following is a valid formula?

    a. `=AVERAGE(B2;C2;D4;G4)`

    b. `SUM(B2:B8)-AVG(D2:D4)`

    c. `=SUM(AVG(C3;C4),(AVG F6:F9`

    d. `=SUM:AVG(SUM,(C3:C9,SUM, (D3:D9))`

3. Which of the following is a valid range name?

    a. `tuitionandfees96`

    b. `tuition 1996`

    c. `tuition+fees`

    d. `96tuitionandfees`

4. When using the IF conditional statement, you can _____.

    a. Set a condition and get one answer if the condition is true and a second answer if the condition is false

    b. Set one condition and one argument to analyze a formula

    c. Enter a condition that performs a calculation on a formula

    d. List between two and six arguments that apply to the IF condition

5. Which of the following could cause the error message #NAME? to be returned as a result?

    a. Using too many functions

    b. Using a nonexistent range name

    c. Using too many parentheses

    d. Using the wrong symbols for operators

6. To delete only data from a range of cells, _____.

    a. Press Del

    b. Choose Edit, Clear, Contents

    c. Choose Edit, Delete

    d. a or b

7. The command used to name a range is located on which menu?

    a. Edit

    b. Insert

    c. Format

    d. Tools

8. To calculate a loan payment, you use which function?

    a. PMT

    b. MAX

    c. MIN

    d. SUM

9. Which cells are totaled in the function =SUM(D10:I10)?

    a. Cell D10 and cell I10

    b. All cells between D10 through I10

    c. All the cells from D10 and I10

    d. None of the above

10. An argument in a function can be which of the following?

    a. A single cell

    b. A range of cells

    c. Any entered value

    d. All of the above

Completion

In the blank provided, write the correct answer for each of the following statements.

1. The _____ in the formula bar lists named ranges.

2. When you use a named range in a formula before you assign the name, Excel returns a _____ in the cell.

3. You can combine or _____ functions within a formula so that you can perform complex calculations at one time.

4. The _____ is always placed within parentheses to indicate which data the function will use to perform its calculation.

5. Click the _____ button on the Standard toolbar to select a function.

6. If you cut a range of cells from a worksheet, the cells are removed and placed on the _____.

7. Functions must begin with a _____.

8. When you use two arguments in a function, separate them with a _____.

9. To use the Paste Name dialog box to insert the name of a range in a function or formula, press _____.

10. To change the name of a worksheet, _____ the sheet tab and then type the new name.

a. >=

b. range name

c. MIN

d. conditional statement

e. parentheses

f. <=

g. MAX

h. nest

I. arguments

j. syntax

Matching

_____ 1. The exact and correct way to type commands and functions

_____ 2. The values on which the function performs its calculations

_____ 3. To place one function within another

_____ 4. A function that returns different results depending on whether a specified condition is true or false

_____ 5. Greater than or equal to

_____ 6. Less than or equal to

_____ 7. A name given to a cell or range of cells

8. Function arguments are enclosed in these

_____

9. Function that finds the largest value in a list of numbers

_____

10. Function that finds the smallest value in a list of numbers

_____

Applying Your Skills

Practice

The following exercises enable you to practice the skills you have learned in this project. Take a few minutes to work through these exercises now.

Create and Use Ranges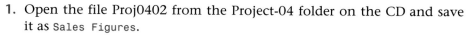

As the owner and business manager of a small coffee shop, you need to evaluate the performance of the merchandise you stock in your store. You want to know if you are buying the right mix of coffees to satisfy your customers.

You have created a worksheet that totals the sales for the first quarter for each type of coffee. Since you plan to use this data in multiple calculations, you decide it would be helpful to use named ranges in the worksheet.

To create and use ranges, follow these steps:

1. Open the file Proj0402 from the Project-04 folder on the CD and save it as `Sales Figures`.

2. Use the Insert, Name, Define command to name the range B4:B10 `January`.

3. Name the `February` and `March` columns also.

4. Use the Name Box drop-down list to select the `January` range.

5. Use the `F5` key to select the `March` range.

6. Save the file, and leave it open for the following exercise.

Printing Ranges

If you do not want to print the entire worksheet, you can print a set area or a named range. In this exercise, you practice doing both.

To print ranges, follow these steps:

1. From the `Sales Figures` file, you want a copy of the worksheet with only the January sales data. To print only this information, select the range of cells from A3:B10.

2. Set this as the print area.

3. Open the Page Setup dialog box and click the Sheet tab.

4. Make sure that the correct range displays in the Print area box and then click the Print button to print this area of the worksheet.

5. Clear the print area.

6. Now you decide to use the range names to print only the numbers for March. Select March from the Name Box on the formula bar.

7. Open the Print dialog box. Choose Selection under Print what to print the selected cells.

8. Print this section of the worksheet and then leave it open for the following exercise.

Editing Ranges

The column headings in this worksheet have been formatted, but you don't like the formatting. You decide to clear and reformat the headings. You also copy the range of data to another section of the worksheet because you want a duplicate copy to experiment with different functions.

To edit ranges, follow these steps:

1. From the Sales Figures file, select the headings in cells B3:E3.

2. Use the Edit, Clear command to clear the formats, but not the contents of the cells.

3. Bold and italicize these headings.

4. Select the cells from A3:E10.

5. Use the Copy and Paste commands to copy the range to cells A15:E22.

6. You later decide that you do not need this additional copy of the data. Select the range of cells from A15:E22.

7. Use the Edit, Delete command to delete this range.

8. Save the worksheet again and then leave it open for the following exercise.

Using Worksheet Functions

You want to total the coffee sales for each month, so you enter a function to perform this calculation. Also, you want a grand total for the quarter, so in this exercise you enter a function to calculate the total sales.

To Use Worksheet Functions, follow these steps:

1. From the Sales Figures file, select cell B11. You want to enter a total for January's sales in this cell.

2. Enter the function =SUM(January). This totals all the data in the range named January.

3. Enter the appropriate functions at the bottom of the February and March columns.

4. Enter the text Quarterly Total in cell A12.

5. Enter the sum function into cell B12 to total all of the sales for the quarter. Use the range names as the arguments.

6. Total the sales for each type of coffee in column E.

7. Save the worksheet again and leave it open for the following exercise.

Using the AVERAGE, MIN, and MAX Functions

To further evaluate the sales data in your worksheet, you decide to use these additional functions.

To use the AVERAGE, MIN, and MAX functions, follow these steps:

1. From the `Sales Figures` file, type `Lowest Sales` in cell A13, `Highest Sales` in cell A14, and `Average Sales` in cell A15.

2. In cell B13 enter the MIN function, using the named range `January` as the argument.

3. Enter this function with appropriate arguments into cells C13 and D13.

4. Enter the MAX function in cell B14, using the named range `January` as the argument.

5. Enter this function with appropriate arguments into cells C14 and D14.

6. In cell B15 enter the AVERAGE function, again using `January` as the argument.

7. Enter the AVERAGE function into cells C15 and D15 using the appropriate arguments.

8. Save the worksheet. Print two copies of the worksheet and then close the file.

Evaluating Utility Expenses

Create a worksheet to calculate the utility expenses for the coffee shop and to see if you can afford air conditioning for the shop.

To evaluate utility expenses, follow these steps:

1. Open the file Proj0403 from the Project-04 folder on the CD and save it as `Utility Expenses`.

2. In column I, calculate the average cost per month of each of the three utilities. Also calculate the average total cost of the utilities.

3. In cell B8, use an IF statement to determine whether or not you can afford air conditioning. For this example, if the average monthly utilities are less than $120, then you can afford air conditioning.

4. Save this file and print two copies. Close the file when you are finished.

Challenge

The following challenges enable you to use your problem-solving skills. Take time to work through these exercises now.

Naming Ranges in a Worksheet

In this exercise, you name ranges in a worksheet.

To name ranges in a worksheet, follow these steps:

1. Open the Proj0404 from the Project-04 folder on the CD file and save it as Profit Loss 2.

2. Name the range of cells from B5:B13 April.

3. Name the columns for May and June.

4. Save the file again and leave it open for the following exercise.

Printing Specified Ranges

In this exercise, you print specified ranges in your worksheet.

To print specified ranges, follow these steps:

1. In the Profit Loss 2 files, print the April range in the Profit Loss 2 worksheet.

2. Set A4:D9 as a print area. Print only this range of data.

3. Clear the print area.

4. Save the workbook and leave it open for the following exercise.

Copying and Formatting Ranges

You practice copying and formatting ranges in this exercise.

To copy and format ranges, follow these steps:

1. In the Profit Loss 2 files, select the April range in the Profit Loss 2 worksheet.

2. Copy this range to Sheet2. (To select Sheet2, click on the sheet tab at the bottom of your screen.)

3. Select the May range on Sheet 1 and copy it to Sheet3.

4. Return to Sheet 1 and select the range of cells from B4:D4.

5. Bold and italicize these cells.

6. Select the range of cells from A5:A13.

7. Bold this range of cells.

8. Save the worksheet again. Print two copies and close the file.

To Check Sales Figures

In this project, you use a function to determine if coffee sales are above a minimum level.

To check sales figures, follow these steps:

1. Open the file Proj0405 from the Project-04 folder on the CD and save it as Sales Figures 2.

2. In the Total column, create a formula to calculate the total sales for January, February, and March for each type of coffee.

3. In the Check column, use a function to return a message that either warns of sales below a minimum level of $500 or reports that sales are OK. Include this check for each type of coffee you sell.

4. Save your work. If requested by your instructor, print two copies of the completed worksheet and then close it.

Calculating Future Salary Requirements

You can use functions and formulas to determine whether your business can support increasing salaries. Use the data provided to calculate the amount of money spent on current salaries and to forecast projected salaries.

To calculate future salary requirements, follow these steps:

1. Open the file Proj0406 from the Project-04 folder on the CD and save it as Salary Forecast.

2. Calculate the projected salaries for each employee.

3. Calculate the average current salary in cell C8 and the average projected salary in cell E8.

4. Calculate the lowest salary in cells C9 and E9.

5. Calculate the highest salary in cells C10 and E10.

6. Calculate the total amount of all current salaries in cell C11 and of all projected salaries in cell E11.

7. In cell B12, use a conditional statement to determine whether you will be able to increase salaries as proposed. To make the decision, assume that if the average projected salary is less that $21,500, you can afford increases.

8. Change all of the increase percentages to five percent to see how the conditional statement is affected.

9. Save your work. If requested by your instructor, print two copies before closing the document.

PinPoint Assessment

You have completed the project and the associated lessons, as well as the Checking Your Skills and Applying Your Skills sections. Now use the PinPoint software evaluation mode to assess your comprehension of the specific exam tasks you have just learned. You can also use the PinPoint Trainer Mode and the Show Me tutorials to practice these specific exam tasks.

Project 5

Five

5

Improving the Appearance of a Worksheet

Formatting a Budget

Objectives   **Required Activities**

In this Project, you learn how to

➤ Use Fonts and Their Attributes   ... ...Apply Font Formats

➤ Change Column Width   ... ...Modify Cell Size and Alignment

➤ Align Text and Numbers

➤ Rotate and Indent Text ... ...Rotate and Indent Text

➤ Format Numbers   ... ...Apply General Numbers Formats

➤ Add Borders and Shading ... ...Apply Outlines

➤ Use Conditional Formatting

➤ Use the AutoFormat Feature

➤ Use the Spelling Checker

Why Would I Do This?

Having completed the first four Projects of *MOUS Essentials: Excel Proficient*, you now know how to build your own Excel worksheet. The budget worksheets you have created contain formulas and functions that provide you with useful information about your expenses.

Formatting

Applying attributes to text and data to change the appearance of a worksheet or to call attention to certain information.

After you create a basic worksheet, however, you may want to improve its appearance by *formatting* it so that it is more readable and attractive. In this project, you learn how to improve the appearance of worksheets by using many of Excel's formatting features. You also learn how to check for spelling errors in a worksheet.

Lesson 1: Using Fonts and Their Attributes

You can dramatically improve the appearance of your worksheet by using different fonts. A *font* is the typeface, type size, and type attributes that you apply to text and numbers.

Font

The typeface, type size, and type attributes of text or numbers.

In this lesson, you use toolbar buttons and the Font dialog box to format with fonts and font attributes. Toolbar buttons let you quickly apply a single formatting characteristic, such as a different font, while the dialog box enables you to preview and apply many formatting characteristics at one time. Try using some different fonts and type attributes in a worksheet now.

To Use Fonts and Font Attributes

❶ From the Project-05 folder on the CD, open the Proj0501 worksheet and save it as Expenses**.**

❷ Select cells B3 through H3 in the Expenses **worksheet.**

This selects the column headings in the Expenses worksheet—the first text you want to change. In Excel, you can change the formatting of a single selected cell or a range of selected cells.

❸ Choose F_o_rmat, C_e_lls.

Excel displays the Format Cells dialog box, in which you can change a number of formatting settings for the selected cells.

❹ Click the Font tab.

The Font options appear, as shown in Figure 5.1.

❺ In the F_o_nt list box, select Times New Roman.

This selects the typeface you want to apply to the selected cells in this example. You may have to use the scroll arrows to scroll down through the list of fonts to get to Times New Roman. Excel displays a sample of the typeface in the Preview box.

Figure 5.1
The Font tab of the
Format Cells dialog box
enables you to choose
font attributes.

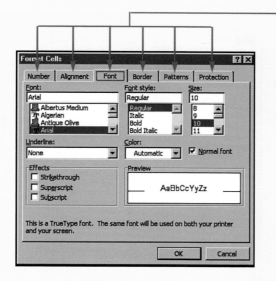

Click a tab to display other formatting options

6 **In the F̲ont style box, select B̲old.**

The text in the Preview box now appears bold.

7 **In the S̲ize list box, select** 12.

Point
A unit of measurement used
in printing and publishing to
designate the height of type.
There are roughly 72 points in
an inch.

Again, you may need to scroll down the list to find 12. The numbers in the Size list refer to *point* size, which is the unit of measurement of font characters. The default type size is 10 points, so changing the size to 12 increases the size of the type. Excel shows how the new type will look in the Preview box.

8 **Choose OK.**

The dialog box closes, and all the formatting changes are applied to the selected cells. All the month headings now appear in the new font and font attributes. Deselect the cells to get a better look at the formatting, as shown in Figure 5.2. Notice that the row height automatically adjusts to accommodate the new type size, although the column widths do not.

Next, format the worksheet's title—Expenses—so that it is obviously the main title. In the following steps, you use the Formatting toolbar's buttons to apply fonts and their attributes.

9 **Select cell A1 and then click the Font drop-down arrow on the Formatting toolbar.**

A list of fonts appears, as shown in Figure 5.3.

continues

To Use Fonts and Font Attributes   (continued)

Figure 5.2
The month headings appear in a new typeface and type size.

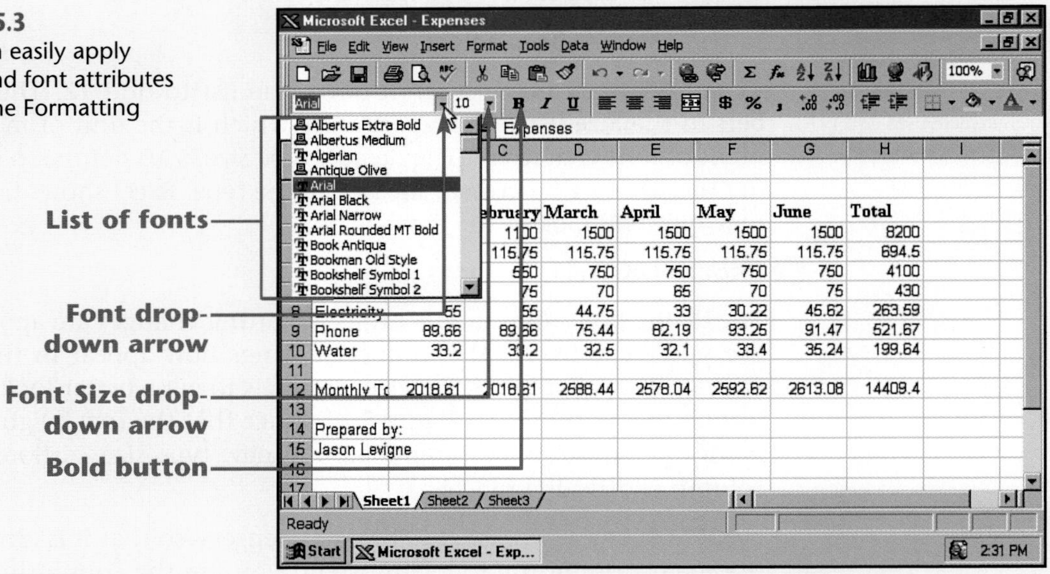

Formatted cells

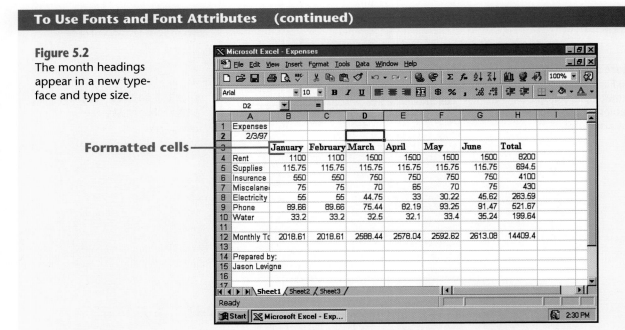

Figure 5.3
You can easily apply fonts and font attributes using the Formatting toolbar.

List of fonts

Font drop-down arrow

Font Size drop-down arrow

Bold button

⑩ **Select Times New Roman from the list.**

Excel changes the font in the selected cell.

⑪ **Click the Font size drop-down arrow on the Formatting toolbar and select 18.**

Excel increases the font size in the selected cell.

B   ⑫ **Click the Bold button on the Formatting toolbar.**

Excel applies the bold attribute to the selected cell.

When you have formatted a cell the way you like, you can use the Format Painter button to copy that formatting to one or more other cells. This tool is extremely handy because it enables you to format cells quickly without opening dialog boxes or making multiple selections from toolbars. Next, use the Format Painter button to copy the type style used for the column headings to the expense labels in column A.

 13 Select cell B3 and click the Format Painter button on the Standard toolbar.

A flashing dotted line appears around cell B3, and the Format Painter button appears pressed in. Note that you only need to select one cell to copy formatting. Just choose one of the cells that already contains the desired formatting and then click the Format Painter.

14 Select cells A4 to A12 and then release the mouse button.

When you release the mouse button, the formatting from cell B3 is applied to the range you selected. When you deselect the range, your worksheet should look similar to the one shown in Figure 5.4.

Figure 5.4
Fonts and their attributes can be applied to a range of cells, using the Format Painter button.

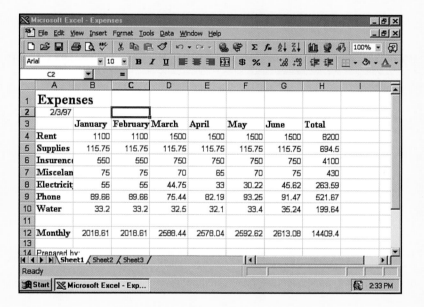

15 Save your work and leave the Expenses **workbook open for the next lesson, where you learn how to change the widths of columns in your worksheet.**

In Excel, you can use the buttons on the Formatting toolbar to italicize and underline characters as well as apply boldface. To change attributes, simply select the cells that you want to format and then click the relevant button on the formatting toolbar, or use the following keyboard shortcuts: Bold is Ctrl+B, italic is Ctrl+I, and underline is Ctrl+U. To remove an attribute, click its button again.

To quickly scroll through the **Font** drop-down list on the Formatting toolbar, start typing the name of the font you want to apply. Excel locates the fonts alphabetically.

continues

To quickly open the **Format Cells** dialog box, press Ctrl+1 or right-click the active cell and choose Format Cells from the shortcut menu.

When you open the Format Cells dialog box, you have a wider choice of font attributes than is available from the Formatting toolbar. In addition to Font, Font style, and Size, you can click Color to select a font color, Underline to choose single or double underlining, Strikethrough to cross out characters, Superscript to position text above the baseline (such as trademark™), and Subscript to position text below the baseline (such as H_2O).

Lesson 2: Changing Column Width

As you may have noticed, several of the column and row labels of the Expenses worksheet don't fit in the default column width. Although row heights adjust automatically when you change fonts, column widths do not. As a result, data entered in one column may be hidden by the data in the column to its right. To make your information fit, you can increase or decrease column widths; you can also change row height, if necessary.

To Change Column Width

❶ In the Expenses worksheet frame, move the mouse pointer to the line to the right of column letter *A*.

The mouse pointer changes to a double-headed black arrow, as shown in Figure 5.5. Column A is the first column you want to change. Notice that several of the expense labels in column A are covered by information in column B. Notice also that when there is no data in column B, Excel simply extends the data in column A across the cell border.

Figure 5.5
The mouse pointer changes to indicate that you can adjust the column width.

Double-headed arrow

	A	B	C	D	E	F	G	H	I
1	**Expenses**								
2	2/3/97								
3		**January**	**February**	**March**	**April**	**May**	**June**	**Total**	
4	**Rent**	1100	1100	1500	1500	1500	1500	8200	
5	**Supplies**	115.75	115.75	115.75	115.75	115.75	115.75	694.5	
6	**Insurenc**	550	550	750	750	750	750	4100	
7	**Miscelan**	75	75	70	65	70	75	430	
8	**Electricit**	55	55	44.75	33	30.22	45.62	263.59	
9	**Phone**	89.66	89.66	75.44	82.19	93.25	91.47	521.67	
10	**Water**	33.2	33.2	32.5	32.1	33.4	35.24	199.64	
11									
12	**Monthly**	2018.61	2018.61	2588.44	2578.04	2592.62	2613.08	14409.4	
13									
14	Prenared hv·								

2 Double-click the left mouse button.

When you double-click the column border between column letters *A* and *B,* the width of column A automatically adjusts to fit the longest entry. Now adjust the widths of columns B and C.

3 Double-click the column border to the right of column B and then double-click the column border to the right of column C.

These actions adjust the widths of columns B and C to fit the longest entry. Your worksheet should now look like Figure 5.6.

Figure 5.6
The adjusted column width fits the longest entry in the column.

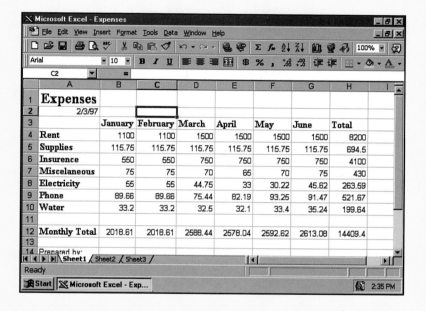

4 Save your work and keep the Expenses **worksheet open. In the next lesson, you learn how to change the alignment of data in a cell.**

When text doesn't fit in the width of a column, the label appears to be cut off or hidden by the next cell. If a number doesn't fit in the width of a column, a series of pound signs (######) appears in the cell. In either case, the data is stored in the worksheet; it just might not be displayed. You can adjust the column width to display the entire cell contents.

Rather than double-clicking the column or row border to force Excel to automatically reset the width or height, you can experiment with widths and heights by using the double-arrow pointer to drag the column and row borders in the worksheet frame. Move the mouse pointer to the border; when the double arrow appears, click and drag the border until you're satisfied with the new width or height.

> To enter a precise **column width**, choose F̲ormat, C̲olumn, Column W̲idth, enter the width (in number of characters) in the C̲olumn Width text box, and choose OK. To enter a precise row height, choose F̲ormat, R̲ow, Row He̲ight, then enter the height (in points) in the Row Height text box, and choose OK. The default row height is 12.75 points.
>
> If you want to reset the column width to the original setting, choose F̲ormat, C̲olumn, S̲tandard Width; make sure that 8.43 is entered in the Standard Column Width box and then choose OK.
>
> To undo the most recent formatting changes, click the Undo button or choose E̲dit, U̲ndo.
>
> You can select several cells, columns, or rows simultaneously to apply any formatting changes to all the selected parts of the worksheet.

Lesson 3: Aligning Text and Numbers

When you enter information into a cell, text aligns with the left side of the cell, and numbers, dates, and times automatically align with the right side of the cell. You can change the alignment of information at any time. For instance, you may want to fine-tune the appearance of column headings by centering all the information in the column. You can also align data across several columns in one step.

To Align Text and Numbers

❶ Select cells A1 through H1 in the Expenses **worksheet.**

You want this title centered over the width of the worksheet.

❷ Click the Merge and Center button on the Formatting toolbar.

Excel merges the selected cells into one cell and centers the text across the width of the worksheet. Even though the worksheet title is centered across the worksheet, it is still located in cell A1. If you want to select the text for further formatting or editing, you must select cell A1. Now, try aligning the column labels.

❸ Select cells B3 through H3.

This selects all the cells you want to align. Notice that the column labels are left-aligned. You can improve the appearance of the worksheet by centering the data in the selected cells.

❹ Click the Center button on the Formatting toolbar.

Excel centers the data in each cell, as shown in Figure 5.7.

❺ Save your work and keep Expenses **open for the next lesson, where you learn how to apply different number formats to cells.**

Figure 5.7
The contents of the selected cells are now centered.

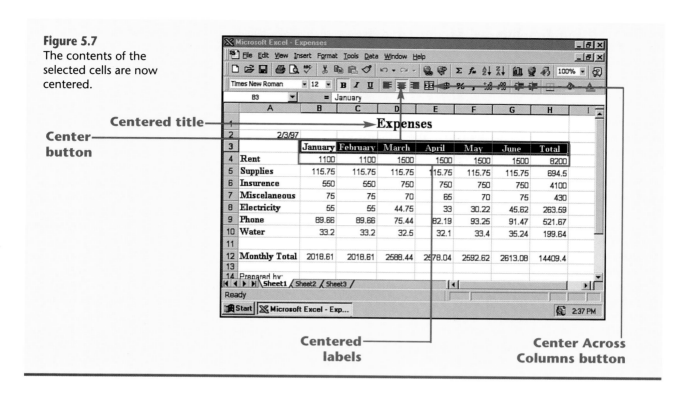

Centered title

Center button

Centered labels

Center Across Columns button

Inside Stuff

The Formatting toolbar has two additional buttons to align text or numbers within a cell. Click Align Left to align the characters to the left of the cell or Align Right to align the characters to the right of the cell.

Lesson 4: Rotate and Indent Text

To save space when you have long column labels, Excel lets you set the text at an angle, put it vertically in the cell (one character below another), or wrap the text onto several lines within the cell.

Using the Align Right feature doesn't always give you the appearance you desire, if you want to show topics as belonging under a main topic in the same column. The characters align to the right side of the cell, but the first letters don't line up one under another in the column. To create this effect, you must indent the text.

To Rotate and Indent Text

❶ Select B3 through H3 in the Expenses **worksheet.**

The selected cells are the ones in which you want to rotate the text. By putting the text on a slant, your columns need less width and the labels are accentuated.

continues

To Rotate and Indent Text   (continued)

② **Right-click anywhere along the selected range of cells and choose Format Cells from the shortcut menu.**

The Format Cells dialog box is displayed.

③ **Click the Alignment tab.**

The Alignment options are displayed, as shown in Figure 5.8.

Figure 5.8
The Alignment tab of the Format Cells dialog box enables you to choose from a variety of text-alignment options.

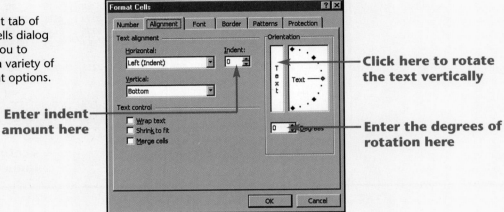

Enter indent amount here

Click here to rotate the text vertically

Enter the degrees of rotation here

④ **In the Orientation area, type** 45 **in the Degrees text box.**

This tells Excel to rotate the text in the selected cells up 45 degrees. To rotate the text down, enter a negative number.

⑤ **Choose OK.**

Excel rotates the text. Deselect the cells so you can see the formatting clearly. Your worksheet should look similar to the one in Figure 5.9.

⑥ **Click A8 and choose Insert, Rows from the menu.**

The Electricity, Phone, and Water labels in Column A all represent utilities. A label in the new blank row will make that clear.

⑦ **In A8, type** Utilities: **as the heading and then press** ⏎Enter.

To make it clear that the labels in the next three cells are included in the Utilities category, you need to indent the text.

⑧ **Select cells A9 through A11. Right-click the selection and choose Format Cells from the menu. Click the Alignment tab.**

If you want to indent characters from the left edge of the cell, select Left alignment and then enter an increment in the Indent text box on the Alignment page of the Format Cells dialog box. Each increment you enter in the text box is equal to the width of one character.

Figure 5.9
Changing the alignment options can improve the appearance of the worksheet.

Rotated Text—

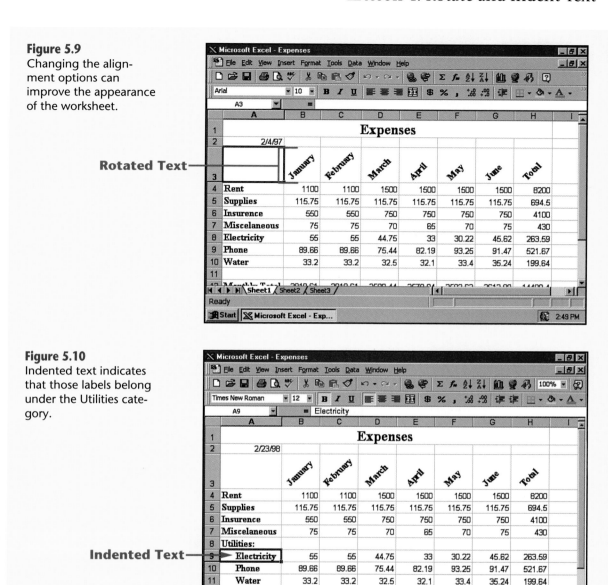

Figure 5.10
Indented text indicates that those labels belong under the Utilities category.

Indented Text—

⑨ **Choose** Left (indent) **from the Horizontal drop-down list. Then set the Indent to 2.**

Setting the indent amount to 2 moves each selected text label 2 characters to the right.

⑩ **Choose OK.**

Your worksheet should now resemble the one in Figure 5.10.

⑪ **Save your work and keep** Expenses **open for the next lesson, where you learn how to apply different number formats to cells.**

If you want text to appear vertically—one character above the next—click the Vertical orientation box on the Alignment page of the Format Cells dialog box.

On the **Alignment** page of the Format Cells dialog box, you can also select a Wrap Text option, a Shrink to Fit option, or a Merge cells option. Choose Wrap Text when you want to enter more than one line of text within a cell. As you type, the text automatically wraps to the next line in the cell. Choose Shrink to Fit when you want to reduce the appearance of the data so it fits within the displayed column width. Choose Merge Cells when you want to combine two or more selected adjacent cells into one larger cell.

Lesson 5: Formatting Numbers

When you enter a number or a formula into a cell, the entry may not appear as you hoped it would. You might type 5, for example, but want it to look like $5.00. You could type the dollar sign, decimal point, and zeros, or you can have Excel automatically format the number for you. When you want to apply a standard format to a number, you format the cell in which the number is displayed.

In Excel, you can format numbers in many ways. You will usually format numbers as currency, percentages, dates, or times of day. Remember that when you apply any kind of formatting, you apply it to the worksheet cell, not to the information itself. This means that if you change the information, the formatting still applies. You can even format empty cells so that when data is entered, it automatically appears with the correct format.

To Format Numbers

❶ Select cells B4 through H13 in the Expenses **worksheet.**

You want to format these cells as currency.

❷ Click the Currency Style button on the Formatting toolbar.

This changes the selected cells to display the default currency format, as shown in Figure 5.11. Note that the blank cells within the selection are formatted as well, even though the formatting doesn't show; if you enter data in those cells, it will appear in the currency style.

❸ With cells B4:H13 still selected, click the Decrease Decimal button twice.

Each time you click the button, Excel removes one decimal place. Because no decimal places are displayed, Excel rounds the values that are displayed to fit this format. However, the actual values will be used in any calculations. You can adjust column widths again to fit the worksheet within the document window (see Figure 5.12).

Now, change the way the date is displayed in the worksheet.

Figure 5.10
You can quickly select a format for the cells by using the Formatting toolbar's buttons.

Currency Style button

Percent Style button

Comma Style button

Increase Decimal button

Decrease Decimal button

Figure 5.12
Use the Decrease Decimal button to decrease the number of decimal places displayed.

Rounded numbers with zero decimal places

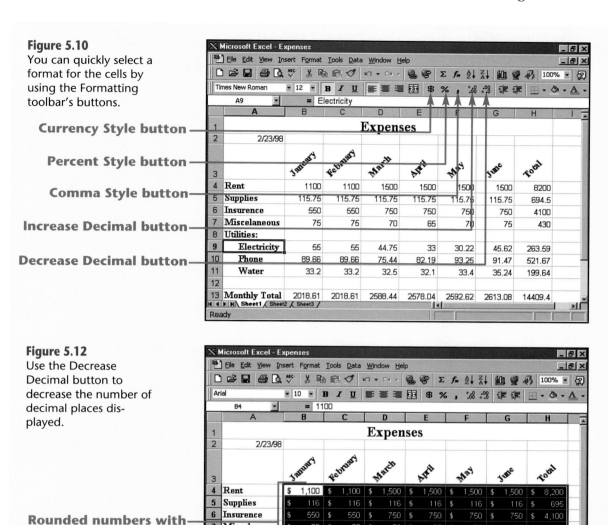

❹ **Move the mouse pointer to cell A2, click the right mouse button, and choose Format Cells from the shortcut menu.**

Excel opens the Format Cells dialog box.

❺ **Click the Number tab in the Format Cells dialog box.**

Excel displays the Number options (see Figure 5.13). Since the selected cell contains a date, the Date category is already selected. You can choose the general type of formatting you want from the Category list and then select the specific format from the Type list.

continues

To Format Numbers (continued)

6 **Select the 4-Mar-97 format from the Type list box.**

Notice that the Sample line shows the date in cell A2 in the format you selected.

Figure 5.13
You can format numbers in a wide variety of categories and styles.

Preview the formatting here

Select the category of number format here

Select the number format here

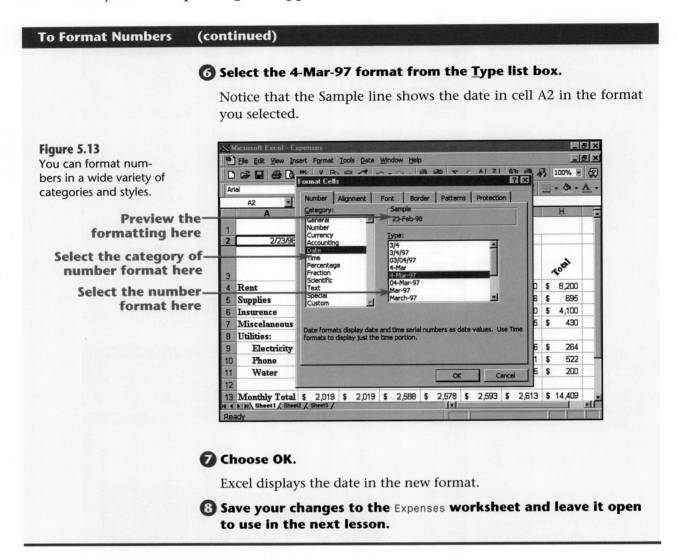

7 **Choose OK.**

Excel displays the date in the new format.

8 **Save your changes to the** Expenses **worksheet and leave it open to use in the next lesson.**

Lesson 6: Adding Borders and Patterns

To call attention to specific cells in a worksheet, you can accent them with formatting. You can make them stand out by changing the font or font attributes of the numbers, as you learned in Lesson 1, or you can change the appearance of the cell itself.

You can add patterns to a cell or range of cells to emphasize important information. For example, you may want to call attention to the highest sales for a month and the grand total. In addition, when you print a worksheet, the grid between columns and rows does not appear. If you want to include lines between cells or outlines around cells, you must add borders.

To Add Borders and Patterns

❶ Select cell G13 in the Expenses **worksheet.**

The monthly expenses for June are the highest in the worksheet. In this example, you decide to emphasize this cell with a pattern and a border.

❷ Choose F̲ormat, C̲ells and then click the Patterns tab in the Format Cells dialog box.

Excel displays the Patterns options in the Format Cells dialog box, as shown in Figure 5.14.

Figure 5.14
The Patterns tab in the Format Cells dialog box enables you to choose cell background textures.

Select a color for cell shading here

View a sample here

Pattern drop-down arrow

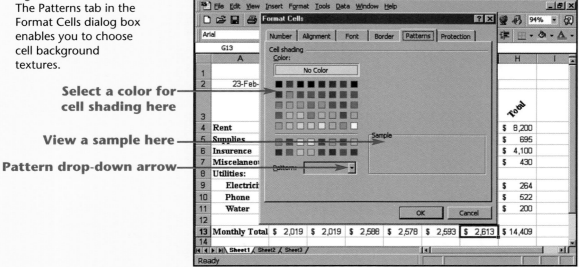

❸ Click the P̲attern drop-down arrow.

A palette of shading patterns appears, as shown in Figure 5.15. You can choose a color or a geometric pattern and then preview a sample in the Format Cells dialog box.

❹ Click the 6.25% Gray pattern at the far right in the first row of the palette.

This selects a light, dotted pattern, which is displayed in the sample box. This simple pattern will not obscure data entered in the formatted cell.

❺ Choose OK.

This confirms the change. You see the shading in cell G13 on-screen (see Figure 5.16). Next, add a border to outline the cell.

 ❻ Click the Borders drop-down arrow on the Formatting toolbar.

A palette of border options is displayed, as shown in Figure 5.16.

continues

To Add Borders and Patterns   (continued)

Figure 5.15
The Pattern palette in
the Format Cells dialog
box offers a wide variety
of patterns and colors.

Choose a pattern here

Choose a color here

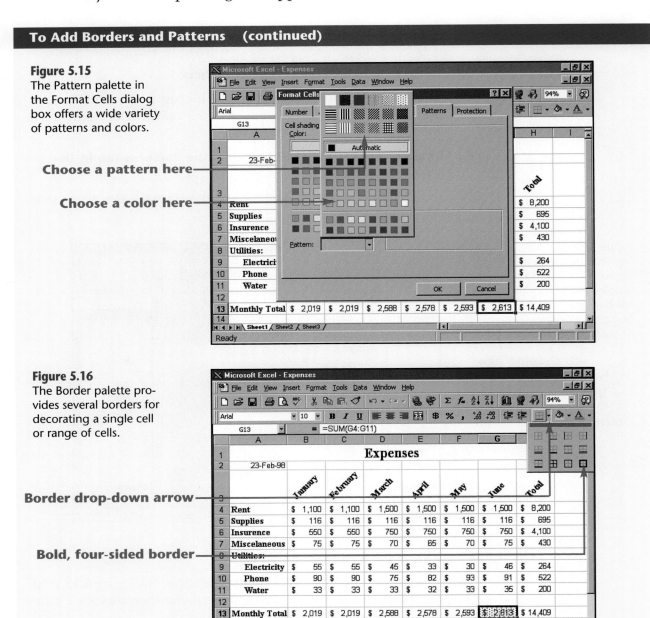

Figure 5.16
The Border palette pro-
vides several borders for
decorating a single cell
or range of cells.

Border drop-down arrow

Bold, four-sided border

❼ Click the bold, four-sided border on the bottom row.

Excel applies the border to the selected cell. Deselect the cell to get a
good look at the formatting. Your worksheet should now look like
the one shown in Figure 5.17.

❽ Save your changes to the Expenses **worksheet and leave it open
to use in the next lesson.**

Figure 5.17
You can add borders
and patterns to any cell
or range of cells

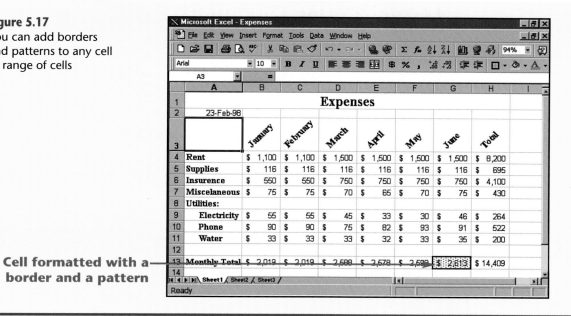

Cell formatted with a—
border and a pattern

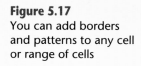 **Inside Stuff**

You can customize borders and lines on the Border tab of the Format Cells dialog box. You can select border placement as well as the type of line you want to use. Simply open the Format Cells dialog box, click the Border tab, make your selections and then choose OK.

One of the most entertaining things about working with Windows 95 applications is being able to use a variety of colors. Excel enables you to personalize your work with color through the Format Cells dialog box. To quickly apply a color to fill a selected cell or range, click the Fill Color drop-down arrow on the Formatting toolbar and select a color from the palette. To quickly apply a color to the data in a selected cell or range, click the Font color drop-down arrow on the Formatting toolbar and select a color from the palette.

Unfortunately, colored letters on a colored background may be clear and attractive on-screen, but hard to read in printed form. Keep in mind that you need to be connected to a color printer to be able to print color worksheets. Without a color printer, colors may turn out to be muddy gray on paper, and all but the simplest patterns can make information on the worksheet hard to read.

Have fun experimenting with the colors and patterns in the Format Cells dialog box, but keep the formatting simple on worksheets that you need to print.

Excel

Lesson 7: Using Conditional Formatting

Using formats to emphasize cells in a worksheet can call attention to specific data. When you format a cell, however, the formatting remains in effect even if the data changes. If you want to accent a cell depending on the value of the cell, you can use conditional formatting.

Like the conditional statements you used in formulas in Project 4, "Calculating with Functions," conditional formats return a result based on whether or not the value in the cell meets a specified criteria. For example, in a worksheet tracking monthly sales, you may want to accent a monthly total only if it is less than the previous month's total or if it is greater than the target sales figure you have set.

To Use Conditional Formatting

❶ In the Expenses **worksheet, select cells B10 to G10.**

This selects the row containing phone expenses. For this example, you want to emphasize any monthly phone expenses that exceed $90.

❷ Choose F̲ormat, Con̲ditional Formatting.

The Conditional Formatting dialog box appears, as shown in Figure 5.18.

Figure 5.18
The Conditional Formatting dialog box enables you to format a cell based on the value in the cell.

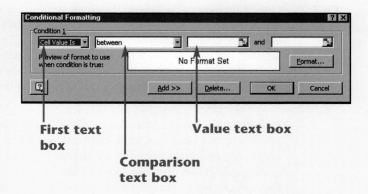

First text box

Comparison text box

Value text box

If you have problems...

If the Office Assistant opens, click the No, Don't Provide Help Now button to close it and continue.

❸ Make sure Cell Value Is appears in the first text box and then press Tab↹**.**

This tells Excel that the condition you are going to specify depends on the constant value entered in the selected cells and then moves the insertion point to the comparison text box. You can also choose to use the value of the formula in the selected cells.

4 **From the comparison drop-down list (the second drop-down list in the dialog box), select greater than and then press** `Tab⇆`.

This identifies the type of comparison you want to use and moves the insertion point to the value text box.

5 **In the value text box, type** 90.

The conditional statement now tells Excel that if the cell value is greater than 90, it should apply the specified formatting. Now, set the formatting.

6 **Click the Format button.**

The Format Cells dialog box is displayed. You can set font style, color, underline, and strikethrough on the Font page, and you can choose border and patterns formatting as well.

7 **Click Bold in the Font style list, click the Color drop-down arrow, click the red square in the color palette and then choose OK.**

This tells Excel to format the data in the cell in red bold type if the condition is met. In this case, if the monthly phone expense is more than $90, it appears in red. In the Conditional Formatting dialog box, you see a sample of the formatting, as shown in Figure 5.19.

Figure 5.19
The conditional statement determines whether a cell is formatted or not.

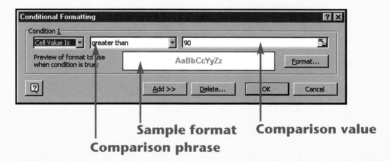

Sample format   Comparison value
Comparison phrase

8 **Choose OK.**

Excel applies the formatting to any of the selected cells that meet the specified criteria, in this case, cells F9 and G9. Deselect the cells so you can get a better look at the result. Your worksheet should look similar to the one in Figure 5.20.

9 **Save the changes you have made to the** Expenses **worksheet and keep it open. In the next lesson, you learn how to use the AutoFormat feature.**

continues

To Use Conditional Formatting   (continued)

Figure 5.20
Only the phone expenses that exceed $90 per month are highlighted.

Highlighted cells

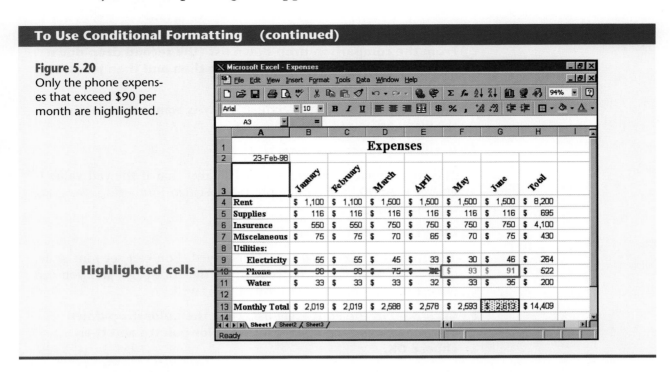

 You can set up to three conditions that must be met in order for the formatting to be applied. Simply click <u>A</u>dd in the Conditional Formatting dialog box to display another set of Condition text boxes. Use the <u>D</u>elete button to remove one or more conditions.

Lesson 8: Using AutoFormat

If you don't want to spend a lot of time formatting a worksheet, or if you want to rely on someone else's flair for design, you can use Excel's AutoFormat feature. The AutoFormat feature contains several predefined table formats that you can apply to selected cells in your worksheet.

Each format contains various alignment, number format, color, and pattern settings to help you create professional-looking worksheets. Generally, you apply one format at a time to a selected cell or range of cells. With a table format, however, you can apply a collection of formats supplied by Excel all at once.

To Use AutoFormat

❶ Select cells A1 through H16 in the Expenses **worksheet.**

This highlights the entire worksheet. Now apply a new format to this range.

❷ Choose F<u>o</u>rmat, <u>A</u>utoFormat.

Excel displays the AutoFormat dialog box (see Figure 5.21). A list of table formats and a Sample area appear in the dialog box. The

Simple table format is currently selected. You can click other table formats to see what they look like in the Sample area.

Figure 5.21
The AutoFormat dialog box enables you to format a range of cells by choosing from a list of standard table styles.

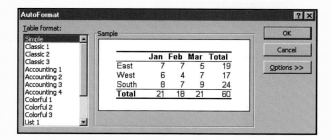

❸ **Scroll down the Table format list box and select the 3D Effects 1 format.**

This selects the 3D Effects 1 table format and displays the formatting in the sample area.

❹ **Choose OK.**

Excel changes the selected cells to the new format. Click any cell to deselect the range so that you can see the formatting clearly, as shown in Figure 5.22. Notice that the previous formatting in the Expenses worksheet has been replaced by the new format. Only the conditional formatting is still in effect. If you plan to use the AutoFormat feature, apply AutoFormat before adding other formatting.

❺ **Save your changes to the Expenses worksheet and leave it open for the next lesson, where you learn how to check for spelling errors.**

Figure 5.22
The worksheet is formatted with the 3D Effects 1 style.

Conditional formatting is still in effect

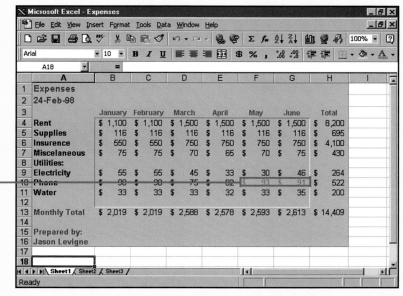

If you have problems...

The table formats in the AutoFormat dialog box can drastically change the appearance of your worksheet. If you don't like the results after closing the AutoFormat dialog box, choose the Edit, Undo command before you take any other action. Alternatively, you can continue making formatting changes to the worksheet.

Lesson 9: Checking the Spelling in a Worksheet

When presenting a worksheet, you should make sure that no misspelled words are in the document. You can use the Excel spelling checker feature to rapidly find and highlight any misspelled words in a worksheet.

The spelling checker highlights words that it doesn't recognize—which, in addition to misspelled words, may be proper nouns, abbreviations, technical terms, and so on, that actually are spelled correctly but aren't in Excel's dictionary. You have the option of correcting or bypassing words that the spelling checker highlights. To personalize the program, you can add proper names, cities, and technical terms to a spelling dictionary file called CUS-TOM.DIC.

The spelling checker won't alert you to a word that is spelled correctly, but used incorrectly, such as "principle" when you mean "principal." You still need to be watchful when creating a document, and not rely on the spelling checker to catch every possible mistake.

Table 5.1 describes the common options used in the Spelling dialog box.

Table 5.1	Spelling Button Options
Option	Description
Change **A**ll	Substitutes all occurrences of the questionable word with the word in the Change To text box.
Change	Substitutes only one occurrence of the questionable word with the word in the Change To text box.
I**g**nore All	Ignores all occurrences of the questionable word in a worksheet.
Ignore	Ignores only one occurrence of the questionable word.
Add	Adds the word to the dictionary (CUSTOM.DIC file).
A**u**toCorrect	Adds the word to the AutoCorrect list so Excel will automatically correct the misspelling as you type.

To Check the Spelling in a Worksheet

❶ In the Expenses **worksheet, select cell A1.**

This makes A1 the current cell so that Excel will begin checking the spelling at the top of the worksheet.

❷ Choose Tools, Spelling.

Excel starts to search the worksheet for spelling errors. When it finds a word it doesn't recognize, it stops, highlights the word in the text, and opens the Spelling dialog box in which it offers suggestions for correcting the word.

In this example, Excel stops on the word *Insurence* and displays the Spelling dialog box, as shown in Figure 5.23. Insurence is misspelled, so it does not appear in the spelling dictionary. Excel makes a guess as to what word you really meant to type and suggests a list of alternative spellings. The correct spelling—*Insurance*—is highlighted at the top of the list. You can select a different alternative, or, if the correct spelling isn't listed, you can type it in the Change to text box.

❸ Choose Change.

Excel replaces the incorrect spelling with the correct spelling and continues to check the spelling of the rest of the worksheet. The Spelling Checker stops at *Miscelaneous,* which is also misspelled, and offers a list of alternatives. The correct spelling is highlighted.

❹ Choose Change.

Excel replaces the word and continues checking the spelling. It stops at *Levigne,* which is a proper noun that is not in the main spelling dictionary, but it is spelled correctly. If you think you will include the name in many workbooks, you should add it to the custom dictionary. If you use the word in the future, Excel won't stop and highlight it if it is spelled correctly, and will suggest a correction if it is misspelled.

❺ Choose Add.

Excel adds the name to the CUSTOM.DIC dictionary and moves on. Excel doesn't find any more misspelled words, so it displays the message The spell check is complete for the entire sheet.

❻ Choose OK.

This confirms that the spelling check is complete. The words *Insurance* and *Miscellaneous* are now spelled correctly in the Expenses worksheet, and the name *Levigne* has been added to the CUSTOM.DIC dictionary.

continues

To Check the Spelling in a Worksheet (continued)

7 **Save your work and close the worksheet.**

If you have completed your session on the computer, exit Excel and Windows 95 before turning off the computer. Otherwise, continue with the "Checking Your Skills" and "Applying Your Skills" sections at the end of this project.

Figure 5.23
Excel highlights the misspelled word and suggests alternatives.

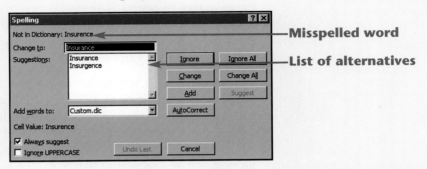

Misspelled word

List of alternatives

If the Spelling dialog box doesn't suggest alternatives to a misspelled word, you need to select the Always Suggest check box in the Spelling dialog box. Conversely, if you don't want it to suggest alternatives, make sure the Always Suggest check box is not selected.

Inside Stuff

To quickly start the Spelling Checker, click the Spelling button on the Standard toolbar or press F7.

If you start the Spelling Checker in the middle of the worksheet, when Excel reaches the end of the worksheet, it asks if you want to continue checking from the beginning. Choose Yes to check the spelling from the beginning of the worksheet. Choose No to close the Spelling Checker.

Excel comes with an AutoCorrect feature that automatically corrects common spelling errors. For example, if you type *adn*, Excel will automatically replace it with *and*. To see the list of words that Excel automatically corrects, choose Tools, AutoCorrect. To add your own spelling bugaboos to AutoCorrect, enter the incorrect spelling in the Replace text box and the correct spelling in the With text box, choose Add and then OK. Alternatively, when the Spelling Checker stops on a misspelled word, you can choose AutoCorrect in the Spelling dialog box to add it to the AutoCorrect spelling list.

Project Summary

To	Do This
Change fonts, font sizes, or font attributes.	Select the cells to format and choose Format, Cells. Click the Font tab, make selections, and choose OK.
Align data.	Select the cells and click the appropriate alignment button on the toolbar or open the Format Cells dialog box. Click the Alignment tab, make selections, and choose OK.
Rotate text.	Select the cells and open the Format Cells dialog box. Click the Alignment tab, enter the number of Degrees, and choose OK.
Indent text.	Select the cells and open the Format Cells dialog box. Click the Alignment tab, choose Left (indent) as the Horizontal alignment, enter a number of characters in the Indent text box, and choose OK.
Change column width.	Drag the column border to the desired width.
Automatically adjust column width.	Double-click the border between columns.
Format numbers as currency.	Select the cells and click the Currency button on the toolbar.
Change the format of numbers.	Select the cells and choose Format, Cells. Click the Numbers tab, select the number type, select the number format, and choose OK.
Add borders to cells.	Select the cells and choose Format, Cells. Click the Borders tab, select the border location, select the border style, and choose OK.
Apply conditional formatting.	Select the cell and choose Format, Conditional Formatting. Select the type of comparison, enter the value to compare, click Format, select the formatting, choose OK and then choose OK again.
Automatically format a range.	Select the cells and choose Format, AutoFormat. Select the table format and choose OK.
Check spelling in a worksheet.	Click the Spelling Checker button on the Standard toolbar and follow the prompts.
Copy formatting.	Select the formatted cell, click the Format Painter button, and select the cells to format.

Checking Your Skills

True or False

For each of the following, check *T* or *F* to indicate whether the statement is true or false.

__T __F **1.** You can quickly adjust the column width to fit the column contents by right-clicking the line between two columns.

__T __F **2.** AutoFormat overrides conditional formatting already in the worksheet.

__T __F **3.** By default, numbers are right-aligned in a cell.

__T __F **4.** You can add a border to one cell or to a group of cells, but you cannot add shading to more than one cell at a time.

__T __F **5.** You can add the name of the city you live in to the Spelling Checker dictionary so that it doesn't question you every time it comes across that name.

__T __F **6.** When using the Alignment option, each increment you enter in the text box is equal to the width of one character.

__T __F **7.** The column width adjusts automatically when you change the type size.

__T __F **8.** When text doesn't fit in the width of the column, a series of pound signs (########) appears in the cell.

__T __F **9.** When you apply formatting, it applies to the worksheet cell, not to the number itself.

__T __F **10.** You should use a lot of different colors for the letters and the background to improve the appearance of your spreadsheets.

Multiple Choice

Circle the letter of the correct answer for each of the following.

1. Which of the following options lets you skip a word that Excel identifies as misspelled?

 a. Ignore

 b. Change

 c. Add

 d. Alternatives

2. Which of the following is *not* a method of adjusting column width?

 a. Format, Column, Width command

 b. Edit, Column, Width command

 c. double-clicking the right column border on the worksheet frame

 d. dragging the column border on the worksheet frame

3. Which of the following *cannot* be formatted using the Formatting toolbar?

 a. fonts

 b. type size

c. column width

d. numerical formatting

4. How many conditions can you apply to each conditional format?

   a. one

   b. two

   c. three

   d. four

5. If pound signs (######) fill a cell, it means that _____.

   a. the cell is not active

   b. the formula is impossible

   c. the column is not wide enough

   d. you must recalculate the formula

6. To copy formatting from one cell to another, you use which of the following?

   a. Formatting toolbar

   b. Font dialog box

   c. Format Painter button

   d. shortcut menu

7. What is the keyboard shortcut to bold selected text?

a. Ctrl+B

b. Ctrl+O

c. Ctrl+L

d. Ctrl+1

8. When you enter the column width in the Column Width text box, you enter the width in which of the following?

   a. points

   b. number of characters

   c. inches

   d. centimeters

9. To rotate text 90 degrees down, you enter what in the Degrees text box?

   a. 90 d

   b. 90

   c. 90 down

   d. 90 d 10.

10. You can set up to how many conditions that must be met for formatting to be applied?

   a. three

   b. four

   c. two

   d. five

Completion

In the blank provided, write the correct answer for each of the following statements.

1. _____-_____ the left mouse button to quickly adjust column width to fit the longest entry.

2. To customize the Spelling Checker, add words to the _____.

3. When formatting a number as currency, you can use the _____ _____ tool to add decimal places.

4. _____ height adjusts automatically to accommodate changes in font size.

5. When aligning data in a cell, use _____ numbers to rotate text down.

6. The numbers in the Font Size list box refer to the _____ size.

7. To enter more than one line of text within a cell, choose the _____ option on the Alignment page of the Format Cells dialog box.

8. To accent a cell depending on the value of the cell, use _____.

9. To quickly start the spelling check, press the _____ function key.

10. The _____ feature automatically corrects common spelling errors.

Matching

a. Ctrl+I

b. Center button

c. Format

d. Merge and Center button

e. numbers

f. custom

g. font

h. Ctrl+U

i. point

j. text

In the blank next to each of the following terms or phrases, write the letter of the corresponding term or phrase.

_____ 1. The typeface, type size, and type attributes of text or numbers

_____ 2. A unit of measurement used to designate the height of type

_____ 3. Keyboard shortcut to italicize text

_____ 4. Keyboard shortcut to underline text

_____ 5. To set a precise column width, use an option on this menu

_____ 6. Aligns with the left side of a cell

_____ 7. Aligns with the right side of a cell

_____ 8. Centers text across columns

_____ 9. Centers text in a cell

_____ 10. You can add words to this spelling dictionary

Applying Your Skills

Practice

The following exercises enable you to practice the skills you have learned in this project. Take a few minutes to work through these exercises now.

Formatting the Sales Worksheet

Practice using different formatting techniques to improve the appearance of the worksheet detailing monthly sales figures.

To format the sales worksheet, follow these steps:

1. Open the file Proj0502 from the Project-05 folder on the CD and save it as Sales Figures 3.

2. Make the column headings stand out by changing the font to Times New Roman, the font size to 14, and the Font Style to Bold Italic.

3. Copy the formatting from the column headings to the row headings.

4. Format all dollar values as currency with two decimal places.

5. Use conditional formatting to highlight all the totals in column E that are below $500. If a number is below $500, have it display in blue.

6. Save the worksheet. Leave the file open for the following exercise.

Modifying the Cell Size and Alignment in the Sales Worksheet

Change the width of columns, and the alignment of data in the Sales Worksheet by completing the following exercise.

To modify the cell size and alignment in the sales worksheet, follow these steps:

1. In the Sales Figures 3 worksheet, center the worksheet heading across all the columns.

2. Change the width of column A so that all the data displays in the cell.

3. Change the width of columns B through F to 10.

4. Center the column headings in columns B through F.

5. Spell check the worksheet. Add the coffee names to your dictionary.

6. Save the worksheet. If requested by your instructor, print two copies and close the worksheet.

Formatting the Job List Worksheet

In this exercise, you format the job list worksheet by changing column widths, and applying number formats.

To format the job list worksheet, follow these steps:

1. Open the Proj0503 file from the Project-05 folder on the CD and save it as Job List 4.

2. Wrap the text in cell E2.

3. Bold all the column headings in row 2.

4. Format the data in the Salary column to Currency, with 0 decimal places.

5. Format the data in the Monthly Rate and Monthly Insurance Premium columns as Currency with two decimal places.

6. Change the insurance percentage in cell B13 to Percentage, with two decimal places.

7. Adjust the width of all the columns so that they are wide enough for the data. If any cell is smaller than the default width (8.43), adjust the width.

8. Add a border to outline the cells in row 2.

9. Save the file and print two copies. Close the file when you have finished.

Formatting the Attendance Worksheet

In this exercise, you format the coffee tasting attendance worksheet by centering and bolding headings, rotating the headings, and indenting labels.

To format the attendance worksheet, follow these steps:

1. Open the file Proj0504 from the Project-05 folder on the CD and save it as Attendance 2.

2. Bold and underline the heading Coffee Tastings.

3. Center this heading across all the columns.

4. Bold all the headings in row 2.

5. Rotate the headings in row 2 down 10 degrees.

7. Indent cells A4:A7 one character.

8. Indent cells A9:A10 one character.

9. Adjust the width of column A so that all the characters display.

10. Save the file, and print two copies. Leave it open for the following exercise.

Using AutoFormat and Spell Check

Practice using AutoFormat by completing the following exercise.

To use AutoFormat and spell check, follow these steps:

1. Spell check the Attendance 2 worksheet. Add any necessary words to the spelling dictionary.

2. Use AutoFormat to format the worksheet. Try different formats until you find one you like.

3. Save the worksheet and print two copies. Close the file when you have finished.

Challenge

The following challenges enable you to use your problem-solving skills. Take time to work through these exercises now.

Formatting the March Orders Worksheet

In this exercise, use various formatting techniques to improve the appearance of the March Orders worksheet.

To format the march orders worksheet, follow these steps:

1. Open the file Proj0505 from the Project-05 folder on the CD and save it as March Orders 2.

2. Bold all the headings in the worksheet.

3. Center the worksheet heading across all the columns.

4. Format the appropriate cells using currency format with 2 decimal places.

5. Make any other changes you think would improve the appearance of the worksheet.

6. Save the file and print two copies. Close the file when you have finished.

Formatting the Salary Worksheet

In this exercise, you improve the appearance of the Salary worksheet by formatting headings, indenting text, and by checking the spelling.

To format the salary worksheet, follow these steps:

1. Open the file Proj0506 from the Project-05 folder on the CD and save it as Salary 2.

2. Format the worksheet heading and column and row headings to make them stand out.

3. Indent all the job positions under the heading Position.

4. Adjust column widths, if necessary.

5. Spell check the worksheet, making any necessary corrections.

6. Save the worksheet. Print two copies and close the file.

Formatting the Ad Costs Worksheet

Format the Ad Costs worksheet by wrapping text, using various numeric formats, rotating text, and applying outlines.

To format the ad costs worksheet, follow these steps:

1. Open the Proj0507 file from the Project-05 folder on the CD and save it as Ad Costs 2.

2. Wrap the text in cells G2 and H2.

3. Format the numbers in columns G and H as percentage with two decimals.

4. Rotate the titles of the ads.

5. Bold all of the headings in the worksheet.

6. Format all the appropriate cells as currency with two decimals.

7. Set up conditional formatting to highlight ad profits that fall between $200 and $300.

8. Save the file and print two copies. Close the file when you have finished.

Formatting the Profit/Loss Statement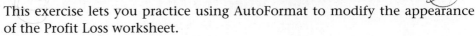

In this exercise, you improve the appearance of the worksheet by using various formatting features, including applying font formats, applying number formats, and shading and outlining cells.

To format the profit/loss statement, follow these steps:

1. Open the Proj0508 file from the Project-05 folder on the CD and save it as `Profit Loss Statement 2`.

2. Increase the font size of the headings in rows 1 and 2.

3. Bold these headings and center them across the columns of the spreadsheet.

4. Bold and italicize the date headings.

5. Bold the headings in column A.

6. Format all the dollar values in currency format, with two decimal places.

7. Format the tax rate in cell B17 as percentage, with two decimal places.

8. Shade the cells that contain the net profit figures.

9. Outline the cell that contains the tax rate.

10. Save the file and leave it open for the following exercise.

Using AutoFormat to Format the Profit Loss Worksheet

This exercise lets you practice using AutoFormat to modify the appearance of the Profit Loss worksheet.

To use autoformat to format the profit loss worksheet, follow these steps:

1. In the `Profit Loss Statement 2` worksheet, use AutoFormat to format this worksheet. You may need to try several formats to find one you like.

2. Make some manual changes to the worksheet to further improve its appearance.

3. Save this file and print two copies. Close the file when you have finished.

PinPoint Assessment

You have completed the project and the associated lessons, as well as the Checking Your Skills and Applying Your Skills sections. Now use the PinPoint software evaluation mode to assess your comprehension of the specific exam tasks you have just learned. You can also use the PinPoint Trainer Mode and the Show Me tutorials to practice these specific exam tasks.

Project 6 / Six

Using Charts and Maps

Charting Expenses and Mapping Offices

Objectives   Required Activities

In this Project, you learn how to

Create a Chart … … … … … … … … … …Create, Format and Modify Charts

Format Text in a Chart

Change the Chart Type

Enhance a Chart

Print a Chart … … … … … … … … … …Preview and Print Charts

Create a Map

Why Would I Do This?

After you create a worksheet, you may want to show the information to someone else. You can simply print the worksheet if you need only numerical detail, or you can transform the information in the worksheet into a chart. With Excel, you can also chart geographical information with maps. Charts and maps are great for visually representing relationships between numerical values while improving the appearance of a presentation.

This project shows you how to use sample data to create and enhance various types of charts. You also learn how to add a map to a worksheet.

Lesson 1: Creating a Chart

Embedded chart
A graphical representation of worksheet data created within the worksheet rather than as a separate worksheet.

In Excel, you can create an embedded chart directly on the worksheet. An **embedded chart** is a graphic *object*—a picture of the data—that appears on the worksheet along with your worksheet data. You can also add a chart of the data on a separate worksheet.

To create a chart, you select the data you want to use in the chart, and then choose Insert, Chart or click the Chart Wizard button on the Standard toolbar. The Chart Wizard provides step-by-step assistance through a series of dialog boxes to choose a chart type and specify chart options, and then automatically creates the chart from the selected data and places it in a box (frame). You can then change or enhance the chart. Now try creating a chart to help you analyze your monthly office expenses.

To Create a Chart

❶ From the Project-06 folder on the CD, open the file Proj0601 and save it as Expenses.

This is the workbook file you use in this Project.

❷ Select cells A2 through G7.

This is the data range you use to create the chart. You can create a chart using any of the information in the worksheet. The range you selected here lets you see how your expense costs change over the course of six months. Note that the data range does not include the totals.

❸ Click the Chart Wizard button on the Standard toolbar.

Excel displays the Chart Wizard - Step 1 of 4 - Chart Type dialog box, as shown in Figure 6.1. This dialog box contains two tabs, Standard Types and Custom Types, which contain chart types from which to make your selection.

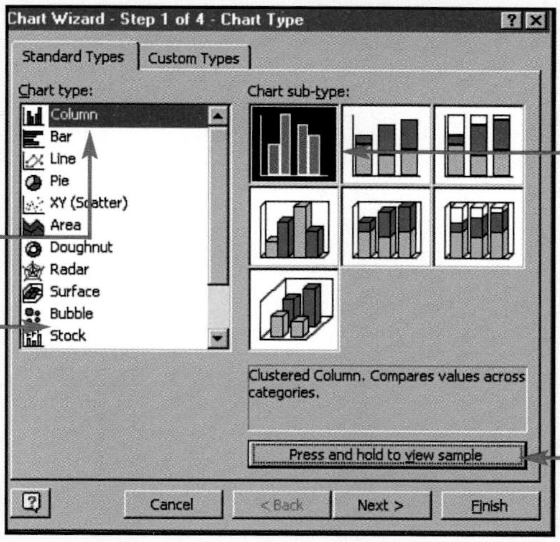

Figure 6.1
The Chart Wizard - Step 1 of 4 - Chart Type dialog box enables you to choose a chart type and subtype.

Default chart type

Choose a chart type and view the available subtypes

Default subtype

Sample button

4 **In the Chart type list, click Column if it is not already selected.**

For this example, the default chart type, Column, is acceptable. Otherwise, you could select a different chart type. Now you can choose a chart subtype. In this case, you will use the default clustered column subtype for the column chart.

5 **Make sure the Clustered Column subtype from the Chart subtype list is selected.**

A description box appears below the subtype choices. When you click a subtype, the description of that choice appears in the box. You can verify your selection of a subtype by checking the description box.

6 **Point to the Press and hold to view sample button, and click and hold down the left mouse button.**

A sample of your chart is displayed in the Sample box.

7 **Release the mouse button, and click the Next button.**

The chart type and subtype are accepted and the Chart Wizard - Step 2 of 4 - Chart Source Data dialog box appears, as shown in Figure 6.2. A sample of the chart you are creating is displayed in the Data Range tab of the dialog box. If necessary, you can change the way the **data series** is displayed from rows to columns, but for this example the default settings are fine. The Series tab allows you to add or remove a series or change the ranges being used for the names and values of each chart series.

continues

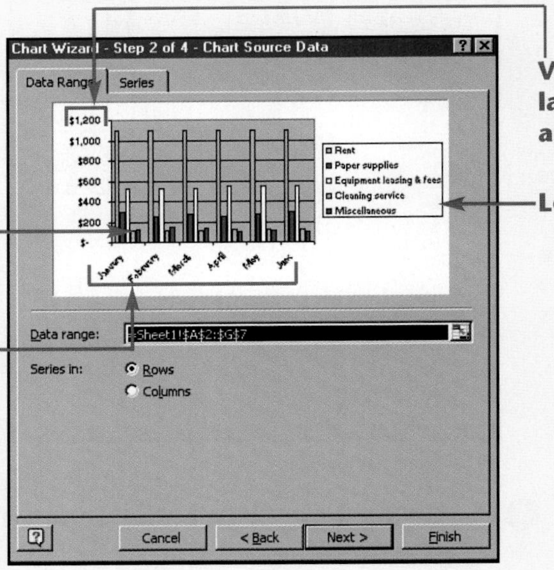

Figure 6.2
The Chart Wizard - Step
2 of 4 - Chart Source
Data dialog box enables
you to change the dis-
play of the data series.

Data series

Category (x) axis
labels list months

Value (y) axis
labels list dollar
amounts

Legend

8 Click the Next button.

The defaults are accepted and the Chart Wizard - Step 3 of 4 - Chart Options dialog box appears. Here, the tabs are displayed so that you can choose to add **chart titles**, label the **axes**, add **gridlines**, hide or change the placement of the **legend**, add **data labels**, or show the **data table**.

9 Click the Titles tab and then the Chart title text box. Type Office Expenses **and press** Tab.

Excel adds the title to the chart and moves the insertion point to the Category axis text box.

10 Type Months **in the Category axis text box, press** Tab, **and then type** Dollars **in the Value axis text box.**

Excel labels the axes on the chart. The Chart Wizard - Step 3 of 4 - Chart Options dialog box should now look like the one shown in Figure 6.3.

11 Click the Next button.

The Chart Wizard - Step 4 of 4 - Chart Location dialog box appears, as shown in Figure 6.4. If you want to see the chart displayed next to its source data, you can embed it as an object on the worksheet. If you prefer to work with the chart separately, place it on its own sheet, and Excel automatically sizes it to fill an entire page.

Figure 6.3
In the Chart Wizard - Step 3 of 4 - Chart Options dialog box, you can change the standard options for the selected chart type.

Type axis titles here

Type the chart title here

Figure 6.4
The Chart Wizard - Step 4 of 4 - Chart Location dialog box enables you to specify the location of your chart.

Click here to place the chart on its own sheet

Click here to embed the chart on the worksheet of your choice

⑫ **Click Finish.**

Excel creates the chart and displays it with eight black squares called *handles* surrounding the box, as shown in Figure 6.5. The Chart toolbar, which you can use to edit the chart, should automatically appear. If it does not, choose View, Toolbars, Chart to display it.

Figure 6.5
Excel creates the chart and embeds it as an object in the current worksheet.

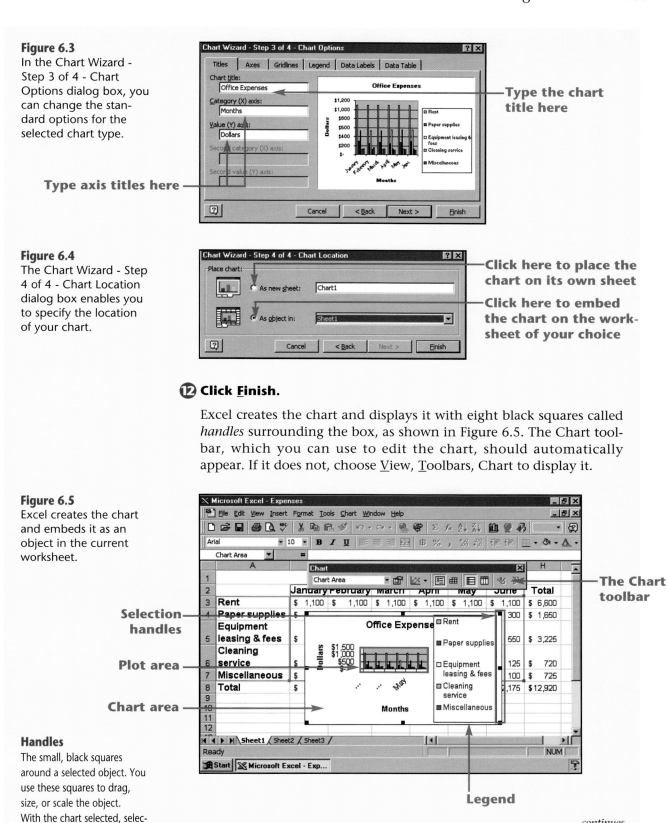

Selection handles

Plot area

Chart area

The Chart toolbar

Legend

Handles
The small, black squares around a selected object. You use these squares to drag, size, or scale the object. With the chart selected, selection handles are displayed, and you can drag the chart to a new position below the worksheet.

continues

To Create a Chart   (continued)

13 **Click inside the chart area (in any blank area) and drag the chart so that the upper-left corner is positioned in cell A10.**

As you drag the chart, the pointer changes to a four-headed arrow. The chart is repositioned, but it needs resizing. It is important to resize the chart before you format it. If you don't resize first, the formatting and added enhancements will be out of proportion with the chart.

14 **Point to the selection handle in the lower-right corner of the chart.**

The pointer changes to a two-headed diagonal arrow.

15 **Drag this selection handle down and to the right until the chart expands through cell G25.**

The chart now fills cells A10:G25.

16 Save your work and keep the Expenses worksheet open for the next lesson, where you learn how to format chart text.

Jargon Watch

Charts and maps are considered to be **objects** in Excel. An object is an item that has its own frame or box and that can be selected, moved, copied, sized, and formatted independently of the worksheet cells behind it. Other objects in Excel include text boxes and clip art.

Charts consist of a number of elements, most of which you can modify or delete. An axis, for example, is a line that serves as a major reference for plotting data on a chart; **axes** is the plural of axis. In a two-dimensional chart, there are generally two axes: one is the y-axis or Value axis where the numbers appear, and the other axis is the x-axis or Category axis where the labels define the categories into which the values fall. The two axes normally meet at the value 0. On a 3-D chart, a second Value axis (z-axis) is included.

The data in your worksheet is plotted against the axes; each value for each category is represented by a data point. A row or column of worksheet data that produces a line on a line chart, a set of columns or bars that share a color on column or bar charts, or an area in an area chart is called a **data series**.

To help a user understand the value of the data points on a chart, you can display **gridlines**. These are lines that extend from the tick marks on an axis through the plot area to make it easier to evaluate data points. There are also axis labels (either values or categories) to help the user understand the chart.

Charts also include text elements. A **chart title** is the text that appears above the chart and defines what the chart is or shows. You can also add axis labels to explain the values or categories displayed. A **legend** is a key that identifies the patterns, colors, or symbols associated with the markers of a data series by the series name. **Data labels** are optional labels that appear at the data points on the chart; they can show the value, category, or percentage of the data point. A **data table** appears with the chart and shows the original values and labels from the worksheet, which is useful if you print the chart separately from the worksheet.

You can move a selected chart or its elements (such as the legend and titles) on the chart by dragging them to a new location. You can also resize a selected chart or element by positioning the mouse pointer over any one of the chart box handles until the pointer changes to a two-headed arrow. Drag the handle away from the center of the chart box to enlarge the box or toward the center of the box to reduce it.

When you drag a handle on the middle of one side of the box, you change the size horizontally or vertically. When you drag a corner handle, you change the vertical and horizontal dimensions at the same time. If you hold down (Shift) while dragging a corner handle, you maintain the original proportions of the chart.

Be careful when increasing the size of a chart, as data series proportions can be misleading. For example, if you stretch the height of a chart without maintaining the original proportions, you visually exaggerate the numerical differences in the data, which can change the impact of the information.

If you want to delete a chart, simply select the chart and press (Del).

You can create a chart on its own sheet in the default (2-D column) chart type by selecting the data and pressing (F11) or the (Alt) + (F1) key combination. You can then modify the chart by using the chart commands.

Lesson 2: Formatting Text in a Chart

After you create a chart, you can format chart text to enhance the chart's title, axes labels, or legend. You can even change the emphasis of the chart's details. You can change text in a chart simply by clicking the text area you want to modify and then making the change, or by formatting the text in the entire chart area at the same time.

You change the format of the text in Excel charts using the same methods you use to format text in worksheet cells. Now try formatting text in the chart you created in Lesson 1.

To Format Text in a Chart

❶ In the Expenses **worksheet, scroll up until you can see the top of the chart. If the handles are not displayed, click somewhere in the chart area.**

The selected chart can be edited and formatted. The Chart Objects text box in the Chart toolbar shows that the Chart Area is selected.

If you cannot see the Chart toolbar on your screen, choose View, Toolbars, and click the Chart option.

 ❷ Click the Format Chart Area button on the Chart toolbar.

The Format Chart Area dialog box is displayed.

continues

Excel

3 Click the Font tab.

This displays the Font options used to change the appearance of text in a chart, as shown in Figure 6.6.

Figure 6.6
The Font tab of the Format Chart Area dialog box enables you to change the appearance of the chart text.

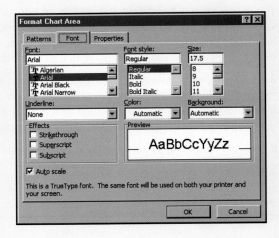

4 In the Font list, select Times New Roman. In the Font style list, select Bold. In the Size list, select 8. Then click OK.

This changes all of the text in the chart to the Times New Roman font with bold style, and reduces the font size to 8 points.

5 Double-click the chart's title.

A selection box appears around the chart's title and the Format Chart Title dialog box appears.

6 Click the Font tab if it is not displayed.

7 In the Size list box, select 24. Click OK.

This increases the size of the chart's title to 24 points and closes the dialog box.

8 Scroll down the worksheet until the bottom of the chart appears. Double-click any Category axis label.

The Format Axis dialog box appears. Now you will change the orientation (direction) of the text for the Category axis. From the Chart toolbar, you can rotate text up or down 45 degrees; however, if you want the text to be rotated 90 degrees, you need to use the Alignment tab in this dialog box.

9 Click the Alignment tab of the Format Axis dialog box.

The alignment options are displayed, as shown in Figure 6.7.

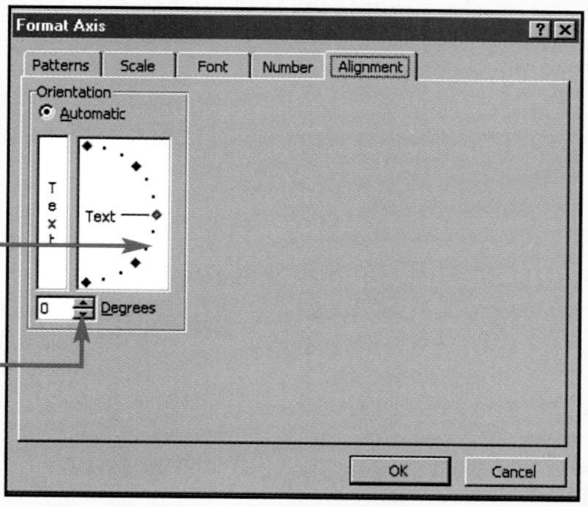

Figure 6.7
The orientation of the text for the chart's titles, except for the legend, can be rotated upward or downward.

Degree indicator —

Spinner to specify the number of degrees

🔟 **Drag the degree indicator up until 90 degrees is displayed in the Degrees box. Click OK.**

The Format Axis dialog box closes. Now view the completed chart in its own window. This eliminates scrolling through the worksheet to view a chart, and chart editing can be done while the chart is open in the window.

⓫ **Choose View, Chart Window.**

The entire chart appears in a chart window that is the same size as the chart on your worksheet, as shown in Figure 6.8.

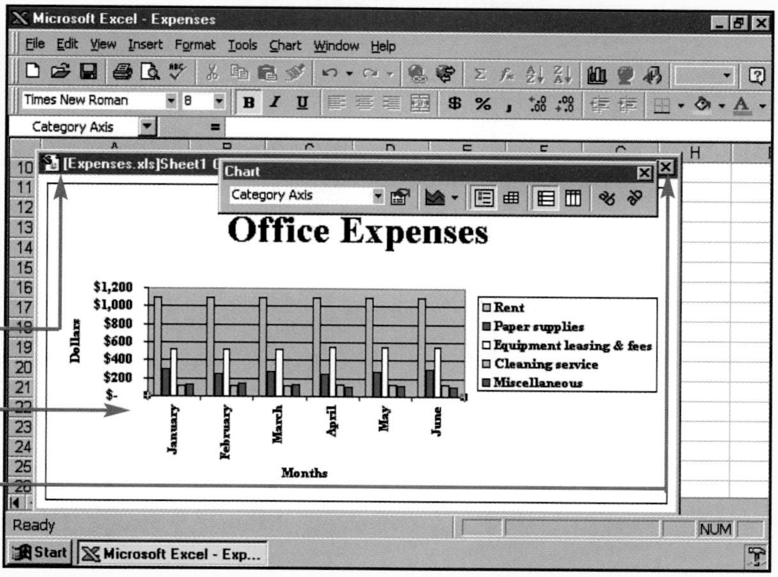

Figure 6.8
The chart title now appears in 24-point Times New Roman. The legend, Value axis, and Category axis text appear in 8-point Times New Roman. The Category axis labels are rotated 90 degrees.

Chart window title —

Chart document window —

Close button —

⓬ **Click the Close button on the chart window.**

The chart window is closed.

⓭ Save your work and keep the Expenses worksheet open. In Lesson 3, you learn how to change chart types.

Lesson 3: Changing the Chart Type

After you create a chart, you may decide that you do not like the type of chart you have selected. Because Excel has a wide variety of chart types, you can display information in a way that best conveys its meaning.

Certain chart types are best for certain situations. It's important to select a chart type that can help you display the information in the most dramatic, appropriate, and meaningful manner possible. For example, you can usually spot trends more easily with a line chart, while a pie chart is best for showing parts of a whole.

Now try changing the Expenses chart to a different type of chart.

To Change the Chart Type

❶ In the Expenses **worksheet, make sure that the chart is selected and the Chart toolbar is displayed.**

Eight selection handles appear on the chart box frame to show that the chart is selected, as shown in Figure 6.9. When you select the chart, the Chart toolbar automatically appears so that the tools associated with charting are available for your use.

Figure 6.9
The selected chart has a border and selection handles.

Chart toolbar ⎯

Chart Type
drop-down
arrow

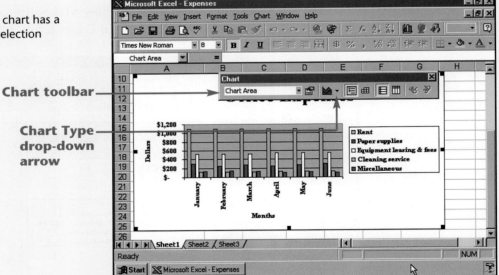

❷ Click the drop-down arrow next to the Chart Type button on the Chart toolbar.

The various chart types are displayed in a three-column, drop-down list, as shown in Figure 6.10. If you can't see the Chart toolbar on your screen, choose View, Toolbars, and then click the Chart option.

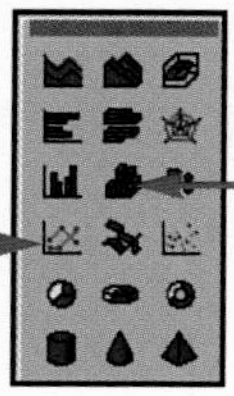

Figure 6.10
Select a chart type from the drop-down list.

Line Chart button ———————→

—— **3-D Column Chart button**

❸ **Click the 3-D Column Chart button (the third button down in the second column).**

Excel changes the chart type to the 3-D column format, as shown in Figure 6.11.

Figure 6.11
The Expenses data appears as a 3-D column chart.

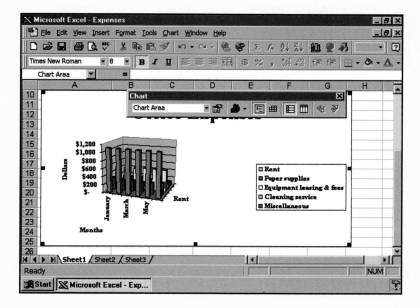

The 3-D column chart does not provide a very good representation of your data. If you want to examine the trends of the source of your income over time, there may be better chart types to use. Consult Table 6.1 to learn more about the different chart types and how they represent your data. Now you will select another type of chart that can more clearly illustrate the trend.

❹ **In the Chart Type drop-down list, click the Line Chart button (the fourth button down in the first column).**

The chart type changes to a line chart, as shown in Figure 6.12.

continues

To Change the Chart Type (continued)

Figure 6.12
In a line chart, you can easily examine trends over time.

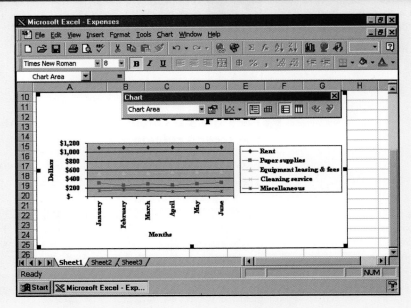

⑤ **Save your work and keep the** Expenses **worksheet open. In Lesson 4, you learn how to enhance your chart's appearance.**

If you have problems... If you aren't sure which chart type to select for a specific job, select one chart type and study the results. Check to see whether the data is accurately represented and conveys the appropriate meaning. Try various chart types until you find the one that best suits your needs.

Table 6.1 describes the various chart types available in Excel.

Table 2.1	Common Chart Types
Chart Type	**Description**
Area	A line chart that shows the area below the line filled with a color or pattern. Use an area chart to compare several sets of data.
Bar or Column	A chart that represents data by the height of the vertical columns or length of the horizontal bars. Use a bar or column chart to compare one item to another or to compare different items over time.
Line	A chart consisting of a series of data at various points along the axis. The points are connected by a line. Use a line chart to indicate a trend over time.
Pie	A circular chart in which each piece (wedge) shows a data segment and its relationship to the whole. Use a pie chart to sort data and compare parts of the whole.

Chart Type	Description
Doughnut	A circular ring-shaped chart that compares the sizes of pieces in a whole. It is similar to a pie chart but can include multiple data series, appearing in concentric rings.
Radar	A line or area chart enclosed around a central point. Use a radar chart to show the uniformity of data.
XY or Bubble (Scatter)	A chart in which data points are placed along the Value axis and a numeric x-axis, similar to a line chart. Use an XY chart to compare trends over uneven time or measurement intervals (scientific data). Use a Bubble chart to plot two variables against the Category and Value axis, similar to the XY chart, adding a third variable represented by the size of the bubble.
Combination	A chart that combines parts from a line, bar, or area chart so that you can plot data in two forms on the same chart. Use a combination chart to show a correlation between two data series.
Surface	A chart that represents optimum combinations between two sets of data. Patterns and colors are added to indicate sections that are in the same range of values.
Stock	A chart to plot stock prices; the data must be organized in the correct order. It can also be used for scientific data.
3-D (Area, Bar, Line, Pie)	A chart that represents data in the same way as its two-dimensional counterpart. Besides displaying height and width, however, a 3-D chart adds depth to the appearance of the chart.
Cone, Cylinder, Pyramid	A chart that enhances the data markers on 3-D column and bar charts.

Lesson 4: Enhancing a Chart

After you have decided which type of chart best conveys the information in your worksheet, you can enhance the chart's appearance in several ways. The most common enhancements include changing chart colors, adding a grid, and formatting the chart labels.

The easiest way to change any part of a chart is to select the chart, move the mouse pointer over the part you want to change, click the right mouse button, and then choose a command from the shortcut menu.

Now try using this easy method to enhance the Expenses chart.

To Enhance a Chart

❶ In the Expenses **worksheet, make sure that the chart is select-ed.**

With the chart selected, the selection handles are displayed and individual elements of the chart can be edited.

❷ Right-click one of the points of the line representing Rent **in the chart.**

A shortcut menu appears and the Rent line is selected, as shown in Figure 6.13.

Figure 6.13
Each element of a chart has its own shortcut menu for editing.

Rent line ────

Shortcut menu ────

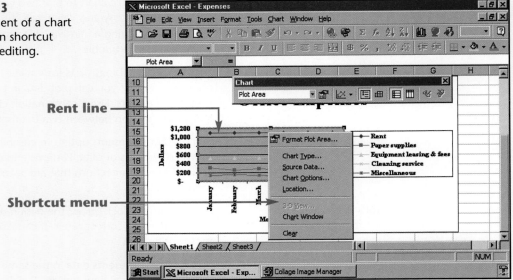

❸ Choose Chart Type from the shortcut menu.

The Chart Type dialog box appears, as shown in Figure 6.14.

Figure 6.14
The Chart Type dialog box enables you to change the chart type and subtype.

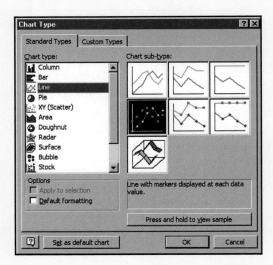

4 **Click Area in the Chart type list, and then click the first chart (Area) in the Chart subtype list and click OK.**

The chart is now a combination area and line chart, as shown in Figure 6.15. Rent, the element you selected to edit, is represented by the large area from $- to the straight black line at $1100 on the Value axis, while the rest of the chart remains unchanged. Now change the color of the total area.

Figure 6.15
This is an example of a combination area and line chart.

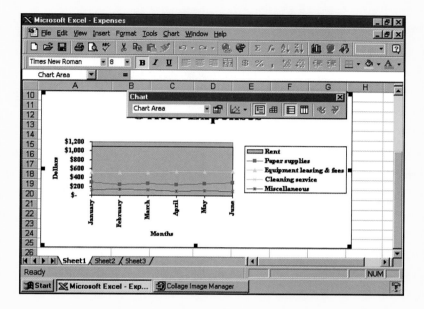

5 **Right-click the Rent area and choose Format Data Series from the shortcut menu.**

The Format Data Series dialog box opens with the Patterns tab selected. In the Area section of the dialog box, a palette of colors is displayed. The current color for the Rent area is shown in the Sample box in the lower-left corner.

6 **Select gray, the third color down in the last column.**

The new color appears in the Sample box, as shown in Figure 6.16.

7 **Click OK.**

The dialog box closes and the new color appears in the chart. Now you will change the number format of the labels on the Value axis to show dollars with two decimal places.

8 **Right-click any of the dollar amounts on the Value axis of the chart and choose Format Axis from the shortcut menu.**

The Format Axis dialog box appears.

9 **Select the Number tab.**

The Number tab and its options appear with the Custom category selected, as shown in Figure 6.17.

continues

To Enhance a Chart   (continued)

Figure 6.16
The Format Data Series dialog box enables you to choose a new color for the selected data series.

Select gray here →

Sample box →

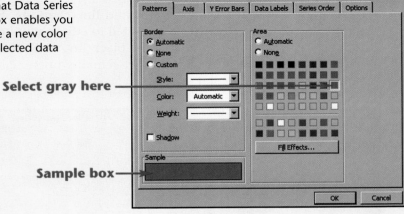

Figure 6.17
On the Number tab of the Format Axis dialog box, you can specify a different number format.

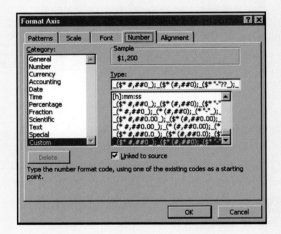

🔟 **Scroll through the Type list and select the type with a dollar sign and two decimal places, $#,##0.00_);($#,##0.00). Click OK.**

Excel applies this format, which includes a $ sign, a comma as a thousands separator, and two decimal places, to the dollar values on the Value axis, as shown in Figure 6.18.

⓫ **Save your work and keep the Expenses workbook open. You use it in the next lesson to learn how to print a worksheet that includes a chart.**

Figure 6.18
The enhanced chart is
easier to read.

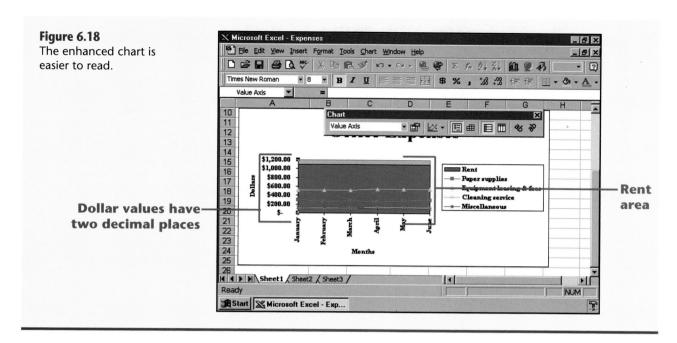

Dollar values have
two decimal places

Rent
area

 **Inside Stuff**

You can modify the format of any element of a chart—the chart title, axis titles, value numbers, axis scale, category axis labels, legend, gridlines, chart area—by right-clicking the element. From the shortcut menu that appears, you select the format command to open the specific format dialog box relating to it.

A quick way to open the specific format dialog box relating to an element is to double-click the element.

 **Exam Notes**

Pie Charts are a little different from charts that have axes. To generate a pie chart, you only need to select a row or column of slice labels from the worksheet and the row or column next to it that contains the values of the slices. Then use the Chart Wizard as you would with any other chart.

Normally, you don't use a legend with a pie chart. Therefore, when you reach the Chart Wizard - Step 3 of 4 - Chart Options dialog box, you should select the Legend tab and remove the check mark from Show legend. To add slice labels to the pie chart, click the Data Labels tab and select Show label or Show label and percent. If you want short lines connecting the label to the appropriate slice on the chart, check Show leader lines.

One other characteristic that pie charts have is the ability to explode or cut a slice, which moves a selected slice away from the center of the pie in order to emphasize that slice. Once the pie chart is complete and embedded in your worksheet or displayed on its own sheet, click the center of the pie once to select it (handles appear on the edge of the pie). Then click once on the slice you want to explode to select just that slice. Point in the middle of the selected slice and drag it a short distance away from the center of the pie.

If you have a 3-D pie chart, you can also tilt or rotate the pie. Select the pie and choose Chart, 3-D View from the menu. Click the two large up and down arrows to change the tilt of the chart; click the circular arrows to rotate the chart. A sample shows the change in position. Choose OK when you have the position you want.

Lesson 5: Printing a Chart

Unless you want to carry around a laptop computer to show your work on-screen, you need to be able to print your worksheets.

Printing lets you view the worksheets you have created, even when you are away from your computer. A printed copy of a chart combined with the worksheet data makes a very effective presentation. Now try printing the entire Expenses workbook file, including the chart.

To Print a Chart

1 **In the** Expenses **worksheet, click anywhere outside the chart.**

This makes sure that no range in the worksheet is selected, not even the chart. The Chart toolbar is removed from the screen.

2 **Choose File, Page Setup.**

The Page Setup dialog box appears, as shown in Figure 6.19. Use this dialog box to adjust the page setup before you print your worksheet. This dialog box provides a wide range of options from which you can choose to customize your printed worksheet. For this example, you will change the margins, header, and footer for the printed worksheet.

Figure 6.19
The Page Setup dialog box.

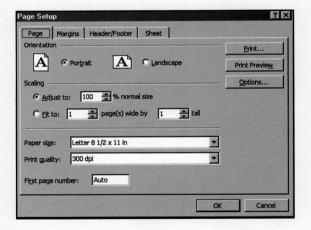

3 **In the Page Setup dialog box, click the Header/Footer tab.**

The Header and Footer options let you specify information to print in the header and footer area of each page. You can choose from predefined headers and footers, or you can create your own.

4 **Click the drop-down arrow next to the Header text box, scroll up, and select (none).**

This removes the default header text, and nothing will print in the header area.

5 Click the drop-down arrow next to the Footer text box and select Expenses.

This footer prints the current file name in the center of the footer area.

6 Click the Margins tab in the Page Setup dialog box.

This displays the Margins options.

7 In the Top text box, click the up arrow twice.

This changes the top margin from 1 to 1.5.

8 In the Bottom text box, click the down arrow once.

This changes the bottom margin from 1 to 0.75. You have now finished setting up the worksheet page for printing. Now preview the page to make sure it is the way you want it to print.

9 Click the Print Preview button in the Page Setup dialog box.

Excel closes the Page Setup dialog box, makes the changes you requested to the page setup, and displays the Print Preview window, as shown in Figure 6.20. In Print Preview, you can see the worksheet as it will look when you print it. (You can also open the Print Preview window by clicking the Print Preview button on the Standard toolbar when the Page Setup dialog box isn't open.) Everything looks all right, so you are ready to print.

Figure 6.20
Print Preview shows you the page as it will print, including the chart.

Click here to print the worksheet

Click here to open the Page Setup dialog box

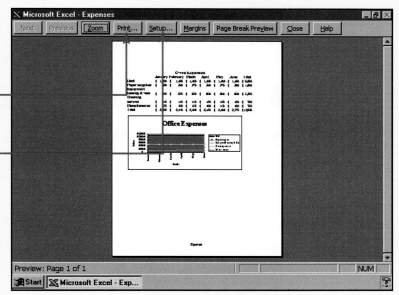

10 Click the Print button on the Print Preview toolbar.

The Print Preview window closes and the Print dialog box appears.

continues

To Print a Chart   (continued)

⑪ In the Number of <u>c</u>opies text box, change the number of copies to 2 and click OK.

Excel prints two copies of the worksheet, including the chart. When you are done printing, save and close the Expenses workbook. In Lesson 7, you learn how to create a map by using data in a different workbook file.

You can print just a chart in Excel without printing the entire worksheet. Select the chart and choose <u>F</u>ile, <u>P</u>rint to open the Print dialog box. Click the Selected Chart option button in the Print What area and then click OK.

If you want to leave additional space between the chart and the worksheet data, simply select the chart and drag it down a few rows. Remember to deselect the chart before printing.

Lesson 6: Creating a Map

Maps are useful for charting information that is defined by state, country, or province. Maps are not one of Excel's built-in chart types, but are a separate feature of Excel. Maps can help you visualize your worksheet information geographically. In this lesson, you compare how many company offices are located in different states in the U.S. By creating a map, you can see where most of the offices are located.

Try creating a map now, using the sample worksheet provided.

To Create a Map

❶ From the Project-06 folder on the CD, open the file Proj0602 and save it as SiteMap**.**

❷ Select cell A3. Hold down ⇧Shift and press Ctrl+End.

This selects all the data in the worksheet so that the information can be used to create your map.

❸ Click the Map button on the Standard toolbar.

The mouse pointer changes to a crosshair, which you can use to specify where in the worksheet Excel should create the map.

❹ Click cell A21 and hold down the left mouse button, then drag the mouse to cell G35.

When you release the mouse button, Excel begins creating the map in the range A21:G35. This may take a few seconds. Excel looks to see which map the data belongs in, based on the geographical data included in the selected data range. If the data could fit in more than one map (which is the case in this example), the Multiple Maps Available dialog box appears, as shown in Figure 6.21.

Figure 6.21
The Multiple Maps
Available dialog box.

⑤ Select United States in North America and click OK.

You may have to wait for several seconds while Excel composes the map. The map appears in the selected cells along with the Microsoft Map Control dialog box, as shown in Figure 6.22. The map is inserted into a frame, which you can use to resize and move the map. You can use the Microsoft Map Control dialog box to change some formatting characteristics of the map. Currently, the # of Offices column is displayed in the map by gray shading—a different shade of gray for a specified range of values. Because the shading values in the map are not easy to discern, try changing the shading to colors now.

Figure 6.22
The map is created,
showing the states in
which offices are
located.

Frame

Show/Hide Microsoft
Map Control

Format buttons

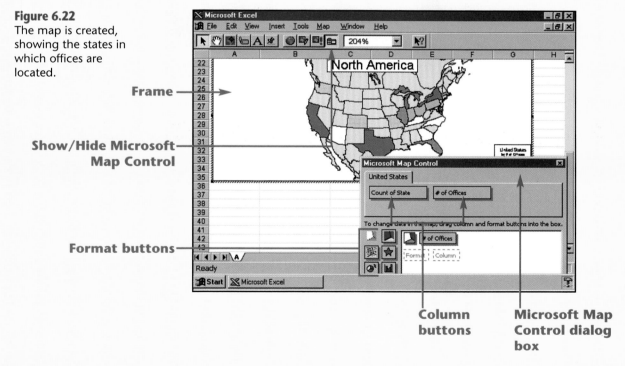

Column
buttons

Microsoft Map
Control dialog
box

continues

To Create a Map (continued)

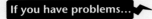

If the Microsoft Map Control dialog box is covering the map so you cannot see the map, simply drag the dialog box out of the way. You can open and close the dialog box by using the Show/Hide Microsoft Map Control button on the toolbar.

6 **In the Microsoft Map Control dialog box, drag the Category Shading button onto the # of Offices button, as shown in Figure 6.23.**

Figure 6.23
Use the Microsoft Map Control dialog box to change the format of the map.

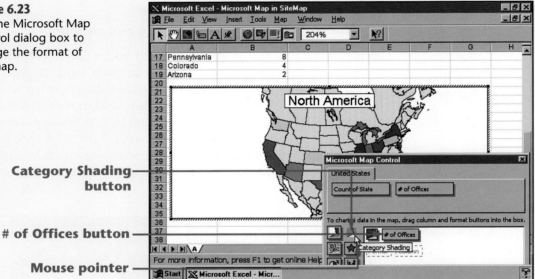

Category Shading button

# of Offices button

Mouse pointer

This takes the values in the # of Offices column of the worksheet and divides them into categories by color. When you release the mouse button, Excel redraws the map, applying a different color to each state to indicate the number of offices in that state.

7 **Close the Microsoft Map Control dialog box.**

The map is complete, as shown in Figure 6.24. The location of offices is now clearly indicated by different colors. The expanded legend is partially hidden in the map frame and is difficult to read.

8 **Drag the legend up to display the entire box.**

9 **Drag the upper-left corner of the legend box up and to the left (approximately even with row 24. Click inside the map to deselect the box.**

You can now see the colors and the numbers in the legend to identify which part of the country has the greatest number of offices (the number identifies the number of offices in each state by color; the number in parentheses identifies how many states have that number of offices). You decide to focus your research on the states surrounding Ohio. Try zooming in on the map now.

Figure 6.24
The map with an expanded legend.

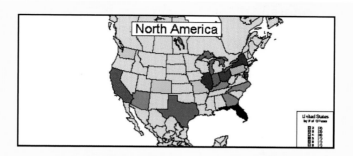

96%

10 Click the Zoom Percentage of Map drop-down arrow and Select 400%.

Excel redraws the map, increasing its magnification. Now change the title of the map.

If you have problems...

If you are unhappy with the view, use the Zoom Percentage of Map button to change the view percentage. You can return to the previous view by opening the View menu and choosing Previous. To view the entire map, choose View, Entire Map.

11 Double-click the Map title.

This selects the map's title and positions an insertion point in the text so that you can enter and edit the title text. You can change the text as well as the text attributes, including font, font size, and font style.

12 Change the text to Office Locations **and press** ⏎Enter.

This changes the map's title. You can drag it to a new location on the map or resize it so that it doesn't cover any of the target states.

13 Drag the map title to the upper-left corner of the map.

The map title is moved. You can also reposition the map within its frame.

14 Click the Grabber button on the Microsoft Map toolbar and click the map and drag it around in the frame until it is positioned to the left of the legend.

Click anywhere outside the map frame to deselect it. The map is complete, as shown in Figure 6.25.

15 Save your work. If requested by your instructor, print two copies of the worksheet with the map. Then close the workbook.

If you have completed your session on the computer, exit Excel and Windows 95 before turning off your computer. Otherwise, continue with the "Checking Your Skills" and "Applying Your Skills" sections.

continues

To Create a Map (continued)

Figure 6.25
The completed map appears below the worksheet data.

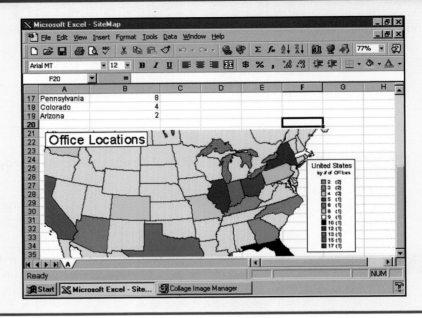

When creating a map, you need to have two columns of data. The first column contains the name of the region, state, or country. You can use abbreviations—such as WV, TN, NC, and so on—or you can use the state's full name. The second column contains the worksheet information. The data in the second column is represented on the map by colors and/or patterns.

As with the elements in a chart, you can right-click elements in a map to open a shortcut menu. You can use the commands on the shortcut menus to quickly edit or enhance the parts of the map.

To print the worksheet with the map, choose File, Print, select the options you want in the Print dialog box and then click OK. To print the map without printing the entire worksheet, select the worksheet cells surrounding the map, click the Selection option in the Print dialog box, and then click OK. You can change options such as the header, footer, and margins by using the Page Setup dialog box, just as you do for all worksheets.

Project Summary

To	Do This
Start the Chart Wizard.	Select the range to be charted and then click the Chart Wizard button on the Standard toolbar or choose Insert, Chart.
Select a chart.	Click the chart.
Format a chart element.	Click the chart element and click the right mouse button. From the shortcut menu, choose the Format option.

To	Do This
Change a chart type.	Select the chart and then choose a chart type from the Chart Type drop-down list on the Chart toolbar.
Print a chart.	Select the chart and click the Print button on the Standard toolbar.
Create a map.	Select the range to be mapped; click the Map button on the Standard toolbar, and then click in the work-sheet where you want the upper-left corner of the map to appear.

Checking Your Skills

True or False

For each of the following, check *T* or *F* to indicate whether the statement is true or false.

__T __F   **1.** A chart can only be placed on the worksheet with the data.

__T __F   **2.** Charts and maps are objects on the worksheet.

__T __F   **3.** An embedded chart must be viewed in a chart window before the elements can be selected, moved, copied, sized, or formatted.

__T __F   **4.** The x-axis usually provides labels to define the categories in the chart.

__T __F   **5.** After a chart is created, you can choose another chart type if you are not satisfied with the representation of your data.

__T __F   **6.** An object has its own frame.

__T __F   **7.** When creating a map, the first column of data should contain the names of regions, states, or countries.

__T __F   **8.** Three ways to create a chart from selected data in Excel are by pressing F11, pressing Alt+F1, and using the Chart Wizard.

__T __F   **9.** Excel cannot create three-dimensional charts.

__T __F   **10.** You should resize a chart before formatting it.

Multiple Choice

Circle the letter of the correct answer for each of the following questions.

1. Which type of chart usually helps you spot trends easily?

   a. area

   b. column

   c. line

   d. pie

2. Which type of chart is best for showing parts of a whole?

   a. area

   b. column

   c. line

   d. pie

3. What is the element of a chart that identifies colors or patterns assigned to a data series or chart categories?

   a. chart area

   b. chart title

   c. legend

   d. value axis

4. What are some common enhancements that are often made to a chart to improve its appearance?

   a. add a grid

   b. change colors

   c. format the chart labels

   d. all the above

5. How many columns of data are needed in your worksheet to create a map?

   a. one

   b. two

   c. three

   d. as many as you want

6. The default chart type is what?

   a. column

   b. bar

   c. pie

   d. line

7. The mouse pointer changes to which of the following when you drag a chart?

   a. 2-headed arrow

   b. 4-headed arrow

   c. hand

   d. pointing finger

8. Three-dimensional charts have a third axis, called what?

   a. x-axis

   b. y-axis

   c. z-axis

   d. d-axis

9. Which of the following is used to identify the data in a chart?

   a. legend

   b. gallery

   c. Chart Wizard

   d. none of the above

10. Use which type of chart to show a correlation between two data series?

   a. column

   b. combination

   c. pie

   d. line

Completion

In the blank provided, write the correct answer for each of the following statements.

1. The _____ button on the Standard toolbar assists you in creating a chart.

2. Excel creates a chart from a _____ you specify on the worksheet.

3. Click the _____ mouse button on a chart or chart element to display a shortcut menu.

4. Select a chart or chart element and then drag a _____ to resize it.

5. Create a _____ to chart information that is defined by state, country, or province.

6. A _____ is a range of values in a worksheet.

7. The labels along the bottom of a chart are the _____ labels.

8. The labels along the left side of a chart are the _____-axis labels.

9. To delete an embedded chart, click it to select it, and press _____.

10. The mouse pointer should be shaped like a _____ on the worksheet cell where you want the upper-left corner of a map to start.

Matching

In the blank next to each of the following terms or phrases, write the letter of the corresponding term or phrase.

a. Category axis

b. data series

c. embedded

d. handles

e. legend

f. line

g. notes

h. object

i. pie

j. Value axis

_____ 1. A range of values in a worksheet

_____ 2. Identifies data series

_____ 3. Black squares surrounding a chart

_____ 4. Vertical axis of a chart

_____ 5. Horizontal axis of a chart

_____ 6. A chart that appears on the worksheet along with the worksheet data

_____ 7. Brief descriptions of the data in a chart

_____ 8. A chart type in which each segment shows a data segment and its relationship to the whole

_____ 9. A chart type consisting of a series of data at various points along the

_____ 10. An item that has its own frame or box

Applying Your Skills

Practice

The following exercises enable you to practice the skills you have learned in this project. Take a few minutes to work through these exercises now.

Creating a Chart and Map Showing Mail Order Sales

In the past six months, you have tried to expand your coffee business by adding a mail order catalog that you send to potential customers in the western United States. Create a chart to show the sales for a mail order catalog business in the first quarter of 1998.

To create a chart and map showing mail order sales, follow these steps:

1. Open the file Proj0603 from the Project-06 folder on the CD and save it as `Mail Chart`.

2. Select the data for both columns and create a line chart embedded in the worksheet.

3. Title the chart `Coffee Sales`. Label the x-axis `State` and the y-axis `Sales`.

4. Move the chart below the worksheet, starting in cell A20. Increase the size of the chart so that it fills the range A20:H45.

5. Change the size of the Plot Area and the font of the labels on the x-axis so that a label for each state displays.

6. Change the font size of the labels on the y-axis so they are the same size as the x-axis labels.

7. Save the file and print a copy of the chart. Leave the file open for the following exercise.

Modifying the Chart Showing Mail Order Sales

Because you plan to print the chart you just made and present it to your supervisor, you want to improve its appearance to create a better impression. You adjust the font size of some of the text, format the chart title, and remove the legend.

To modify the chart showing mail order sales, follow these steps:

1. In the `Mail Chart` worksheet, change the font size of the x- and y-axis titles to a 12-point font.

2. Change the Chart Title to a 20-point, bold and italic font.

3. Delete the chart legend.

4. Preview the chart to see how it looks on the page.

5. Print two copies of the chart. Save the file again and leave it open for the following exercise.

Creating a Map Showing the Location of Mail Order Sales

To help target future markets and improve sales, you need to create a map for your sales force that shows where your mail order sales are being made. You want the map to also display how much is being ordered by state based on current sales.

To create a map showing the location of mail order sales, follow these steps:

1. In the `Mail Chart` worksheet, select the data for both columns and create a map, starting in cell A50 through cell G65 of the worksheet.

2. Experiment with some of the map features to enhance the map. For example, change the colors on the map. Change the zoom percentage. Resize the legend so that it doesn't cover any of the map.

3. Change the map title to `Mail Order Sales`. Try editing the font and font size in the title text.

4. Save your work. If requested by your instructor, print two copies of the worksheet with the chart and map before closing the file.

Comparing Sales Using a Chart

In order to help your distribution network understand how well one type of coffee is selling in comparison to the rest, create a pie chart to demonstrate the percentage of sales each coffee type has.

To compare sales using a chart, follow these steps:

1. Open the file Proj0604 from the Project-06 folder on the CD and save it as `Charting Sales`.

2. Create a pie chart using the total sales data in the worksheet. Title the chart `Coffee Sales`.

3. Move the chart below the worksheet data.

4. Now change the chart type to an exploded pie chart.

5. Delete the legend from the pie chart.

6. Choose to display data labels and percentages next to each slice of the pie.

7. Save your work. If requested by your instructor, print two copies of the worksheet with the exploded pie chart.

Creating a Line Chart on a Chart Sheet

In this exercise, you have the opportunity to create a chart on a separate chart sheet and then change the chart type and add titles.

To create a line chart on a chart sheet, follow these steps:

1. Open Proj0605 from the Project-06 folder on the CD and save it as `Beverages`.

2. Select the data range of A4:D7 and then press F11 to create a chart on its own sheet.

3. When the chart sheet appears, right-click to display a chart shortcut menu.

4. Choose the Chart Type command to change the column chart to a line chart.

5. Right-click to display a chart shortcut menu and then select the Chart Options command to insert a chart title and an x-axis title. The chart title is `1st Quarter Sales`. The x-axis title is `Beverage Sales`.

6. If requested by your instructor, print two copies of the worksheet and chart.

7. Save and then close the workbook.

Challenge

The following challenges enable you to use your problem-solving skills. Take time to work through these exercises now.

Creating an Embedded Pie Chart

To show your employees the sales results for July, you create an embedded pie chart.

To create an embedded pie chart, follow these steps:

1. Open Proj0606 from the Project-06 folder on the CD and save it as July Sales.

2. Use the data range A5:B11 to create the chart.

3. Position the chart in rows 14 through 25 below the data area.

4. Insert the chart title July Sales.

5. If requested by your instructor, print two copies of the worksheet and chart. Save and then close the workbook.

Formatting a Chart

Your boss has asked you to create a sales chart that he plans to use in a meeting. You have the data in a worksheet, but you need to create a column chart and format it to make the best possible impression at the meeting.

To format a chart, follow these steps:

1. Open Proj0607 from the Project-06 folder on the CD and save it as Formatted Chart.

2. Position the chart below the data area (rows 11 through 22).

3. Insert the chart title Sales. Label the x-axis as 1998 and the y-axis title as in thousands.

4. Change the Model B data series to the color yellow. Change the Model C data series to red.

5. Change the chart type to bar. Adjust the chart area size and font sizes, if necessary.

6. If requested by your instructor, print two copies of the worksheet and chart. Save and then close the workbook.

Creating a Map

In this project, you create a map showing the number of state agents located throughout the United States.

To create a map, follow these steps:

1. Open Proj0608 from the Project-06 folder on the CD and save it as Company Agents.

2. Create a map using the State and Agents data columns.

3. Add the map title Agents by State.

4. Apply Category Shading to the Agents column.

5. If requested by your instructor, print two copies of the worksheet and map; then save and close the workbook.

Changing Chart Type

In this exercise, you create a chart showing non-salary compensation for company employees.

To change chart type, follow these steps:

1. Open the Proj0609 from the Project-06 folder on the CD and save it as Garnet & Gold.

2. Create a column chart using the data in columns A and B.

3. Move the chart to the range A15:E30.

4. Add a chart title Garnet & Gold Industries.

5. Adjust the size of the chart and the font size so that all x-axis labels display.

6. Delete the legend

7. If requested by your instructor, print two copies of this chart.

8. Change the chart type to a clustered column with a 3-D visual effect.

9. If requested by your instructor print two copies of the worksheet; save and then close the workbook.

Creating Embedded Charts

In this exercise, you create multiple imbedded charts in a worksheet.

To create embedded charts, follow these steps:

1. Open Proj0610 from the Project-06 folder on the CD and save the workbook with the name Motor Pool.

2. Create six embedded column charts, one for each car in the motor pool. Include appropriate chart titles.

3. If requested by your instructor, print two copies of the worksheet. Save and then close the workbook.

PinPoint Assessment

You have completed the project and the associated lessons, as well as the Checking Your Skills and Applying Your Skills sections. Now use the PinPoint software evaluation mode to assess your comprehension of the specific exam tasks you have just learned. You can also use the PinPoint Trainer Mode and the Show Me tutorials to practice these specific exam tasks.

Project 7

Seven

Creating Advanced Charts and Graphics

Adding a Logo to a Worksheet and Improving a Graph

Objectives   **Required Activities**

In this Project, you learn how to
- ➤ Import a Graphic Image
- ➤ Copy a Graphic Image to a Chart
- ➤ Draw and Format a Freeform Object … … … …Create and modify lines and objects
- ➤ Draw and Format an Oval Object
- ➤ Group Graphic Objects
- ➤ Create and Modify 3-D Shapes … … … … …Create and modify 3-D shapes
- ➤ Rotate a 3-D Chart
- ➤ Create a Picture Chart
- ➤ Add a Text Box to Annotate a Chart

Why Would I Do This?

T he phrase, "A picture is worth a thousand words," can apply to Excel. You can often summarize pages of complex data in one or two easily understandable charts. With the charts and graphics features of Excel, you can help your audience interpret the data you present to them. You can create reports and presentations to provide information (to sell your ideas, sell your products, or provide details of your company's sales and profits, for example). Enhancing the appearance of a report or presentation by using graphics can help capture the attention of the reader or listener and drive home your point with more emphasis.

Graphic image
A picture file or drawing saved to a file and available for your use.

In this project, you learn how to enhance worksheets or charts with a *graphic image*. Because at times you may not find just the right image from another source, you learn how to draw your own graphics by using the Excel drawing tools. You also learn how to enhance charts—rotate a 3-D chart and create a 2-D picture chart.

Lesson 1: Importing a Graphic Image

Examples of graphic images include clip art picture files that come with Microsoft Office, photographs scanned into the computer as a graphic file, or artwork created with a graphics software program and saved in a file for your use. Table 7.1 lists graphic files that can be used with Excel.

Table 7.1	Types of Graphic Files for Use with Excel
File Extension	**Software File Type**
.BMP	Windows Paintbrush, Windows 95 Paint, or Bitmap
.CDR	CorelDRAW
.CGM	Computer Graphics Metafile
.DRW	Micrografx Designer/Draw
.DXF	AutoCAD Format 2-D
.EMF	Enhanced Metafile
.EPS	Encapsulated PostScript
.GIF	Graphics Interchange Format
.JPG	Joint Photographic Experts Group (JPEG)
.PCD	Kodak Photo CD
.PCT	Macintosh Picture (PICT)
.PCX	PC Paintbrush
.PNG	Portable Network Graphics
.TGA	Targa
.TIF	Tagged Image File Format (scanned images)
.WMF	Windows Metafile
.WPG	WordPerfect Graphics

If you have problems...

In order to import some of these file formats, you may need to install a separate graphics filter. If you have difficulty importing the file, close all your programs and choose Settings, Control Panel from the Start menu. Click the Add/Remove Programs icon in the Control Panel (you'll need your original installation disks or CD). Click the Microsoft Office tab if you installed the Office suite or the Microsoft Excel tab if you only installed Excel. Look for Converters and Filters, or Graphics Filters. Then follow the onscreen instructions to add the needed graphics filters to your system.

Import
When you retrieve a file from a source other than Excel, you import the file.

A sample company logo was designed for you and saved to a .BMP file. In order to use this logo, you *import* the graphic image into Excel.

To Import a Graphic Image

1 **From the Project-07 folder on the CD, open the file Proj0701 and save it as** `Ice Cream Sales`.

This workbook contains two worksheets, labeled `Annual Sales` and `Chart`.

2 **Click cell A1 of the** `Annual Sales` **sheet tab, if it isn't already selected.**

You would like to place the logo in this area of the worksheet.

3 **Choose Insert, Picture, and click From File in the submenu.**

The Insert Picture dialog box is displayed, as shown in Figure 7.1. The drive from which you have been opening the project data files should be listed in the Look in text box. There should be two picture files available, and they appear in the Name list. If you don't see the preview of the graphics, click the Preview button on the dialog box toolbar.

Figure 7.1
The Insert Picture dialog box displays a list of available graphic files, with a view of the highlighted file name.

List of available files

Look in text box

Preview button

View of picture

4 **Click the** `Icecream` **file if it is not already highlighted and then click Inset.**

If you have problems...

If you cannot find the Icecream graphic file, ask your instructor in which drive and folder to look.

continues

To Import a Graphic Image (continued)

Handles

When a graphic is selected, small white squares, called selection handles, surround the object. When you drag a handle, the object is resized.

If you have problems... ◀

Figure 7.2
The graphic is displayed with eight white squares, known as handles, located around the border.

The picture of an ice-cream sundae, which is your company logo, is pasted into your worksheet. The Picture toolbar is also displayed, as shown in Figure 7.2. The graphic is displayed with eight white squares, called *handles*, located around the border. These handles are used to resize the image.

Make sure that the Picture toolbar is displayed on-screen. If it isn't, choose View, Toolbars and click Picture in the submenu.

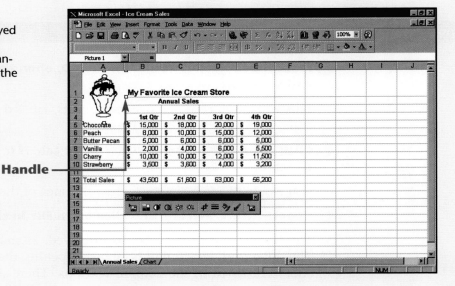

Handle ——

⑤ Using the mouse, point to the handle at the lower-right corner of the graphic.

The mouse pointer changes to a double-headed arrow.

⑥ Drag the handle diagonally up to the bottom of row 1 and then to the left under the column heading A. Now, release the mouse button.

The graphic is proportionately resized and the handles are still displayed around the border of the graphic, as shown in Figure 7.3.

⑦ Click the middle of the graphic and drag the graphic to the middle of cell A1.

The mouse pointer changes to a four-headed arrow, indicating that you are moving the graphic instead of sizing it. After you release the mouse button, the graphic is positioned in the center of cell A1.

⑧ Click the Format Picture button in the Picture toolbar. The Format Picture dialog box is displayed.

You use the Format Picture dialog box to draw a border around your logo.

Choose Insert, Picture to import graphics into a worksheet or chart. When the graphic is imported, it becomes an independent object on the worksheet or chart. The graphic can then be copied, moved, and formatted (the color or pattern, however, cannot be changed) within Excel.

⑨ Click the Colors and Lines tab (see Figure 7.4).

Figure 7.3
The graphic is resized to fit in cell A1.

Corporate logo——

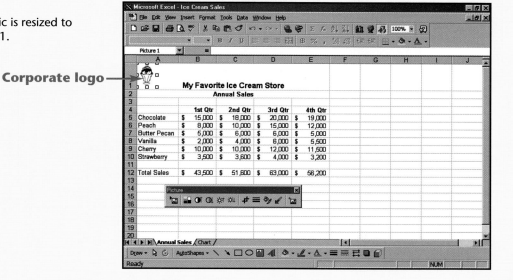

Figure 7.4
Line options are listed in the Colors and Lines tab of the Format Picture dialog box.

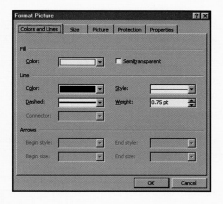

⑩ Under Line, click the down arrow next to Color. From the color palette, select Automatic. Choose OK.

⑪ Click in cell A3 to deselect the graphic.

A border is displayed around the graphic, as shown in Figure 7.5.

⑫ Save the workbook and keep it open for the next lesson, where you learn how to copy this graphic to a chart.

continues

To Import a Graphic Image   (continued)

Figure 7.5
The ice cream graphic is
displayed with a border.

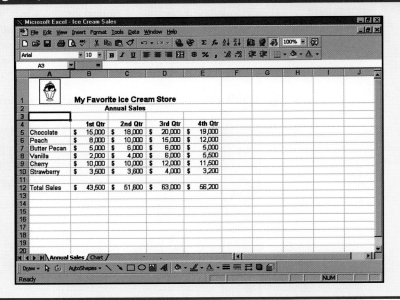

 **Inside Stuff**

Make sure that you don't move graphic images over worksheet data or areas of a chart that contain pertinent information. If you do so, the graphic hides the information behind it.

Lesson 2: Copying a Graphic Image to a Chart

After you import a graphic image, you can use it on another worksheet or chart. In Excel, you can select the graphic and copy it to the Windows Clipboard. After you place the graphic on the Clipboard, you can paste it to a new location.

Now try to copy the graphic you imported into your worksheet from Lesson 1 so that you can use it in your chart.

To Copy a Graphic Image to a Chart

1 **Click the graphic in cell A1 of the** Annual Sales **sheet in the Ice Cream Sales workbook.**

The graphic is selected, and handles display around the border of the graphic.

 2 **Click the Copy button on the Standard toolbar.**

The graphic is copied to the Clipboard.

3 **Click the** Chart **sheet tab.**

④ Click the Paste button on the Standard toolbar.

The graphic is pasted in the upper-left corner of your chart, as shown in Figure 7.6.

Figure 7.6
The graphic is pasted in the upper-left corner of your chart.

Pasted graphic ——

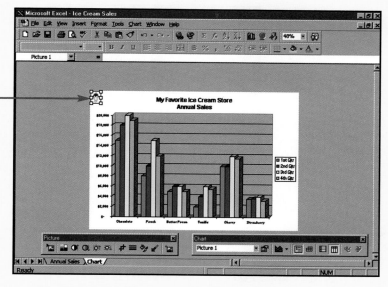

⑤ Click the middle of the graphic and drag the graphic to the upper-right corner of the chart.

The graphic is positioned at the upper-right corner of the chart. Now you want to make the graphic larger.

⑥ Drag the bottom-left handle of the graphic down and to the left to the edge of the Plot area of the chart.

This action makes the logo proportionately larger.

⑦ Click outside the chart area to deselect the graphic.

Your chart is complete, as shown in Figure 7.7.

⑧ Save the workbook and keep it open for the next lesson, where you will learn to draw a filled freeform object.

You can protect an object, such as the company logo, from any editing or formatting changes by protecting the worksheet. First, you must identify any objects that you want to remain unprotected and then turn on the worksheet protection feature.

To do so, select the object to be unprotected. Choose Format, Picture; choose the Protection tab and make sure the Locked option is checked. Click OK. Now choose Tools, Protection, Protect Sheet. Make sure that only the Objects box is checked. If you would like to prevent unauthorized users from removing sheet protection, assign a password up to 255 characters long. Then choose OK. You cannot select a protected object. To turn off the protection, choose Tools, Protection, Unprotect Sheet.

continues

To Copy a Graphic Image to a Chart (continued)

Figure 7.7
The completed chart with company logo.

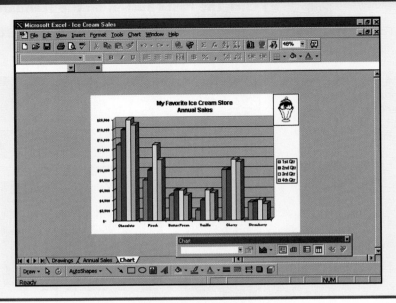

Lesson 3: Drawing and Formatting a Freeform Object

Suppose that you looked through several clip art packages to find the right graphic for a chart but you didn't find one that you wanted. Because Excel provides drawing tools, you can create your own graphic image and save it in a separate worksheet.

The Drawing toolbar displays buttons for the most commonly needed drawing objects—lines, arrows, 3-D shapes, and so on. You access the less commonly needed drawing objects via menus or dialog boxes associated with the Drawing toolbar. Table 7.2 lists and briefly describes the purpose of the buttons on the Drawing toolbar.

Table 7.2   Excel's Drawing Tools

Button Name	Description
Draw	Displays a menu of drawing commands
Select Objects	Selects drawing objects
Free Rotate	Rotates objects to any angle
AutoShapes	Displays a pop-up menu of different shapes
Line	Draws straight lines
Arrow	Draws arrows
Rectangle	Draws rectangles and squares
Oval	Draws ovals and circles
Text Box	Creates text anywhere without attaching it to an object

Button Name	Description
Insert WordArt	Lets you create a WordArt object in your document
Fill Color	Applies fill colors or attributes to selected objects
Line Color	Applies color or patterns to selected lines or outlines
Font Color	Applies color to selected text
Line Style	Applies a line thickness or style to a selected line or outline
Dash Style	Applies a dashed line style to a selected line or outline
Arrow Style	Applies an arrow style or direction to a selected line or arrow
Shadow	Applies a shadow to a selected object
3-D	Applies a three-dimensional (3-D) setting to a selected object

In this lesson, you use the Filled Freeform drawing tool to create a triangle-shaped graphic object.

To Draw and Format a Freeform Object

❶ **Click the** `Annual Sales` **sheet tab in the** `Ice Cream Sales` **workbook.**

❷ **Choose Insert, Worksheet.**

A new worksheet is added to the workbook, to store drawings you create.

❸ **Double-click the** `Sheet1` **tab; type** `Drawings` **and press** ⏎Enter.

The sheet tab is renamed.

❹ **Click the Drawing button on the Standard toolbar.**

The Drawing toolbar is displayed at the bottom of the worksheet above the status bar, as shown in Figure 7.8. Depending on how the toolbar was last used, the Drawing toolbar may appear as a floating toolbar or docked above the Status bar. Table 7.2 lists a quick explanation of what each tool does.

Cross hair
The small, thin cross mouse pointer used for drawing. Drawing is done from the center of the cross hair, so to start at a new point directly over one you just completed, make sure the center of your cross hair is over that point.

❺ **Choose AutoShapes, Lines and click the Freeform icon on the Drawing toolbar, as shown in Figure 7.9.**

The mouse changes to a small, thin cross (also called a *cross hair*), which you use to begin drawing the first line for the triangle.

continues

To Draw and Format a Freeform Object   (continued)

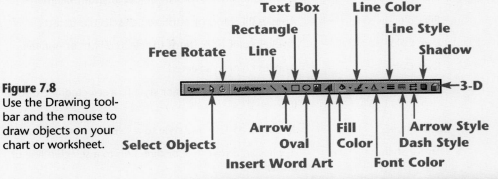

Figure 7.8
Use the Drawing toolbar and the mouse to draw objects on your chart or worksheet.

Figure 7.9
Use the Freeform tool to draw curved and straight lines on your chart or worksheet.

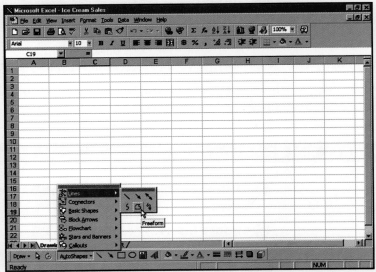

6 **Move the pointer to the top of cell B4. Click the worksheet and release the mouse button.**

This action sets your starting point for the line that you will be drawing, as shown in Figure 7.10. As you move the mouse pointer in the next step, the line length and position change. You click the mouse button again to end a line.

If you have problems...

If you start drawing and a pencil appears, click the worksheet and release the mouse button.

7 **Move the mouse pointer down and to the right, to the bottom of cell B5; click to end the line.**

8 **Move the mouse pointer up and to the right, on the line at the top of cell B4; click to end the line.**

9 **Move the mouse pointer to the left to draw a line that will close the triangle.**

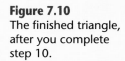

Figure 7.10
The finished triangle,
after you complete
step 10.

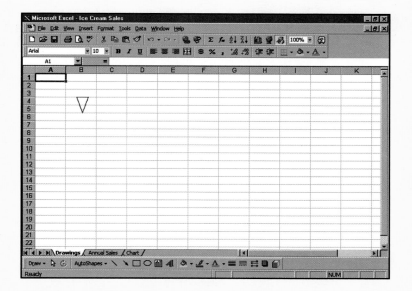

⑩ Click to end the drawing. Click outside of the drawing area on the worksheet to deselect the object.

The triangle object is complete and the handles are removed (refer to Figure 7.10).

If you have problems...

If you do not like the object that you have drawn, click any border to select the object. The handles surround the border of the graphic. Press Del or choose Edit, Clear, All to remove the object. Then try again.

⑪ Click the triangle object.

Handles are displayed around the triangle object.

⑫ Click the arrow next to the Fill Color button in the Drawing toolbar.

The Fill Color palette is displayed.

⑬ Click the brown color in the third row (second button in the color palette). Click outside of the palette area on the worksheet to deselect the object.

The triangle object is filled with the color you selected and the handles are removed.

⑭ Save the workbook and keep it open for the next lesson, where you learn to draw another object.

- To draw a line or arrow, click the Line or Arrow button on the Drawing toolbar, position the mouse pointer (cross hair) where you want the line or arrow to start, hold down the mouse button and drag to the end of the line or arrow, and release the mouse button. Hold down ⬆Shift as you drag to make a straight horizontal or vertical line or arrow.

- To draw a rectangle, click the Rectangle tool on the Drawing toolbar, position the mouse pointer (cross hair) where you want one corner of the rectangle to be, hold down the mouse button and drag diagonally to the opposite corner, and then release the mouse button. Hold down ⬆Shift as you drag if you want to draw a square.

- To draw an oval, click the Oval tool on the Drawing toolbar, position the mouse pointer (cross hair) where you would imagine one corner of a rectangle surrounding the oval to be, hold down the mouse button and drag diagonally to the opposite corner, and then release the mouse button. Hold down ⬆Shift as you drag if you want to draw a circle.

- To draw a shape, click the AutoShapes button on the Drawing toolbar, select the category of shape you want, click the shape, and then position your mouse pointer (cross hair) where you would imagine one corner of a rectangle surrounding the shape to be. Hold down the mouse button and drag diagonally until your shape is the desired size and then release the mouse button. Hold down ⬆Shift as you drag to keep the shape in proportion to the original in the AutoShapes palette.

- To add a text box, click the Text Box button on the Drawing toolbar, position the mouse pointer (cross hair) where you want one corner of the box to be, hold down the mouse button and drag diagonally to the opposite corner, and then release the mouse button. Hold down ⬆Shift as you drag if you want to draw a square text box. After the box is drawn, enter your text. The paragraphs wrap within the margins of the box, and you can format the text using the formatting tools or the menu commands.

Lesson 4: Drawing and Formatting an Oval Object

In Excel, the Drawing toolbar provides several types of objects to assist you in creating your objects. You can draw circles with the Oval tool.

Now try drawing a circle to be combined with the triangle you created in Lesson 3. The combined objects will form an ice-cream cone graphic. You use the new graphic to enhance an existing chart later in this project.

To Draw and Format an Oval Object

❶ Click the Drawings **sheet tab in the Ice Cream Sales workbook, if it isn't already displayed.**

❷ Click the Oval button on the Drawing toolbar.

The mouse pointer changes to a small, thin cross.

❸ **Position the pointer at the left corner of the top border of cell B2.**

❹ **Click and hold down the left mouse button; hold down the ⇧Shift key while you drag down until the circle slightly overlaps the top of the triangle in cell B4. Then drag to the right to complete the circle.**

When you release the left mouse button, the drawn circle object is displayed with handles surrounding it, as shown in Figure 7.11.

Figure 7.11
The circle after completing step 4.

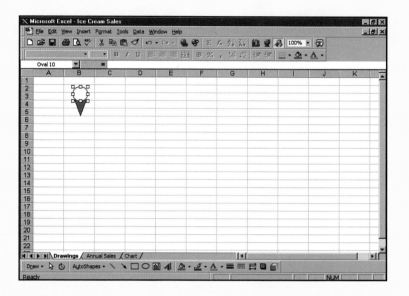

 If you have problems...

If you want to restart the circle drawing, click the object to display the selection handles and press Del, or choose Edit, Clear, All to remove the object. Then try again. If the circle isn't positioned correctly on top of the triangle, you can drag the circle object to reposition it instead of redrawing it.

 ❺ **Click the arrow next to the Fill Color button in the Drawing toolbar.**

The Fill Color palette is displayed.

❻ **Click the dark brown color in the first row (second button in the color palette).**

The second object is complete.

❼ **Click the triangle object.**

Handles are displayed around the border of the object.

Draw ▾ ❽ **Click the Draw button on the Drawing toolbar and choose Order, Bring to Front. Click outside the drawing area to deselect the object.**

continues

To Draw and Format an Oval Object (continued)

The triangle object is now placed in front of the circle, overlaying the bottom of the circle. The ice-cream cone is complete and should look similar to the graphic shown in Figure 7.12.

9 Save the workbook and keep it open for the next lesson, where you group these two objects into one object.

Figure 7.12
The triangle object goes in front of the circle to complete the ice-cream cone graphic.

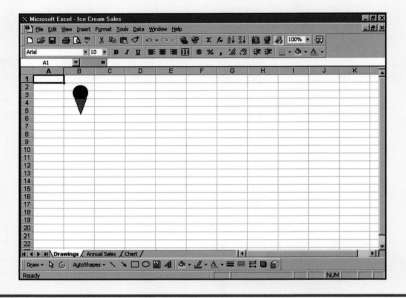

Don't worry if the object you created is not perfect. You can resize and move objects. Click the object to display the handles; drag the handles in any direction to make the object smaller or larger. To move an object, point inside the object and drag it into position.

To edit a freeform object's shape, select the object, click the Draw button on the Drawing toolbar, and choose Edit Points from the menu. Point handles appear at each corner in the shape. Move your mouse pointer over a point until it becomes a miniature, four-headed arrow. Then drag the point to adjust its position. To add another point along a line, hold down Ctrl and click on the line. To remove a point, hold down Ctrl and click on the point. Click away from the object to deselect the object and end the point editing.

Lesson 5: Grouping Graphic Objects

You may want to treat the graphic objects you create as one object for future editing and formatting. In Excel, you can use the Group command from the Draw button on the Drawing toolbar to combine separate objects.

In the following steps, you learn to select the two objects created in Lessons 3 and 4 and group them as one ice-cream cone object.

To Group Graphic Objects

❶ Click the triangle object on the `Drawings` **worksheet in the Ice Cream Sales workbook.**

❷ Press ⇧Shift **and click the circle object.**

Handles surround the objects separately to show they are both selected.

❸ Click the D̲raw button on the Drawing toolbar and click G̲roup.

Handles now surround the entire object—the circle and the triangle—showing that they are now one object and can be treated as such for future editing and formatting.

❹ Click outside of the drawing area on the worksheet to de-select the object.

The handles are removed from the object.

❺ Save the workbook. If requested by your instructor, print two copies, and then leave the workbook open for the next lesson. In the next lesson, you learn to create and modify 3-D shapes.

If you change your mind about grouping objects, you can select the object and click the U̲ngroup option from the D̲raw button on the Drawing toolbar.

Lines have characteristics such as thickness, style, dash, arrowheads, and color. Some of these attributes can also be applied to the outlines of rectangles, ovals, and shapes. To apply a line attribute to a selected line, arrow, or shape outline:

- Click the Line Style button on the Drawing toolbar to select line thickness or style (double, thin-thick, thick-thin, and so on). Click M̲ore Lines on the Line Style palette to open the Format AutoShapes dialog box, which offers a greater selection of line style options.

- Click the Dash Style button on the Drawing toolbar to select a dashed or dotted line style.

- Click the Arrow Style button on the Drawing Toolbar (not applicable to object outlines) to set the style and direction of arrowheads. Click M̲ore Arrows on the Arrow Style palette to open the Format AutoShapes dialog box, which offers a greater selection of arrowhead options.

- Click the Line Color button on the Drawing toolbar to apply the current color to the line, arrow, or outline. Click the down arrow next to the button to see a greater selection of colors. Choose No Line to remove a line. Choose P̲atterned Lines to add dot, crosshatch, diagonal line, and other patterns to the line. Choose M̲ore Line Colors to see a greater selection of colors.

- Double-click the line, arrow, or outline to open the Format AutoShape dialog box that offers all the line attribute options and allows you to set the line thickness in ¼-point increments.

continues

Ovals, rectangles, and shapes have fill attributes. The available types of fills include:

■ **No fill**—Leaves the item empty.

■ **Solid color**—Fills the item with one color.

■ **Pattern**—Fills the item with a pattern (dots, crosshatch, diagonal lines, horizontal lines, vertical lines, and so on) in two colors—one for the pattern (Foreground) and one for the Background behind the pattern.

■ **Gradient**—The fill varies from light to dark shades of the same color (One-Color), from one color to another color (Two-Color), or in a preset pattern of many colors (Preset). You then pick the Shading Style to specify in what direction the gradient should display.

■ **Texture**—Fills the item with textured graphics such as green marble or granite.

■ **Pictures**—Fills the item with repeated copies of a picture you have on file (such as a logo or the Windows wallpaper graphics).

To apply fill attributes to a selected object:

■ Click the Fill Color button on the Drawing toolbar to apply the current fill color.

■ Click the arrow next to the Fill Color button to choose from a palette of colors. Choose No Fill if you don't want the item to have a fill. Choose More Fill Colors if you want to see a larger selection of colors.

■ To choose a fill other than a solid color, click the arrow next to the Fill Color button, and then select Fill Effects. This opens the Fill Effects dialog box from which you can select gradient, texture, pattern, or picture fills.

Excel offers more drawing tools to enhance the objects you've drawn. Here are some of the other features you might want to use:

■ **Free Rotate**—To rotate a selected object, click the Free Rotate button on the Drawing toolbar, position the mouse pointer over one of the four rotating handles at the corners of the object, and drag in a circular motion until the object is at the desired angle.

■ **Rotate 90°**—To rotate a selected object 90° clockwise or counterclockwise, click Draw on the Drawing toolbar, choose Rotate or Flip from the menu, and then select Rotate Right or Rotate Left.

■ **Flip**—To flip an object horizontally (so it looks like its mirror image) or vertically (so it's upside down), click Draw on the Drawing toolbar, choose Rotate or Flip from the menu, and then select Flip Horizontal or Flip Vertical.

■ **Shadow**—Apply a shadow to a selected object by clicking the Shadow button on the Drawing toolbar and selecting the style of shadow you want from the pop-up palette. To adjust the position of the shadow, choose Shadow Settings from the pop-up palette to make the Shadow Settings toolbar appear. Use the buttons on the toolbar to set the shadow position or color.

■ **Order**—As you draw additional objects, they appear on top of the ones you drew first and sometimes they cover up the objects you want to appear on top. To change the order of an object in the stack, click the Draw button on the Drawing toolbar to see a pop-up menu, select Order, and then pick an ordering command—Bring to Front, Send to Back, Bring Forward, Send Backward.

■ **Align or Distribute**—To line up two or more selected objects or space them evenly apart, click the D<u>r</u>aw button on the Drawing toolbar, choose <u>A</u>lign or Distribute from the menu. Then select one of the alignment or distribution options from the submenu, such as Align <u>C</u>enter, Align <u>T</u>op, Distribute <u>H</u>orizontally, and so on.

Lesson 6: Create and Modify 3-D Shapes

The objects you drew in Lessons 3 and 4 were flat objects. Excel can give your objects a three-dimensional (3-D) appearance, so they seem to stand out from the screen.

In this lesson, you create an AutoShape arrow to indicate how well chocolate sales are doing. You have to fill the arrow with color, rotate it, and size it to fit on the worksheet. You'll also make the arrow appear three-dimensional.

To Draw and Modify a 3-D Object

❶ **Click the** Drawings **sheet tab in the Ice Cream Sales workbook if it isn't already displayed.**

❷ **Choose A<u>u</u>toShapes, Block <u>A</u>rrows from the Drawing toolbar and select the Striped Right Arrow (the first arrow in the fifth row) as shown in Figure 7.13.**

Your mouse pointer becomes a cross hair.

Figure 7.13
The AutoShapes menu has a variety of ready-made shapes ready for you to use.

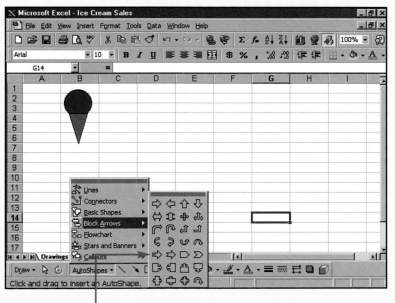

Striped Right Arrow

continues

To Draw and Modify a 3-D Object (continued)

❸ **Move the mouse pointer to E6, hold down the left mouse button, and drag to F9. Release the mouse button.**

When you release the mouse button, the arrow is displayed with handles around it (see Figure 7.14). An additional diamond-shaped handle appears. You use this handle to control the depth of the arrowhead and the thickness of the arrow line. Now you're going to add color to the arrow.

Figure 7.14
Some shapes, like the Striped Right Arrow, have an adjustment handle to help you change the shape.

Drag this handle to change the shape of the arrowhead

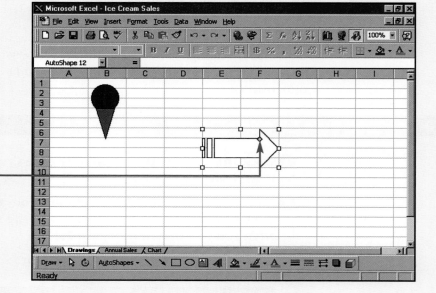

❹ **Click the down arrow next to the Fill Color button on the Drawing toolbar and select bright red (first box in third row).**

Excel offers a variety of colors. If you don't see a color you want, click More Fill Colors to see a wider selection.

❺ **Choose Draw, Rotate or Flip, Rotate Left from the Drawing toolbar.**

Rotate Left rotates a selected object 90 degrees counter-clockwise. When you want to turn an object so it's vertical, this is much easier and more precise than using the Free Rotate tool.

❻ **Click the 3-D button on the Drawing toolbar and select the third option in the second row.**

The 3-D palette offers several options to give your objects depth and perspective. You click the one most suitable to your purposes. To customize the 3-D look of your object, click 3-D Settings to display the 3-D Settings toolbar. With the buttons on that toolbar, you can change the tilt of the object, its depth and direction, the lighting and shadows, the appearance of the object's surface, and the 3-D color.

7 Click Cut on the Standard toolbar.

This removes the arrow from the Drawings sheet. In the next step, you paste it onto the Annual Sales sheet.

8 Click the Annual Sales sheet tab and then click the Paste button on the Standard toolbar.

The arrow now appears on the Annual Sales sheet. It needs to be positioned and sized to fit at the end of the data.

9 Move the arrow by dragging it into the F column, so the tip is at the top of F5. Then size the arrow to fit in cells F5 through F12.

With the arrow fitting into the F column, you need a label to make it obvious what the arrow means.

10 Click G5 and type CHOCOLATE!. Then press ↵Enter.

11 Select G5 and then choose Format, Cells. Select the Font tab and change the font to 14-point Arial Bold Italic and the font color to red.

12 Click the Alignment tab and set the Degrees to 90. Choose OK.

The text now has the same orientation as the arrow, but it doesn't fit in the cell. You need to center the text in the cells next to the arrow.

13 Select the cells G5 through G12 and click the Merge and Center button on the Formatting toolbar.

The text now runs alongside the arrow (see Figure 7.15). You may want to adjust the size of the column to bring it closer to the arrow and the size of row 5 so it matches the height of the nearly rows.

Figure 7.15
The arrow and text communicate excitement about the figures.

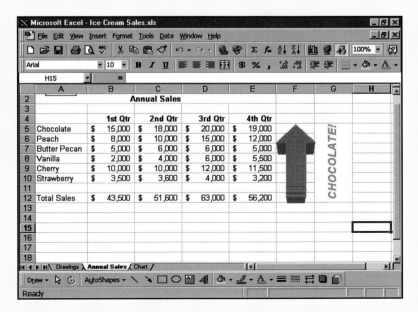

continues

To Draw and Modify a 3-D Object (continued)

⑭ **Choose View, Toolbars and click Drawing in the submenu.**

The Drawing toolbar is removed from the screen (you could also click the Drawing tool on the Standard toolbar to remove the Drawing toolbar).

⑮ **Save the workbook. If requested by your instructor, print two copies, and then close the workbook. In the next lesson, you use a 3-D chart and learn how to rotate its view.**

Lesson 7: Rotating a 3-D Chart

You may want to fine-tune a 3-D chart you created from your worksheet. Sometimes, for example, a data series on the chart may be blocked from view. In Excel, you can create a different view of your 3-D chart by rotating it using the mouse, or through the Chart, 3-D View command. The 3-D View options are shown in Table 7.3, at the end of this lesson. Changes can be made to the chart height or perspective depending on the chart type.

Now try using both methods to rotate the 3-D chart provided in the data file and adjust it to a new view.

To Rotate a 3-D Chart

① **From the Project-07 folder on the CD, open the file Proj0702 and save it as** Charts.

② **Click the** Chart **sheet tab if it isn't already selected.**

This sheet contains a 3-D column chart with a data series that is difficult to view.

③ **Choose Chart, 3-D View.**

The 3-D View dialog box is displayed, as shown in Figure 7.16.

Figure 7.16
The 3-D View dialog box enables you to tilt, rotate, and stretch 3-D charts.

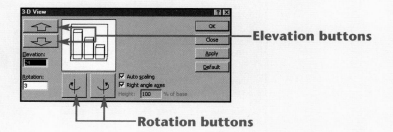

④ **Decrease the Elevation to** 4 **and change the Rotation to** F. **Click OK.**

The new view for the 3-D chart is displayed, as shown in Figure 7.17. For more information on the elevation and rotation options refer to Table 7.3 at the end of this lesson.

Figure 7.17
The 3-D chart displayed from a new angle.

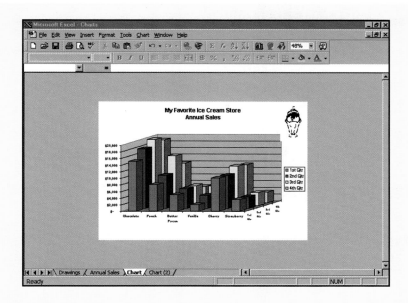

If you have problems...

After changing the elevation and rotation in step 4, the sundae graphic may slightly overlap the chart. Simply resize the graphic by dragging the lower-left handle toward the upper-right corner of the chart.

❺ Click the axis at the top-right corner of the chart.

Black handles appear on each of the eight axes tips, as shown in Figure 7.18.

Hint: You'll know where to click the mouse when you see the Corners ScreenTip pop up on-screen in the axis corner.

Figure 7.18
Black handles appear on the eight tips.

Handle—

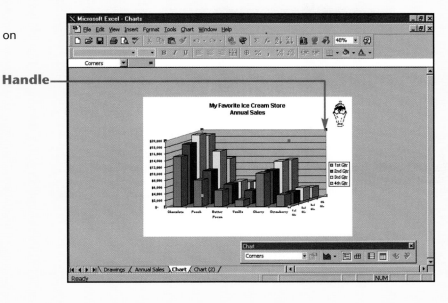

continues

To Rotate a 3-D Chart **(continued)**

6 **Using the mouse, point to the black handle in the top-right corner of the chart.**

Make sure that you are pointing to the handle in the top-right corner of the chart (refer to Figure 7.18). The mouse pointer changes to a small, thin cross.

7 **Click and hold down the left mouse button while you drag the mouse straight up approximately 1/4-inch.**

As you drag the mouse a wire-frame outline of the chart is displayed, as shown in Figure 7.19.

Figure 7.19
The chart outline shows the new orientation.

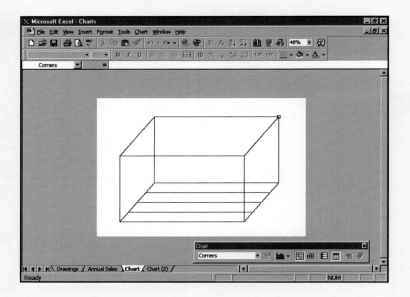

8 **Release the left mouse button.**

The new 3-D view, with all data series visible, is displayed, as shown in Figure 7.20.

9 **Save the workbook and keep it open for the next lesson, where you create a picture chart.**

If you have problems...

If the new 3-D view does not appear similar to Figure 7.20, click the Undo button to return to the previous view so you can start over.

Figure 7.20
The chart is displayed in the new 3-D view.

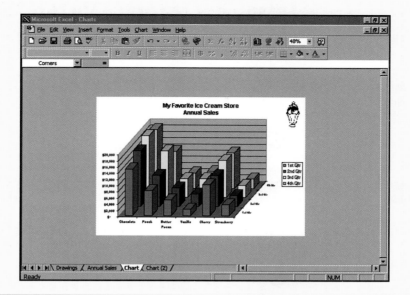

 **Inside Stuff**

To apply a perspective you created to another chart, note the settings for this perspective, as shown in the 3-D View dialog box. Then display the chart that you want to change. To change the settings select Chart, 3-D View and then click the Apply button. The 3-D View options are described in Table 7.3.

Table 7.3 Format, 3-D View Options

Option	Changes Made to Chart
Elevation	The angle can be from –90 to +90 degrees except for pie charts. Acceptable pie chart angles are from 10 to 80 degrees.
Rotation	The chart can rotate from 0 to 360 degrees around the vertical axis. For 3-D bar charts, the rotation ranges from 0 to 44 degrees.
Auto Scaling	With this check box cleared, you can change the z-axis height (vertical) as a percentage of the x-axis (chart width). A number between 5 and 500 can be used.
Right Angle Axes	With this check box cleared, you can set the Perspective (sense of depth) and Height. With this check box selected, you can auto scale the height or set the height. 3-D bar charts always have the Right Angle Axes check box selected.

Lesson 8: Creating a Picture Chart

Picture chart
A chart in which a column, bar, or line marker on a chart has been replaced with a graphic from a Windows graphic or drawing program.

With Excel, you can replace the column, bar, or line markers in a data series with a picture, drawn with Excel's built-in drawing tools or from a graphics program. With this feature, you are sure to grab the attention of your audience and the result can be very effective and appealing when used in a report.

Now you replace a chart column marker with the ice-cream cone object you created in the previous lessons for your *picture chart*.

To Create a Picture Chart

1 **Click the** Chart **sheet tab of the** Charts **workbook.**

The 2-D chart is displayed.

2 **Click any one of the column markers in the 3rd Qtr data series.**

A black square is displayed in the 3rd Qtr columns for each ice-cream product, as shown in Figure 7.21.

Figure 7.21
The 3rd Qtr data series is selected.

A black square identifies the selected data series

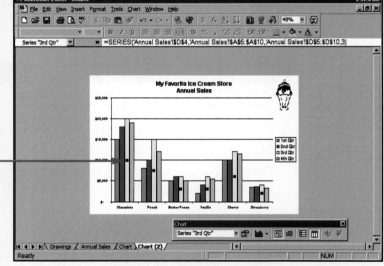

3 **Click the** Drawings **sheet tab.**

The Drawings worksheet is displayed with the ice-cream cone graphic.

4 **Click the object (the ice-cream cone) to select it.**

Remember that the two objects were grouped into one.

5 **Click the Copy button on the Standard toolbar.**

The object is copied to the Clipboard.

6 **Click the** Chart **sheet tab.**

The 2-D chart is displayed.

❼ Click the Paste button on the Standard toolbar.

The object replaces the column markers for the 3rd Qtr data series and the ice-cream cone picture is stretched to the value it represents. The data series is still selected.

If you have problems... ◄

If only one column marker is replaced with the picture, the entire data series (3rd Qtr column markers for each product) was not selected prior to pasting the picture from the Clipboard. Select the 3rd Qtr data series again and paste the picture or select the column markers individually and paste the picture.

❽ Point the mouse to one of the selected data series pictures and right-click.

The shortcut menu is displayed.

❾ Choose Format Data Series and click the Patterns tab.

The Patterns tab of the Format Data Series dialog box is displayed.

❿ Click the Fill Effects button.

The Fill Effects dialog box is displayed.

⓫ Click the Stack option and choose OK.

This option stacks the pictures in the data series and returns you to the Format Data Series dialog box.

⓬ Click the Data Labels tab and click the Show value option. Choose OK.

⓭ Click outside the chart to deselect the data series.

The completed chart includes a stacked picture for the 3rd Qtr data series and data labels displaying the values, as shown in Figure 7.22.

⓮ Save the workbook and keep it open for the next lesson, where you annotate the chart with a text box.

Figure 7.22
The third quarter is represented by ice-cream cones to complete the picture chart.

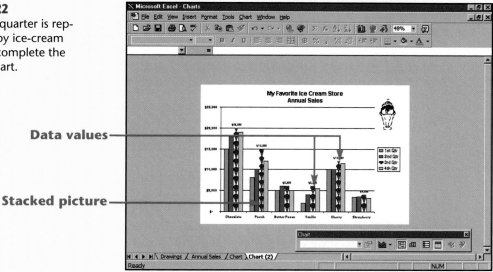

To remove a picture from the data series, select the data series; then choose <u>E</u>dit, Cl<u>e</u>ar, <u>F</u>ormats.

Lesson 9: Adding a Text Box to Annotate a Chart

In Excel, you can add comments to a chart to emphasize specific information by creating a text box. The text box can draw special attention to data on the chart.

In this lesson, you add a text box to the completed chart to emphasize the top selling product.

To Add a Text Box to Annotate a Chart

❶ Click the Chart **sheet tab of the** Charts **workbook if it isn't already selected.**

 ❷ Click the Drawing button on the Standard toolbar.

The Drawing toolbar is displayed.

 ❸ Click the Text Box button on the Drawing toolbar.

The mouse pointer changes to a small, thin cross (cross hair).

❹ Move the mouse pointer to the Plot area of the chart, located below the letter U in the word Annual.

❺ Hold down the left mouse button and drag the mouse down and to the right, almost to the end of the Plot area, to draw a box. Release the mouse button.

The insertion point is now positioned in the top-left corner of the box.

❻ Type Chocolate is still our best selling ice cream.

The text is displayed in tiny print as you are typing.

❼ Press Ctrl **to select the text box. Click the Font Size box on the Formatting toolbar and click 12 pt.**

The text size is increased and the text box is selected (the handles still appear around the border of the box).

If you have problems...

If the text box is not large enough to display all the text you typed, select the box to display the handles and drag the handles to resize the box.

❽ Double-click the text box border.

The Format Text Box dialog box is displayed.

❾ Click the Colors and Lines **tab. Under Line, click the down arrow next to** C<u>o</u>lor. **Click Automatic and choose OK.**

⑩ Click outside of the text box to deselect it.

A thin border is added to the text box.

⑪ Click the Arrow button on the Drawing toolbar.

The mouse pointer changes to a small, thin cross.

⑫ Point the mouse at the left edge of the text box; then click and drag the mouse to the $20,000 data value. Release the mouse button.

When you release the mouse button, an arrow, which points to the $20,000 data value, is displayed.

⑬ Deselect the arrow. Click the Drawing tool on the Standard toolbar to remove the Drawing toolbar.

If you do not like the size or position of the arrow after you draw it, make sure the handles appear around the object and press Del. If the handles do not appear, just click the arrow to display them.

The chart is complete, as shown in Figure 7.23. If requested by your instructor, print two copies of the chart.

⑭ Save the workbook and close it.

Figure 7.23
The chart has been enhanced with an arrow and text box.

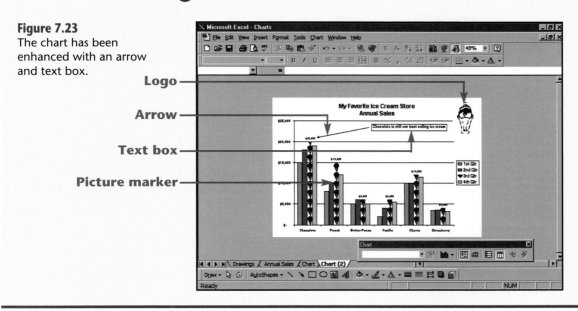

Logo

Arrow

Text box

Picture marker

Excel

Project Summary

To	Do This
Import a graphic.	Choose Insert, Picture, From File. Change folders, if needed, and click file name. Click OK.
Copy a graphic.	Select the graphic and click the Copy button. Move to new location and click the Paste button.
View the Drawing toolbar.	Click the Drawing button on the Standard toolbar, or choose View, Toolbars, and click Drawing in the submenu.
Draw a line, arrow, rectangle, or oval.	Click the appropriate button on the Drawing toolbar. Click the worksheet and drag the mouse to draw the object.
Draw a freeform object.	Click the AutoShapes tool on the Drawing toolbar. Click Lines and choose a shape. Click where a line is to begin and click where a line should end. If the lines do not meet, double-click to end the drawing. If the lines close an object, click to end the drawing.
Format an object.	Double-click the object.
Group objects.	Click the first object to select it and hold down (⬆Shift) while clicking successive objects. Click the Draw button on the Drawing toolbar and click Group.
Ungroup objects.	Select object; then click Ungroup, from the Draw button on the Drawing toolbar.
Create 3-D shapes.	Select an object and then click the 3-D button on the Drawing toolbar. Choose the direction of the 3-D effect.
Rotate objects.	Select the object, choose Draw on the Drawing toolbar. Then select Rotate or Flip, and then Rotate Left or Rotate Right.
Change the rotation of a 3-D chart.	Choose Chart, 3-D View and select the desired option, or select an axis on the chart and drag the handles to rotate the chart.
Add a picture (object) to a data series of a chart.	Copy the object to the Clipboard. Click the marker for the data series in the chart to select it and click the Paste button.
Stack a data series picture.	Click the data series marker in the chart to select it. Click the right mouse button on the selected series and choose Format Data Series. Choose the Patterns tab and click Fill Effects, Stack.
Add a text box object to your chart or worksheet.	Click the Text Box object on the Drawing toolbar and type the text at the insertion point.

Checking Your Skills

True or False

For each of the following, check *T* or *F* to indicate whether the statement is true or false.

__T __F **1.** You cannot import a picture directly into a worksheet or chart.

__T __F **2.** A graphic imported into a worksheet can be copied to the Clipboard and pasted into a chart.

__T __F **3.** The only way to change the rotation of a 3-D chart is through Chart, 3-D View.

__T __F **4.** If you add a picture to a data series on a chart, the legend, by default, is updated to reflect the picture.

__T __F **5.** You can include only one graphic object on a chart.

__T __F **6.** If an object you create is not perfect, your only option is to delete it and start over.

__T __F **7.** Hold down the Ctrl key while drawing a line to make the line straight.

__T __F **8.** Paragraphs do not wrap within a text box.

__T __F **9.** You can use scanned photographs in an Excel worksheet if they are saved in a TIF file.

__T __F **10.** If you move graphic images over worksheet data, the graphic hides the information behind it.

Multiple Choice

Circle the letter of the correct answer for each of the following:

1. Which tool on the Drawing toolbar is used to fuse multiple objects as one for editing or formatting?

   a. Bring to front

   b. Group

   c. Ungroup

   d. Drawing selection

2. Which of the following short-cut menu options enables you to stack your chart's data series picture?

   a. Format Column Group

   b. AutoFormat

   c. Format Data Series

   d. Format Plot Area

3. You can add text to which of the following drawing tools?

   a. Rectangle

   b. Oval

   c. Arrow

   d. Text Box

4. To move a graphic object, you

   a. use the mouse to select the object; point to any one of the eight handles (the mouse is a two-headed arrow) and drag the mouse in the direction to be moved.

   b. use the mouse to select the object; point to the object (with the mouse pointer) and drag it to its new location.

   c. use the mouse to double-click the object; point to the object and then drag it to its new location.

   d. both b and c are correct.

5. To resize an object and keep it in proportion, you

   a. drag a corner handle.

   b. hold down ⬆Shift while dragging a corner handle.

   c. hold down Alt while dragging a corner handle.

   d. hold down Ctrl while dragging a corner handle.

6. The first step in protecting an object from any editing or formatting changes is to

   a. identify any objects you want to remain unprotected.

   b. turn on the worksheet protection feature.

   c. disable the worksheet protection feature.

   d. mark all the objects you want to protect.

7. What happens when you hold down the ⬆Shift key while drawing a rectangle?

   a. The rectangle is deleted from the worksheet.

   b. The rectangle remains proportional as you draw.

   c. You draw a square.

   d. You draw a straight horizontal line.

8. Which of the following range of elevations is acceptable for 3-D pie charts?

   a. –90 to +90 degrees

   b. 10 to 80 degrees

   c. 0 to 90 degrees

   d. –10 to 100 degrees

9. Use the _____ tool to draw curved and straight lines on your chart or worksheet.

   a. Freeform

   b. Curve

   c. Scribble

   d. Line

10. To color a graphic object, click the _____ button on the Drawing toolbar.

    a. Color Object

    b. Color Graphic

    c. Color Fill

    d. Fill Color

Completion

In the blank spaces provided, write the correct answer for each of the following statements.

1. When a graphic object is selected, eight _____ are displayed around the border.

2. To select several objects for grouping, click the border of the first object and then press _____while _____ the border of the other objects.

3. If you have problems with a drawing, you can remove it from the screen by selecting it and pressing _____.

4. Using the mouse, click the _____ on a chart and drag a handle to rotate the 3-D chart view.

5. To remove a picture from a data series, first select the series, and then click the _____ menu, _____ option, and _____ option.

6. Use the Windows _____ to copy a graphic to a new location.

7. To add dot patterns to a line, choose the _____ option on the Line Color palette.

8. The _____ option allows you to customize the rotation of an object.

9. A _____ _____ lets you create text anywhere without attaching it to an object.

10. A method of making a 3-D chart easier to read is to _____ the chart.

Matching

In the blank next to each of the following terms or phrases, write the letter of the corresponding term or phrase.

a. a texture fill

b. cross hair

c. graphic image

d. gradient fill

e. BMP

f. import

g. selection handles

h. TIF

i. PCX

j. picture chart

_____ 1. When a graphic is selected, these surround the object

_____ 2. The small, thin cross mouse pointer used for drawing

_____ 3. To retrieve a file from a source other than Excel

_____ 4. A picture file or drawing saved to a file and available for your use

_____ 5. Replace a column, bar, or line marker on a chart with a graphic

_____ 6. Fills the item with graphics such as marble or granite

_____ 7. The fill varies from light to dark shades of colors

_____ 8. A bitmap file extension

_____ 9. A Paintbrush file extension

_____ 10. A file extension used for scanned images

Applying Your Skills

Practice

The following exercises enable you to practice the skills you learned in this project. Take a few minutes to work through these exercises now.

Drawing a Freeform Object

In this project, you practice using the drawing tools to create a graphic object.

To draw a freeform object, follow these steps:

1. Open a new, blank worksheet in Excel.

2. Using the drawing toolbar, create a drawing of a coffee cup. You need to use various shapes, lines, and curves to create the coffee cup. Don't worry about your drawing being perfect; just try to create a close approximation of a coffee cup.

3. Select each drawing object in the coffee cup. (Remember to hold down the ⬆Shift key while selecting additional objects.)

4. Click the <u>D</u>raw button on the Drawing toolbar and click <u>G</u>roup.

5. Resize the object so it takes up no more than three cells in your work sheet.

6. Save the worksheet as `Coffee Cup Drawing`. Leave the worksheet open for the following exercise.

Copying a Graphic Image to a Chart

Now that you have created a coffee cup graphic image, you want to copy it to a chart to enhance the appearance of the chart.

To copy a graphic image to a chart, follow these steps:

1. Open file Proj0703 from the Project-07 folder on the CD and save it as `Coffee Sales`.

2. Select the `Chart 1` sheet tab if necessary.

3. Use the <u>W</u>indow menu to select the `Coffee Cup Drawing` worksheet.

4. Select the Coffee Cup object and copy it to the Clipboard.

5. Use the <u>W</u>indow menu to select the Coffee Sales worksheet.

6. Paste the coffee cup graphic into the chart worksheet.

7. Move the coffee cup so it is immediately to the right of the heading, `1st Quarter Sales`.

8. Save the file again and leave it open for the following exercise.

Creating a Picture Chart

Use the coffee cup graphic you created to add interest to your chart.

To create a picture chart, follow these steps:

1. Copy coffee cup object at the top of the chart to the Clipboard.

2. Click any one of the Mocha column markers.

3. Click the Paste button on the Standard toolbar.

4. Right-click on one of the Mocha column markers.

5. Choose Format Data Series and click the Patterns tab.

6. Click the Fill Effects button and choose the Stack option.

7. Save the file and leave it open for the following exercise.

Inserting a 3-D Shape and a Text Box

In this exercise, you insert a 3-D arrow. You then insert a text box to describe this arrow.

To insert a 3-D shape and a text box, follow these steps:

1. Insert an upward pointing block arrow into the top-right corner of the 1st Quarter Sales chart.

2. With the arrow selected, click the 3-D button on the Drawing toolbar.

3. Choose the first 3-D option in the palette.

4. Insert a text box below the arrow.

5. Type the following text into the text box:

   Sales continued on an upward trend

6. Format the text so the font is large enough to read, and it appears to the right of the chart. (Move the legend down to the bottom of the chart, if necessary.)

7. Save the file and leave it open for the following exercise.

Rotating a 3-D Chart

In this exercise, you change the 1st Quarter Sales chart to a 3-D chart and then rotate it to improve its appearance.

To rotate a 3-D chart, follow these steps:

1. Right-click on the chart and choose Chart Type from the shortcut menu.

2. Choose the Clustered Column chart with 3-D visual effect.

3. Click the axis at the top-right corner of the chart.

4. Using the mouse, rotate the chart by dragging it to the left.

5. Try several different rotations of the chart until you find one you like.

6. Save the worksheet file. If directed by your instructor, print two copies and then close it.

Challenge

The following challenges enable you to use your problem-solving skills. Take time to work through these exercises now.

Importing a Graphic

A new sporting goods company has asked for your help in using Excel to enhance some of their spreadsheets. Using your new skills, enhance the Sports Equipment Distributors worksheet and chart with a corporate logo by importing a graphic.

To import a graphic into your chart, follow these steps:

1. Open the Proj0704 file from the Project-07 folder on the CD and save it as `Sports Equipment Sales`.

2. Make sure that the Sales sheet tab is displayed and click cell A1.

3. Insert the tennis picture file from the drive from which you have been opening the project data files into this worksheet. You might need to ask your instructor in which drive and folder to look.

4. Resize the graphic so that it fits into cell A1 and add a border.

5. Copy the graphic to the Clipboard and paste it in the Chart1 sheet. Move the graphic to the top-right corner of the chart.

6. Resize the graphic to make it larger.

7. Save the workbook and keep it open for the next exercise. If requested by your instructor, print two copies of the chart.

Drawing an Object

The line chart was already created to compare quarterly sales for the Sports Equipment Distributors and will be used in a presentation. Now you need to draw a tennis ball for use in your picture chart.

To draw the object, follow these steps:

1. Insert a new worksheet in front of the Sales sheet in the `Sports Equipment Sales` workbook by selecting the Sales sheet and choosing Insert, Worksheet. This worksheet will contain your drawing.

2. Use the Oval tool on the Drawing toolbar to draw a circle to represent the tennis ball (approximate the size to fill three cells vertically).

3. Use the Scribble tool from the AutoShapes button on the Drawing toolbar to draw two arcs inside the circle.

4. Select and group the three objects.

5. Reduce the size of the object to fit in approximately one cell.

6. Save the workbook and keep it open for the next exercise. If requested by your instructor, print two copies of the worksheet.

Creating a Picture Chart

You can use the tennis ball object (which you created in the preceding exercise) in a picture chart to enhance your presentation.

To create a picture chart, follow these steps:

1. Copy the tennis ball object to the Clipboard; then paste it to the data series on the line chart in the Chart1 sheet.

2. Insert Data labels on the chart (values only).

3. If the data values overlay the object, select the data value and drag it to a new location above the object.

4. If requested by the instructor, print two copies of the chart. Save the workbook and keep it open for the next exercise.

Creating a 3-D Shape and Adding a Text Box

You want to insert a 3-D arrow into the chart to draw the reader's attention to the excellent 4th quarter sales.

To create a 3-D shape and add a text box, follow these steps:

1. Select the Chart 1 worksheet.

2. Insert a Bent Arrow into the worksheet, choosing from the Block Arrows option on the Auto Shapes menu.

3. Flip the arrow horizontally, so it points to the left.

4. Move the arrow to the right edge of the worksheet, so it points to the numbers for the 4th quarter.

5. Choose an appropriate 3-D format for the arrow.

6. Under the arrow, add a text box with the text Great finish!

7. Move the legend out of the way, if necessary.

8. Save the workbook and keep it open for the next exercise. If requested by your instructor, print two copies of the worksheet.

Rotating a 3-D Chart

A 3-D pie chart was created, showing the percentage of sales represented by each quarter this year. You change the elevation of the 3-D chart using Chart, 3-D View. Then, you use the mouse to change the view of the pie.

To rotate a 3-D chart, follow these steps:

1. Click the Chart2 sheet tab.

2. Use the Chart 3-D View dialog box to change the elevation to 25.

3. Select Qtr 4 (the largest piece of the pie) and drag it out to the left to explode it from the whole.

4. If requested by the instructor, print two copies of the chart. Save the workbook and close it.

PinPoint Assessment

You have completed the project and the associated lessons, as well as the Checking Your Skills and Applying Your Skills sections. Now use the PinPoint software evaluation mode to assess your comprehension of the specific exam tasks you have just learned. You can also use the PinPoint Trainer Mode and the Show Me tutorials to practice these specific exam tasks.

Project 8

Eight

Working with Worksheets

Tracking Monthly Expenses

Objectives

Required Activities

In this Project, you learn how to

➤ Select a Worksheet

➤ Insert a New Worksheet

➤ Delete a Worksheet ... ...Delete Worksheets

➤ Move and Copy Worksheets

➤ Change Worksheet Tab Names

Why Would I Do This?

The Excel file where you work and store your data is called a **workbook**. When you start a new workbook, three **worksheets** are included. These worksheets help you organize your data into a single file by being able to separate it into several sheets. You may add up to a total of 255 sheets to a workbook, including the **chart sheets** you create to display charts and graphs. However, you should be aware that large workbooks do require more **RAM** when you're working with them and that worksheet operations may slow perceptibly.

 Jargon Watch

A **workbook** is the Excel file where you enter and store data. Sometimes called a 3-D workbook, the file can contain several **worksheets**. A worksheet is a single page (or sheet) within a workbook, on which you enter data, perform calculations, and set up printable pages. It's sometimes referred to as a spreadsheet.

A workbook can also contain **chart sheets**. A chart sheet is a workbook sheet created when you choose to store a chart or graph on a separate sheet instead of embedding it into a worksheet.

When you open Excel, the application and the workbook you have open are kept in the **RAM** (random access memory) of your computer. This is the working memory of your computer that keeps track of your current operation—each character you type or delete and each calculation you perform—and any other applications you have open. The larger your computer's RAM (in megabytes or gigabytes), the more operations the computer can handle at the same time and the faster it can perform functions for you. However, RAM isn't permanent storage. Should the power to your computer fail, everything you are working on will be lost unless you save it to a storage area, such as your hard disk or a floppy disk.

In this project, you learn to add and delete worksheets, change the order of the worksheets by moving sheets, duplicate worksheets, and change the names of the worksheets.

Lesson 1: Selecting Worksheets

At the bottom of your screen, above the Status bar, Excel displays a tab for each of the sheets in your workbook (see Figure 8.1). The currently displayed sheet is white with bold text. To switch from one sheet to another, you click on the name of the sheet you want to see. Use the tab scrolling buttons to the left of the tabs to go to the first sheet, the previous sheet, the next sheet, or the last sheet.

Before you can perform any worksheet operations (copy, move, and delete), you must be able to select the worksheet on which you want to perform the operation. Select a worksheet now.

Figure 8.1
A tab appears for each worksheet in the workbook; the active worksheet name is bolded.

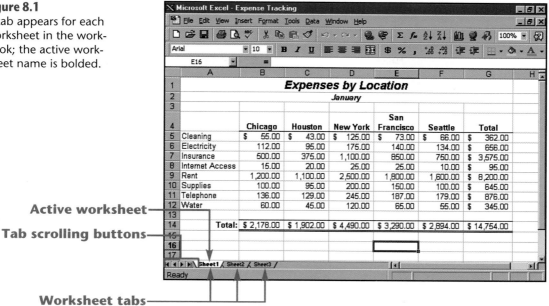

Active worksheet

Tab scrolling buttons

Worksheet tabs

To Select Worksheets

① From the Project-08 folder on the CD, open the file Proj0801. Save the file as Expense Tracking.

This workbook has only three worksheets. The worksheet tabs still have the default names Sheet1, Sheet2, and Sheet3.

② Click the Sheet2 **tab.**

Active Worksheet
The worksheet that is currently selected and displayed on your screen.

The tab turns white and the tab name becomes bold. This is now the *active worksheet*. Now select another sheet.

③ Hold down ⇧Shift **and click the** Sheet1 **tab.**

Both tabs are white, indicating that they are both selected. However, Sheet2 is in bold but Sheet1 is not. That's because Sheet2 is still the active worksheet. Using ⇧Shift to select additional sheets only works if the worksheets you want to select are adjacent to each other, or if you want to select all the sheets between the two sheet tabs you click (see Table 8.1 for a description of how to select multiple sheets).

TABLE 8.1   Selecting Sheets

Do This	To Select
Click the sheet tab.	A single sheet
Right-click any of the tab scrolling buttons and click the name of the sheet from the shortcut menu.	A single sheet when you can't see the tab

continues

To Select Worksheets   (continued)

Do This	To Select
Click the first tab you want to select, hold down ⇧Shift, and then click the last tab.	Adjacent sheets (selects all sheets between the first and last tabs you click)
Click the first tab you want to select, hold down Ctrl, and click the other tabs you want selected.	Non-adjacent sheets
Right-click any sheet tab and choose Select All Sheets from the shortcut menu.	All sheets in the workbook

4 Click on the Sheet3 **tab.**

To deselect the sheets, click on any other tab or perform an operation on the selected tabs.

5 Hold down Ctrl **and click the** Sheet1 **tab.**

Holding down Ctrl lets you select sheets that aren't next to each other.

6 Right-click the Sheet2 **tab and choose Select All Sheets from the shortcut menu.**

All the worksheets in the workbook are selected.

7 Right-click any of the tab scrolling buttons and choose Sheet1 from the shortcut menu.

Keep this worksheet open to use in the next lesson.

Inside Stuff

The default number of worksheets included in a new workbook is three. To change that default, choose Tools, Options to open the Options dialog box. Select the General tab. Enter a number in the Sheets in new workbook box. Choose OK.

Lesson 2: Inserting Worksheets

The workbook you are preparing contains data for the twelve months of the year. Each month has a separate worksheet, and there is an additional sheet for the year-end totals. Only the figures for January are entered so far, although Sheet2 contains the labels and formulas for February. In this lesson, you add the other sheets needed for the workbook.

To Insert a Worksheet

❶ Select Sheet3 **in the** Expense Tracking **workbook.**

❷ Choose **I**nsert, **W**orksheet from the menu.

The new worksheet tab, automatically named Sheet4, appears before the Sheet3 tab (see Figure 8.2). Since both Sheet3 and Sheet4 are blank worksheets, you don't have to worry about the order of the tabs at this time. However, you may realize that adding nine more worksheets will go slowly if you continue to add them one at a time.

Figure 8.2
The newly inserted worksheet appears before Sheet3.

New worksheet

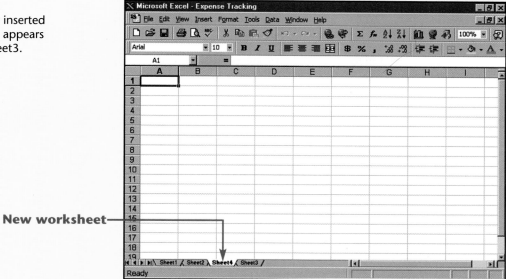

❸ Right-click the Sheet4 **tab and choose** **S**elect All Sheets **from the shortcut menu.**

❹ Choose **I**nsert, **W**orksheet from the menu.

Another four worksheets were added to the workbook, the same number as you had selected when you chose the **I**nsert, **W**orksheet command. You still need to add five worksheets.

❺ Hold down ⇧Shift **and click five worksheet tabs and then choose** **I**nsert, **W**orksheet.

To add a specific number of worksheets, select the number of tabs. You now have thirteen tabs.

❻ Save the workbook, but do not close it.

Lesson 3: Deleting Worksheets

Because you may have too many sheets in a workbook, or you want to remove a sheet that contains data you no longer need, deleting a worksheet or worksheets is a simple operation. However, when you delete a worksheet, be sure that the data on that sheet is no longer necessary because it will be removed as well.

In this lesson, you learn how to remove any worksheets you no longer need.

To Delete a Worksheet

1 **In the** Expense Tracking **workbook, select all the worksheet tabs except** Sheet1 **and** Sheet2**.**

Use the techniques you learned in Lesson 1 for selecting adjacent sheets.

In the previous lesson, you added a number of sheets to the workbook because you anticipated a need for enough sheets to cover the entire year's expenses plus a year-end total sheet. Except for Sheet1 and Sheet2, all the remaining worksheets are blank. Instead of copying the range from Sheet2 to the other worksheets, it might make more sense to copy the entire sheet. Before you do that, however, you need to remove the blank sheets you created.

2 **Choose** E̲dit, De̲lete Sheet **from the menu.**

Excel requests confirmation of your command to delete the sheets you selected (see Figure 8.3). Once the sheets are deleted, you cannot undo the action.

Figure 8.3
Microsoft Excel asks whether you want to delete the selected sheets.

3 **Choose OK to delete the sheets.**

Only two worksheets remain—Sheet1 and Sheet2. You have removed the worksheets you added but you also lost the label you entered on Sheet13. Undo is not able to recover that information (it is grayed out). You should always check your worksheets carefully before you delete them to be sure that no important data is stored on one of them.

4 **Save the workbook but leave it open for the next lesson.**

Inside Stuff   A quick way to delete a selected worksheet is to right-click the worksheet tab and choose <u>D</u>elete from the shortcut menu.

Lesson 4: Moving and Copying Worksheets

A workbook that contains similar data for different locations or time periods contains some sheets that closely resemble others in the workbook. One way to place the information from one sheet into a new sheet is to create a duplicate of the sheet by copying it. When you're starting a new workbook file, you may even want to copy existing sheets from another workbook as a basis for the new one.

As you insert, copy, and delete worksheets, the sheets in your workbook may no longer follow a logical order. You need to be able to shuffle the sheets around until order is achieved. You do this by moving sheets. You can even move sheets from one workbook to another.

This lesson shows you how to copy and move sheets within one workbook and also from one file to another.

To Copy and Move Worksheets

❶ Select Sheet2 **in the** Expense Tracking **workbook.**

Sheet2 contains the labels and formulas you will need for each monthly worksheet.

❷ Choose <u>E</u>dit, <u>M</u>ove or Copy Sheet from the menu.

The Move or Copy dialog box appears (see Figure 8.4).

Figure 8.4
The Move or Copy dialog box enables you to specify where you want the copy to go.

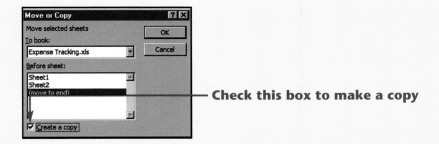

Check this box to make a copy

❸ In the <u>B</u>efore sheet: box, select (move to end).

This choice instructs Excel to place the copy of the sheet after all the other worksheets in the workbook.

❹ Click <u>C</u>reate a copy to place a check mark there.

If you don't enable this option, Excel moves the sheet.

continues

To Copy and Move Worksheets   (continued)

5 **Choose OK.**

A new sheet appears with Sheet2 (2) on the tab. The labels and formulas are the same as the original Sheet2. Now you need to create another copy of Sheet2.

6 **Select** Sheet2, **hold down** Ctrl, **and drag.**

The mouse pointer changes to a small page icon with a plus (+) sign in it (see Figure 8.5). As you move the mouse pointer along the sheet tabs, a small arrow appears above the tabs. The arrow indicates where the copy will appear when you release the mouse button.

Figure 8.5
When you drag a sheet tab, the worksheet moves to a new position. Hold down Ctrl to copy the worksheet.

Mouse pointer—

Arrow—

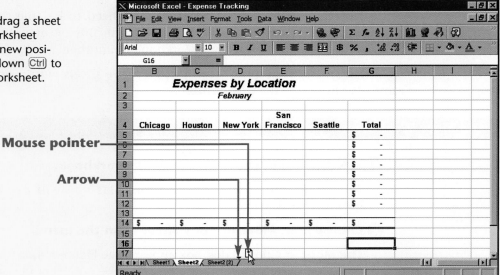

7 **Release the mouse button when the arrow appears after the last sheet tab.**

Another copy of Sheet2 appears. The tab label reads Sheet2 (3).

8 **Select Sheet2, Sheet2 (2), and Sheet2 (3). Choose <u>E</u>dit, <u>M</u>ove or Copy. In the <u>B</u>efore sheet box, select** (move to end). **Click <u>C</u>reate a copy and then choose OK.**

Three more copies of Sheet2 appear. You need six more copies to have a complete set of worksheets for the year.

9 **Select all six copies of Sheet2. Choose <u>E</u>dit, <u>M</u>ove or Copy. In the <u>B</u>efore sheet box, select** (move to end). **Click <u>C</u>reate a copy and then choose OK.**

Currently, Sheet1 contains the data for January. Organizationally, however, your colleagues would prefer that the "totals" page be the first sheet. This means you need to move one of the sheets without any figures into the first position.

⑩ Right-click the Sheet2 (3) **tab. Choose Move or Copy from the shortcut menu.**

⑪ Choose Sheet1 **from the Before sheet list. Make sure Create a copy is not checked, and then choose OK.**

Sheet2 (3) is now the first worksheet in the workbook.

⑫ Save the workbook.

You need to create a similar workbook for your boss, who wants to keep quarterly information instead of monthly. However, he needs the same labels and formulas as you have on Sheet2. In the next few steps, you start the new workbook and copy the Sheet2 worksheet to it.

You can easily move a worksheet tab by dragging it to a new position. Point to the tab you want to move and hold down the mouse button. The mouse pointer changes to an arrow with a page icon next to it. A small arrow appears, pointing between the nearest tabs. As you drag, the arrow moves to indicate where the tab will stay when you release the mouse button. When the arrow is in the correct position, release the mouse button.

This same drag-and-drop method can be used for copying the tabs, except you hold down the Ctrl key as you drag. The page icon next to the mouse pointer displays a plus sign (+) when you're copying.

⑬ Choose File, New from the menu. Select the blank Workbook icon and choose OK.

⑭ Save the new file as Quarterly Expenses.

Now that you've created the new workbook, you want to switch to the Expense Tracking workbook so you can copy Sheet2 to the new workbook.

⑮ Choose Window, 2 Expense Tracking.

⑯ Right-click the Sheet2 **tab and choose Move or Copy from the shortcut menu.**

The Move or Copy dialog box appears (see Figure 8.6).

Figure 8.6
Select the name of the workbook to which you want to copy the worksheet.

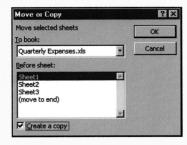

continues

To Copy and Move Worksheets   (continued)

⑰ **From the To book drop-down list, select** Quarterly Expenses.xls.

⑱ **Select** Sheet1 **from the Before sheet list.**

⑲ **Click Create a copy to place a check mark there and then choose OK.**

When you check the title bar, you see that Excel automatically switches you to the Quarterly Expenses workbook. Note that Sheet2 (2) has been added to that workbook and that it appears before the other worksheets.

⑳ **Save the** Quarterly Expenses **workbook and close it.**

You are automatically returned to the Expense Tracking workbook.

㉑ **Save the workbook but leave it open for the next lesson.**

Lesson 5: Changing Worksheet Tab Names

Dealing with worksheet names such as Sheet1, Sheet2, and Sheet2 (3) is confusing when you have more than two worksheets. You can assign your own names to the sheet tabs to help you distinguish the worksheet contents from other sheets in the workbook.

In this lesson, you change the tab names in the Expense Tracking workbook to make one for each month of the year and one for the year's totals.

To Change the Name of a Worksheet Tab

❶ **In the** Expense Tracking **workbook, right-click the first worksheet tab,** Sheet2 (3). **Choose Rename from the shortcut menu.**

The tab name is highlighted.

❷ **Type** Total **and press** ⏎Enter.

The name of the tab is now Total.

❸ **Double-click the** Sheet1 **tab.**

The tab name is highlighted.

❹ **Type** January **and press** ⏎Enter.

❺ **Change the Sheet2 tab to** February. **Then name each of remaining worksheets for each of the months of the year.**

After you finish changing the tab names, your workbook looks similar to the one shown in Figure 8.7.

Figure 8.7
Each tab after the first one has the name of a month.

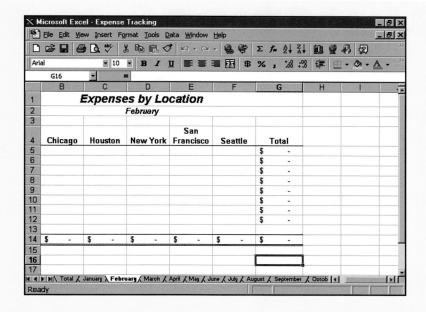

If you make a mistake entering a tab name, double-click on it again to highlight the name and then single-click to see an insertion point. Move the insertion point using ← and →. Enter new characters as needed. Use Del or ←Backspace to remove characters. Press ↵Enter after you have corrected the name.

6 **Save your changes to the** Expense Tracking **workbook and print two copies, if requested by your instructor. Then close the file.**

With a large number of worksheet tabs in a workbook, the size of the horizontal scroll bar shrinks to accommodate more tabs at the bottom of the screen. To adjust the size of the horizontal scroll bar or to see more or fewer tabs, drag the separator between the tabs and the scroll bar.

If you have completed your session on the computer, exit Excel and Windows 95. Otherwise, continue with the "Checking Your Skills" and "Applying Your Skills" sections at the end of this project.

Project Summary

To	Do This
Select a worksheet.	Click the sheet tab.
Select two or more adjacent worksheets.	Click the first tab, hold down (⇧Shift), and click the last tab.
Select two or more nonadjacent worksheets.	Click the first tab, hold down (Ctrl), and then click each tab you want to select.
Select all the worksheets in a workbook.	Right-click any worksheet tab and select Select All Sheets from the shortcut menu.
Insert a worksheet.	Click the worksheet tab before which you want the new worksheet to appear. Choose Insert, Worksheet.
Delete a worksheet.	Click the tab for the worksheet you want to remove and then choose Edit, Delete Sheet.
Move a worksheet.	Right-click the tab for the worksheet you want to move and choose Move or Copy from the shortcut menu. Select the name of the workbook to which you want to move the sheet from the To book drop-down list (use the name of the current workbook if you only want to move the sheet within the same workbook). From the Before sheet list, set the position of the moved worksheet by selecting the name of the sheet that will follow it. Choose OK.
Copy a worksheet.	Right-click the tab for the worksheet you want to copy and choose Move or Copy from the shortcut menu. Select the name of the workbook to which you want to copy the sheet from the To book drop-down list (use the name of the current workbook if you only want to copy the sheet within the same workbook). From the Before sheet list, set the position of the duplicate worksheet by selecting the name of the sheet that follows it. Click Create a copy to place a check mark there. Choose OK.
Change the name on the worksheet tab.	Right-click the tab and choose Rename from the shortcut menu, or double-click the tab. Type the new name and press (↵Enter).

Checking Your Skills

True or False

For each of the following, check *T* or *F* to indicate whether the statement is true or false.

__T __F   **1.** You can add up to 15 sheets to a workbook file.

__T __F   **2.** You cannot change the default number of sheets that are included in a new workbook.

__T __F   **3.** You cannot undo the deletion of a worksheet.

__T __F   **4.** Large workbooks require more RAM and can slow down worksheet operations.

__T __F   **5.** When you copy a worksheet, the data in the worksheet is also copied.

Multiple Choice

Circle the letter of the correct answer for each of the following:

1. When you start a new workbook, _____ worksheets are included.

    a. three

    b. five

    c. ten

    d. one

2. What is a quick way to delete a worksheet?

    a. Click the worksheet tab and press Del.

    b. Right-click the tab and choose <u>D</u>elete from the shortcut menu.

    c. Select the worksheet tab and choose <u>E</u>dit, <u>D</u>elete.

    d. Double-click the worksheet tab.

3. How can you move a worksheet within a workbook?

    a. Drag the worksheet tab to the new location.

    b. Use the Move or Copy Sheet command on the Edit menu.

    c. Double-click the worksheet tab and then select Move from the shortcut menu.

    d. a and b

4. When you are copying a worksheet, the mouse pointer changes to a small page icon with a_____ in it.

    a. arrow

    b. four-headed arrow

    c. plus sign

    d. minus sign

5. You can tell which worksheet is active because

    a. the word `active` displays in the title bar.

    b. the worksheet name displays in the title bar.

    c. the sheet tab is red.

    d. the sheet tab is white, and the sheet name is in bold.

Completion

1. A _____ sheet is a workbook sheet created when you choose to store a chart or graph on a separate sheet.

2. To copy a worksheet, hold down the _____ key when dragging a sheet tab.

3. When editing a tab name, use the _____ or _____ key to remove characters.

4. To adjust the size of the horizontal scroll bar to see more or fewer tabs, drag the _____ between the tabs and scroll bar.

5. Use the _____ _____ buttons to display different sheet tabs.

Matching

In the blank next to each of the following terms or phrases, write the letter of the corresponding term or phrase.

a. Ctrl

b. Select All

c. worksheet

d. 3-D workbook

e. workbook

f. ⬆Shift

g. active worksheet

_____   1. The Excel file where you enter and store data

_____   2. A single page within a file where you enter data

_____   3. The worksheet currently selected and displayed on your screen

_____   4. Hold down this key to select two or more adjacent worksheets

_____   5. Hold down this key to select two or more non-adjacent worksheets

_____   6. Another name for an Excel workbook

_____   7. Choose this to select all the worksheets in the workbook

Applying Your Skills

Practice

The following exercises enable you to practice the skills you have learned in this project. Take a few minutes to work through these exercises now.

Selecting a Worksheet and Inserting New Worksheets

In this exercise, you practice selecting worksheets and inserting new worksheets into a workbook file.

To select a worksheet and insert new worksheets, follow these steps:

1. Open the Proj0802 from the Project-08 folder on the CD and save it as Salary 3.

2. Select Sheet2 to see the information entered.

3. Select Sheet3. This worksheet is still blank.

4. You know you need three more worksheets to enter all the salary data. Select the three worksheet tabs, and choose Insert Worksheet. This adds three worksheets to the workbook.

5. Use the tab scrolling buttons to display the different worksheet tabs.

6. Select Sheet1.

7. Save the file again and leave it open for the following exercise.

Deleting Worksheets

You realize that you need only four worksheets instead of six. In this exercise, you practice deleting extra worksheets from the Salary 3 workbook.

To delete worksheets, follow these steps:

1. Select Sheet6 and choose Edit, Delete Sheet to delete the worksheet.

2. Right-click Sheet5. Choose Delete from the shortcut menu to delete this worksheet.

3. Select the first tab in the workbook.

4. Drag the separator between the tabs and horizontal scroll bar to the right until you can see all four tabs in the workbook.

5. Save the file again and leave it open for the following exercise.

Moving and Copying Worksheets

In this exercise, you practice moving worksheets within the workbook and making duplicates of worksheets.

To move and copy worksheets, follow these steps:

1. To move Sheet1 to the beginning of the workbook, select this sheet.

2. Drag it to the left until the triangle points to the location at the beginning of the workbook.

3. Release your mouse button to move the worksheet.

4. Move Sheet2 by right-clicking on the Sheet2 tab.

5. Choose Move or Copy from the shortcut menu.

6. Select Sheet4 in the Before Sheet box and choose OK.

7. Use either method to move Sheet3 in front of Sheet4.

8. Make a copy of Sheet1 by right-clicking the Sheet1 tab.

9. Choose Move or Copy from the shortcut menu.

10. Choose Sheet1 in the Before Sheet box.

11. Check the Create a copy check box and then choose OK.

12. Save the file and leave it open for the following exercise.

Changing Worksheet Tab Names

You want to make the worksheet tabs more descriptive, so you decide to change the names. In this exercise, you change the tab names of your worksheets.

To change worksheet tab names, follow these steps:

1. Right-click on the Sheet1 tab.

2. Choose Rename from the shortcut menu.

3. Type Raises as the tab name.

4. Double-click on the Sheet1 tab.

5. Type Salary Info as the tab name.

6. Rename the Sheet2 tab to 401K Contributions.

7. Save the changes to the Salary 3 file, and print two copies if directed by your instructor. Close the file.

Challenge

The following challenges enable you to use your problem-solving skills. Take time to work through these exercises now.

Selecting and Inserting New Worksheets

You select worksheets and insert blank worksheets into a workbook.

To select and insert new worksheets, follow these steps:

1. Open the file Proj0803 from theProject-08 folder on the CD and save it as Sales and Orders.

2. Select each of the worksheet tabs to see what data is in each worksheet.

3. Insert three blank worksheets into the workbook file.

4. Save the file and leave it open for the following exercise.

Deleting Worksheets

In this exercise, you delete extra worksheets from the Sales and Orders file.

To delete worksheets, follow these steps:

1. Delete the Sheet6 worksheet from the Sales and Orders file.

2. Select the Sheet3, Sheet4, and Sheet5 worksheets and delete all three at one time.

3. Save the file and leave it open for the following exercise.

Moving and Copying Worksheets

In this exercise, you rearrange the worksheets in the Sales and Orders file, and make duplicate copies of worksheets.

To move and copy worksheets, follow these steps:

1. Change the order of the worksheets so that Sheet2 appears to the left of Sheet1.

2. Make a copy of the Sheet1 worksheet and place it at the end of the workbook.

3. Save the file and leave it open for the following exercise.

Changing Worksheet Tab Names

You change the worksheet tab to more descriptive names.

To change worksheet tab names, follow these steps:

1. Change the Sheet1 tab name to March Orders.

2. Change the Sheet2 tab name to Sales Figures.

3. Change the Sheet1 (2) tab name to Order Worksheet.

4. Save the changes to the Sales and Orders file, and print two copies if directed by your instructor. Close the file.

PinPoint Assessment

You have completed the project and the associated lessons, as well as the Checking Your Skills and Applying Your Skills sections. Now use the PinPoint software evaluation mode to assess your comprehension of the specific exam tasks you have just learned. You can also use the PinPoint Trainer Mode and the Show Me tutorials to practice these specific exam tasks.

Project 9

Nine

Creating and Printing Reports

Reporting on Employee Sales

Objectives   **Required Activities**

In this Project, you learn how to
- ➤ Install the Report Manager Add-In
- ➤ Create a Custom View
- ➤ Create a Report with Report Manager
- ➤ Edit and Print a Report

Why Would I Do This?

Throughout this book, you have worked with Excel workbooks, and when you have printed anything, it has been just one area of a worksheet. Sometimes, however, you may want to print information from different sources or different sets of worksheet data. Suppose you need to create a single printed report from different worksheets in order to make comparisons between them more easily. It's much easier to create a report if the pages are numbered sequentially than by opening one worksheet and printing it, opening another and printing it, and so forth. After you create a report, it will go through all the printing setups for you. Using the View, Report Manager command, you can compile, print, and edit your reports.

Lesson 1: Installing the Report Manager Add-In

Like many spreadsheet and database programs, Excel can utilize supplemental programs called **add-ins**. An add-in extends a program's basic capabilities by adding specific new functionality to the program. You must install an add-in before the primary program (such as Excel) can use the add-in. To complete this project, you need to install the Report Manager add-in. The View, Custom Views command enables you to store the area and the page setup information for the data you want to print. The Report Manager enables you to create reports from the views you have saved. You can still print worksheet data without using custom views and the Report Manager. However, if you use these Excel features, additional printing options are available to you.

 Jargon Watch

Excel can use several add-ins. These programs are stored in files ending with the .XLA extension. Additional files needed by the add-ins use the extension .XLL. You can find these files in the Library folder, which is in the Excel folder. (If you use Microsoft Office 97, the Excel folder is typically stored in the MS Office folder.)

To Install the Report Manager Add-In

1 Start Excel if it is not already open.

2 Choose Tools, Add-Ins.

The Add-Ins dialog box opens, as shown in Figure 9.1.

3 Select Report Manager by placing a check mark in its check box. If a check mark already appears beside this option, proceed with step 4.

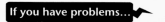

If you do not find the add-in in the list or if you try to access an add-in and receive a **Cannot Find** message with the name of the add-in file, you need to install the add-in. If you chose Typical from the installation option list when you originally installed Excel, the Report Manager add-in was not installed. The default for the Complete and Custom installations is all the add-ins; however, some might have been deselected upon installation. If any add-ins are missing from your system, you should ask the instructor for guidance in installing them. Then, after installing the add-ins, you might need to go back and start the add-ins by using the previous procedure.

The View Manager was an add-in in the previous version of Excel, but now is accessed by choosing <u>V</u>iew, Custom <u>V</u>iews.

Figure 9.1
Use the Add-Ins dialog box to install (or uninstall) any of the add-in programs listed.

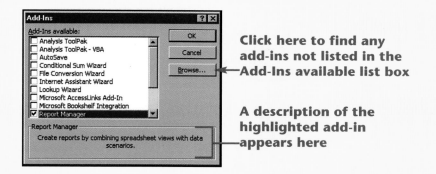

Click here to find any add-ins not listed in the Add-Ins available list box

A description of the highlighted add-in appears here

 Click OK.

The Add-Ins dialog box closes. Other than that, it might seem that nothing has happened, but you have opened the Report Manager to be used. If you click the <u>V</u>iew menu, you will notice that the <u>R</u>eport Manager option appears along with Custom <u>V</u>iews in the menu.

Lesson 2: Creating a Custom View

View
A saved set of display and print settings for a worksheet.

When you work with a worksheet, you probably return to certain areas frequently to get information or to print. You might want to set up the screen so a data range always appears in a certain way; then you do not have to set it up when you want to view it that way. Or you might need to display the same data in different ways, depending on what information you are trying to convey. By using Custom <u>V</u>iews from the <u>V</u>iew menu, you can save a lot of time in creating specific on-screen views of your data.

With the <u>V</u>iew, Custom <u>V</u>iews feature, you can store the range, display, and print settings for the worksheet areas you frequently view or print. If there is a particular way in which you want to see your data on-screen, you can use this feature to set up the *view* and then give it a name. In fact, you can create as many views of your worksheet as you want. When you save your workbook, the named views are also saved. These views are particularly useful when you repeatedly use the same data but display it differently for different reports.

❶ **Open the file Proj0901 from the Project-09 folder on the CD and save it as** My Report.

❷ **Activate the Month 1 worksheet.**

This worksheet has the individual sales totals for four weeks and the shift totals for the same four weeks.

Suppose you need to produce several different printouts from this data. By creating views, you can simply open the view and print, without setting up the page the way you want it again. This is true even if you edit the data in the view. Start by creating a view that shows only the shift subtotals for the month of January.

❸ **Select columns C through F.**

These are the columns to be hidden.

❹ **Choose F̲ormat, C̲olumn, H̲ide.**

If you prefer, you can right-click the selection and choose H̲ide from the shortcut menu.

❺ **Press** Ctrl+Home.

Columns C through F are now hidden so that only the January monthly totals show for each employee.

❻ **Click Row Level button 2. This is the button with 2 on it, located to the left of the column letters in the worksheet frame.**

Your screen appears as shown in Figure 9.2. The Row Level buttons display hidden rows within the worksheet. In this worksheet you click the Row Level 1 button to see only the Grand Total. Each subsequent button reveals more data, organizing it differently for printing and viewing. This organization by levels is a result of outlining the worksheet, a procedure discussed fully in the Expert level book, Project 10, "Creating Summary Reports."

❼ **Choose F̲ile, Page Set̲up.**

If you prefer, you can right-click the workbook icon on the menu bar and choose Page Set̲up from the shortcut menu.

The Page Setup dialog box appears. When you set up a view, you can set up specific page-layout options for the range you are viewing. Excel assumes that you will want to print this data in a certain way, just as you want to view it in a certain way.

❽ **On the Page tab, select L̲andscape in the Orientation area.**

This step tells Excel to print the data across the paper's length, rather than across its width.

Figure 9.2
After you click Row Level button 2, the worksheet displays only shift subtotals.

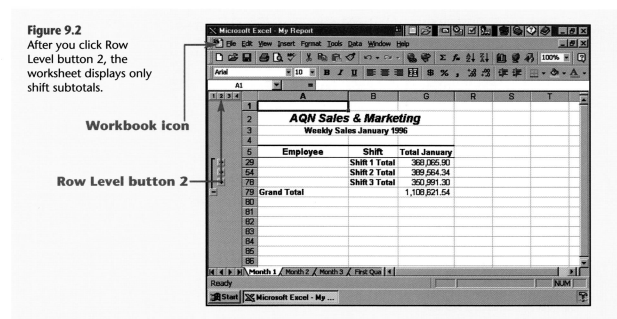

Workbook icon

Row Level button 2

⑨ **Click the Margins tab and check to make sure that the following settings are selected:**

Top and Bottom margins should be 1 inch.

Left and Right margins should be .75 inch.

Both the Header and Footer settings should be .5 inch from the paper's edges.

⑩ **Select the Horizontally check box to center the data horizontally on the page.**

⑪ **Click the Header/Footer tab.**

Here you can specify a *header* and *footer* to appear on the printed worksheet.

Header
Information—such as page number, date, sheet name—to be repeated automatically at the top of each printed page.

⑫ **Click the arrow button next to the Header drop-down list and choose the (none) option at the top of the list.**

This tells Excel not to place a header across the top of the page when printing.

Footer
Information—such as page number, date, sheet name—to be repeated automatically at the bottom of each printed page.

⑬ **Click the arrow button next to the Footer drop-down list and choose** Page 1 of ?, **near the top of the list.**

If your report has eight pages, for example, the footer on the first page reads Page 1 of 8.

⑭ **Click the Sheet tab and make sure that the Gridlines check box is deselected; then choose OK.**

If Gridlines is selected, Excel prints horizontal and vertical gridlines on your report. Reports usually do not need printed gridlines, and they can be unattractive.

continues

Excel

To Create a Custom View   (continued)

You have just set all the settings for this view. The columns you want hidden are hidden, and the print settings are set the way you want them. Now you can give this view a name.

⑮ Select cells A1 through G79.

These are the cells you want to include in this view.

⑯ Choose View, Custom Views.

The Custom Views dialog box appears, displaying views already created for individual data (the original view shows all the data) and monthly data, as shown in Figure 9.3.

Figure 9.3
The Custom Views dialog box enables you to add new views to the worksheet or to display existing views.

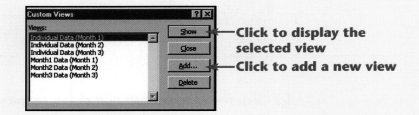

Click to display the selected view

Click to add a new view

⑰ Choose Add.
The Add View dialog box appears, as shown in Figure 9.4.

Figure 9.4
The Add View dialog box lets you name the views you create.

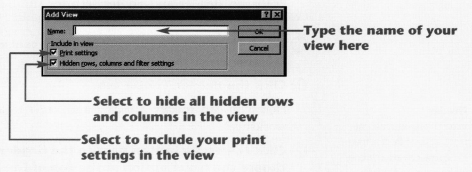

Type the name of your view here

Select to hide all hidden rows and columns in the view

Select to include your print settings in the view

⑱ In the Name text box, type Shift Subtotals.

This is your new view's name.

⑲ In the Include in view area, select the Print settings check box (if it is not already selected).

This step ensures that your print settings are included in the view.

⑳ Select the Hidden rows, columns and filter settings check box (if it is not already selected) and choose OK.

This step ensures that any hidden rows and columns will be hidden when you open the view.

Your view is saved with its name and all attributes. Now you can return to that view when you are in the worksheet—simply by specifying the view. Return to the original view of the worksheet; then display the new view.

㉑ **Choose View, Custom Views.**

㉒ **Select Individual Data (Month 1) from the Views list.**

㉓ **Click the Show button.**

Your screen returns to its original view. The original view was already saved as a named view, so it was easy to return the worksheet to that view.

㉔ **Choose View, Custom Views again.**

㉕ **Select Shift Subtotals from the Views list and click the Show button.**

The screen changes to show the Shift Subtotals view.

㉖ **Save the changes and keep the workbook open for the next lesson.**

Inside Stuff

Before creating new views, it is a good idea to create a view that shows all your data. You might want to save that view with a name such as Original Data. With this view handy, you can quickly return the worksheet to its original form instead of re-creating the original view (unhide columns and rows, and so on). If you save your workbook with a custom view displayed on a worksheet, the file opens, showing that view.

When you create a view, that view is saved only with the worksheet in which it was created. You cannot use that view with another worksheet.

To change a view you have already named, display the view. Modify the display and print settings as needed. Repeat the process of naming a view; use the same name to overwrite the original.

To delete a view, choose View, Custom Views and select the view you want to delete from the Views list. Click the Delete button. When finished, click the Close button.

Lesson 3: Creating a Report with Report Manager

In Lesson 2, you displayed your data with the various views you created. These views can be very helpful because they enable you to jump quickly from one display to another. If your worksheet's data changes very frequently, however, you might spend a lot of time changing to different views and printing them.

If you use the Report Manager, you can save time by telling the computer what views to print and in what order. Report Manager prints the chosen views as one report, and with only one command.

Before you can create a report, you must have created your views already (refer to Lesson 2).

To Create a Report with Report Manager

① Make sure that the My Report **workbook is open, with the** Month 1 **worksheet active.**

② Choose View, Report Manager.

The Report Manager dialog box appears, as shown in Figure 9.5.

Figure 9.5
Use the Report Manager dialog box to add and print reports.

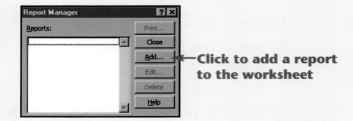
Click to add a report to the worksheet

③ Choose the Add button.

The Add Report dialog box appears, as shown in Figure 9.6.

Figure 9.6
The Add Report dialog box enables you to name the report and specify the contents of the report.

Choose the contents of each report section here

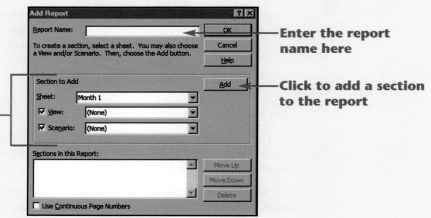
Enter the report name here

Click to add a section to the report

④ In the Report Name text box, type Individual Sales**.**

Just as you can name a view, you can give a name to a report.

⑤ In the Section to Add area, click the Sheet arrow button and select Month 1 from the drop-down list (if it is not already selected).

The Sheet drop-down list displays the names of all sheets in the active workbook.

⑥ Select the View check box if it is not selected.

⑦ Click the View arrow button and select Individual Data (Month 1) from the drop-down list.

The View drop-down list displays all views available in the active workbook.

Because you do not have any scenarios in this workbook, you can leave (None) in the Scenario list box.

8 Choose the Add button.

The view is added to the Sections in this Report list at the bottom of the dialog box.

9 Choose Month 2 from the Sheet list, choose Individual Data (Month 2) from the View list, and then click the Add button.

10 Choose Month 3 from the Sheet list, choose Individual Data (Month 3) from the View list, and then click the Add button.

11 Select the Use Continuous Page Numbers check box.

Selecting this option tells Excel to number all pages in the report consecutively, rather than restarting the numbering at the beginning of each section.

The Add Report dialog box now appears as shown in Figure 9.7.

Figure 9.7
The completed Add Report dialog box now includes the report name as well as the sections that you have added to the report.

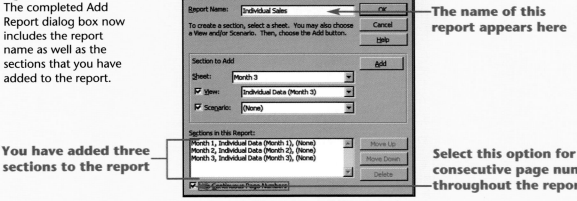

The name of this report appears here

You have added three sections to the report

Select this option for consecutive page numbers throughout the report

12 Click OK.

The Add Report dialog box closes.

13 Click Close.

The Report Manager dialog box closes.

14 Save the changes and keep the workbook open for the next lesson.

Lesson 4: Editing and Printing a Report

After you create a report, you might want to add a view to it or delete a view. You might find that the data is not in the order you wanted. This lesson shows you how to edit and print a report in Report Manager.

To Edit and Print a Report

1 **Choose View, Report Manager.**

The Report Manager dialog box appears.

2 **Select Individual Sales from the Reports list.**

3 **Click the Edit button.**

The Edit Report dialog box appears, as shown in Figure 9.8.

Figure 9.8
The Edit Report dialog box enables you to modify the settings in an existing report.

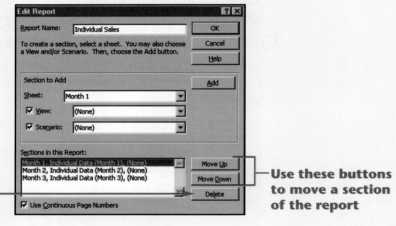

Click here to delete the selected section from the report

Use these buttons to move a section of the report

For this example, you change the order of the sections in your report.

4 **In the Sections in this Report list, select Month 1, Individual Data (Month 1), (None).**

Change the order in which the report is printed by moving this item to a different position.

5 **Click the Move Down button twice.**

The selection moves to the bottom of the list.

6 **In the Sections in this Report list, select Month 3, Individual Data (Month 3), (None).**

Now move this item to the top of the list.

7 **Click the Move Up button once.**

The selection moves to the top of the list. Moving the order of these items in the list changes the order in which they print.

8 **Click OK.**

The Edit Report dialog box closes and your changes are saved.

9 **Click Close.**

The Report Manager dialog box closes.

10 **Save the changes to your workbook.**

Now that you have created and edited your report, you can print it.

⓫ **Choose View, Report Manager.**

The Report Manager dialog box appears.

⓬ **Select Individual Sales from the Reports list.**

⓭ **Click the Print button.**

The Print dialog box appears, as shown in Figure 9.9.

Figure 9.9
In the Print dialog box, specify the number of copies you want to print.

Type the number of copies you want to print

⓮ **In the Copies text box, type 1 and click OK.**

This step creates your report and prints it to your default printer with the print settings you chose for each view.

⓯ **Save the changes and then close the workbook.**

If you have completed your session on the computer, exit Excel and Windows 95 before turning off your computer. Otherwise, continue with the "Checking Your Skills" and "Applying Your Skills" sections.

Project Summary

To	Do This
Install Report Manager.	Open Excel and choose Tools, Add-Ins. Select the Report Manager add-in by placing a check mark in the check box. Click OK.
Create a view.	Set up your worksheet the way you want it to appear (hidden columns, level of detail, and so on). Set up the way you want the view to be printed, using File, Page Setup. Then choose View, Custom Views. Choose Add and name the view. Click OK to save the view.
Create a report.	Your worksheet must be open and have views defined to use Report Manager. Choose View, Report Manager and click the Add button. Enter the name of the report in the Report Name text box. Use the Sheet and View drop-down lists to select the worksheets and views to include in each section. Use the Add button to complete each section. Choose the Use Continuous Page Numbers check box, if desired. Click OK to save the Report definition, and click Close to exit Report Manager.

continues

To	Do This
Edit a report.	With the worksheet open, choose View, Report Manager and select the report to edit from the list. Click the Edit button. Reorder, delete, and add sections as required. Click OK when done and click Close to exit Report Manager.
Print a report.	With the worksheet open, choose View, Report Manager and select the report to print from the list. Click Print, select the number of copies desired, and click OK.

Checking Your Skills

True or False

For each of the following statements, check *T* or *F* to indicate whether the statement is true or false.

__T __F **1.** The Custom Views and Report Manager features are both Excel add-ins.

__T __F **2.** Before adding a view, set up the way the worksheet should look and how it should be printed.

__T __F **3.** You can add or delete a view, but you cannot modify it.

__T __F **4.** If you create a view showing all your worksheet data, you can return quickly to that original view.

__T __F **5.** When you create a view, it can be used with any worksheet.

Multiple Choice

Circle the letter of the correct answer for each of the following questions.

1. Which Excel command is used to set up the way you want a view to be printed?

   a. File, Print

   b. File, Page Setup

   c. View, Custom Views

   d. View, Report Manager

2. Which options are included in the Add View dialog box?

   a. Name

   b. Print Settings

   c. Hidden Rows, Columns and Filter settings

   d. All of the above

3. Which buttons from the Add Report or Edit Report dialog box can be used to reposition sections of a report?

   a. Add

   b. Move Down

   c. Move Up

   d. Both b and c

4. How many views of a worksheet can you create?

   a. As many as you want

   b. One

   c. Two

   d. Three

5. How would you print a Report Manager report?

    a. Choose <u>F</u>ile, <u>P</u>rint

    b. Choose <u>F</u>ile, Prin<u>t</u> Area

c. Choose <u>V</u>iew, <u>R</u>eport Manager, select a report, and then choose <u>P</u>rint.

d. Choose <u>V</u>iew, Custom <u>V</u>iews

Completion

In the blank provided, write the correct answer for each of the following statements.

1. A saved set of display and print settings for a worksheet is called a _____.

2. To use the Report Manager, the _____ must be open and a _____ must already be defined.

3. Using the _____ command from the <u>V</u>iew menu, you can compile, edit, and print your reports.

4. In the Add Report dialog box, you can use the Section to Add area to add a _____ and _____ to your report.

5. Choosing the Use <u>C</u>ontinuous Page Numbers option ensures that page numbers will print _____ throughout the report instead of restarting numbering at the beginning of each section.

Matching

In the blank next to each of the following terms or phrases, write the letter of the corresponding term or phrase.

a. .XLL

b. Tools

c. view

d. header

e. Report Manager

f. <u>V</u>iew

G. .XLA

h. footer

i. <u>F</u>ile

j. add-in

_____ 1. A program that extends a programs basic capabilities

_____ 2. A saved set of display and print settings for a worksheet

_____ 3. Information repeated automatically at the top of a page

_____ 4. Information repeated automatically at the bottom of a page

_____ 5. The file extension for add-in files

_____ 6. Additional files needed by add-ins use this extension

_____ 7. Use this dialog box to add and print reports

_____ 8. Select this menu to install the Report Manager

_____ 9. Select this menu to use the Report Manager

_____ 10. Select this menu to display the Page Setup dialog box

Applying Your Skills

Practice

The following exercises enable you to practice the skills you have learned in this project. Take a few minutes to work through these exercises now.

Creating Views

Create a set of custom views in a workbook to display various sales information for your coffee shop.

To create views, follow these steps:

1. Open the Proj0902 from the project-09 folder on the CD and save it as `Custom Report`.

2. Select the print settings first. Use the Page Setup dialog box to have the worksheet centered on the page both horizontally and vertically. Make sure that gridlines are not turned on. Use the remaining default settings.

3. Create a view of the entire worksheet. Choose View, Custom Views.

4. Choose Add.

5. In the Name text box, type `Original Data`.

6. In the Include in view area, select the Print Settings check box, if necessary, and then choose OK.

7. Click the Row Level button 1. This collapses the worksheet so that only the subtotals and grand total display.

8. Using steps 3–6, save this as `Totals View`.

9. Click Row Level button 2 to redisplay all of the worksheet.

10. Click Column Level button 1 (above the row numbers). Now the worksheet displays only the Total column for each category.

11. Save this view as `Quarterly Total View`.

12. Save the workbook and leave it open for the following exercise.

Creating a Report

In this exercise, you use the views you created to generate a report.

To create a report, follow these steps:

1. Choose View, Report Manager.

2. Choose the Add button.

3. In the Report Name text box, type `Coffee Shop Sales`.

4. Make sure Sheet1 is selected in the Section to Add area.

5. Select the View check box if it is not selected.

6. Click the View arrow button and choose Quarterly Total View.

7. Choose the Add button.

8. Add the Totals View and Original Data views to the report.

9. Select the Use Continuous Page Numbers check box.

10. Click OK and then click Close from the Report Manager dialog box.

11. Save the workbook again, and leave it open for the following exercise.

Editing and Printing the Coffee Shop Sales Report

In this exercise, you change the order of the views and print a copy of the coffee shop sales report.

To edit and print the coffee shop sales report, follow these steps:

1. Choose View, Report Manager.

2. Click the Edit button.

3. Select Original Data from the Sections in this Reports list at the bottom of the dialog box.

4. Move this view up to the beginning of the report.

5. Move the Quarterly Total View to the end of the report and then click OK.

6. Click the Print button.

7. In the Copies text box, type 2 and click OK.

8. Save the changes and close the workbook.

Challenge

The following challenges enable you to use your problem-solving skills. Take time to work through these exercises now.

Creating a View

Create a set of views in a workbook that assist in the presentation of projects to managers and investment bankers.

To create a view, follow these steps:

1. Open Proj0903 from the Project-09 folder on the CD and save it as Annual Project Cash Flow.

2. Set up a custom view for the Beauty Supplies, Accessories, Gifts, and Custom Jewelry sheets by hiding rows 6–7, 9–12, 14–18, and 20 on all these sheets. Set up the pages to print in landscape view, centered on the page horizontally, without gridlines or headers, and with page numbers in the form Page 1.

3. Select the Beauty Supplies tab and set up a view that includes cells A1 to F22. Name this view Beauty Supplies Annual Summary. Now set up identical views for the Accessories, Gifts, and Custom Jewelry sheets, with view names to differentiate them. (Notice that the person who

created the workbook has already created a Cash Flow Details view for each sheet.)

4. Switch to the Cash Flow Details view on all worksheets. Save the changes and leave the workbook open for the following exercise.

Creating Reports

Now that your views are set up, you can create reports that cover only one project or that cover any combination of projects.

To create reports, follow these steps:

1. In the `Annual Project Cash Flow` workbook select the `Beauty Supplies` tab. Switch to the Annual Summary view. Notice that the other tabs switched to the same view.

2. Create a report called `Beauty Supplies Annual Summary Report` that includes only the Beauty Supplies Annual Summary view.

3. Switch to the `Master CFA` tab of the workbook. Create a report called `All Projects Annual Summary Report`. This report should include one section for each of the projects in which the project's Annual Summary view is included. Use continuous page numbers.

4. Save the changes and leave the workbook open for the following exercise.

Editing and Printing Reports

You now have views and reports defined. However, your CFO likes to see project reports in alphabetical order by project name. In this exercise, you reorder the sections in the `All Projects Annual Summary Report` and print the report.

To edit and print a report, follow these steps:

1. Select any tab in the `Annual Project Cash Flow` workbook. Edit the `All Projects Annual Summary Report` to put the sections in alphabetical order.

2. Print the `All Projects Annual Summary Report`.

3. Save the changes and then close the workbook.

PinPoint Assessment

You have completed the project and the associated lessons, as well as the Checking Your Skills and Applying Your Skills sections. Now use the PinPoint software evaluation mode to assess your comprehension of the specific exam tasks you have just learned. You can also use the PinPoint Trainer Mode and the Show Me tutorials to practice these specific exam tasks.

Project 10

Ten

Creating More Complex Formulas and Functions

Calculating Sales Bonuses

Objectives

Required Activities

In this Project, you learn how to

➤ Round a Formula's Results

➤ Create a Decision-Making Formula

➤ Create a Formula with Nested Functions

➤ Create a Formula with Multiple IF Statements

Excel

Why Would I Do This?

So far, your exposure to Excel has included some simple mathematical formulas and a couple of basic functions. In this project, you explore more complex functions and learn how useful they can be. But first, pause for a quick refresher on some of the terms you need to know when dealing with formulas and functions in Excel.

Functions
Built-in formulas in Excel that perform simple to complex calculations.

Microsoft's programmers have spent years developing and testing many formulas that can be used in accounting, engineering, statistics, real estate, and many other fields. These formulas have been given names (such as SUM and AVERAGE) and are referred to as *functions*. Functions can be extremely useful because they can perform complicated calculations for you; all you have to do is choose the function you want to use and provide Excel with data relevant to your problem—sort of a "fill-in-the-blanks" solution. By typing a single function, you can replace a series of formulas or expressions that would otherwise be required to achieve the same result.

Arguments
The inputs you supply for a function so that it can perform the calculation.

The pieces of data you provide to a function are called *arguments*. For example, suppose you want to determine the average of the values in cells A1 through A5 of your worksheet. You can simply use Excel's AVERAGE function and type only the range of cells you want to average—in this case, A1:A5 (A1 through A5). The function would look like this: **=AVERAGE(A1:A5)**. The specified cells (A1:A5) are the arguments for the function.

Relative reference
A cell reference in a formula that adjusts to the new location when you copy the formula.

Also remember that the cells referenced in the formula example are called *relative references*. When you copy the formula to another column on the worksheet, the cell references automatically change to reflect the formula's new location. On the other hand, when an *absolute reference* is used in a formula like **=AVERAGE($A$1:$A$5)**, it always refers to a specific cell address, no matter what. When you copy or move the formula to a new location, the absolute cell reference in the formula does not change.

Absolute reference
A cell reference in a formula that doesn't change when you copy or move the formula to a new location.

By using functions, you avoid typing data incorrectly, you can work faster, and you don't have to worry about miscounting the amount of data. A more complex example is the NPV function. The NPV function calculates the net present value of a series of cash flows—an operation that most people would not even know how to perform with standard formulas. By using the built-in functions, Excel eliminates your need to know and understand complex formulas, but still allows you to utilize them.

Lesson 1: Rounding a Formula's Results

The worksheet in this lesson calculates January employee bonuses at five percent of the employee's monthly sales. However, suppose that the Accounting department wants you to round the bonuses to the nearest ten dollars. Now you must go back to this January worksheet and edit the original formula so that it rounds the bonus amounts. To do this, you can use Excel's ROUND function.

The ROUND function looks like this:

```
=ROUND(value,decimal_place)
```

Here is what the arguments mean:

> *value* is the number or formula you want to round.
>
> *decimal_place* is the number of decimal places you want your value rounded to. Following are some typical examples:

0	0 decimal places
2	2 decimal places to the right of the decimal
–2	2 decimal places to the left of the decimal

To Round a Formula's Result

❶ From the Project-10 folder on the CD, open the file Proj1001 and save it as Bonus**.**

❷ Activate the January worksheet.

❸ Select cell C7 and press Ctrl+Shift**.**

Holding down the Ctrl key while pressing the Shift key (grave accent mark—on the same key as the ~ (tilde), usually located next to the ① key on the keyboard) is a shortcut to view your formulas in their cells, as shown in Figure 10.1. The columns in your worksheet should expand, and the formulas should become visible in their cells.

Figure 10.1
The formulas, rather than the formula results, are displayed in Column C.

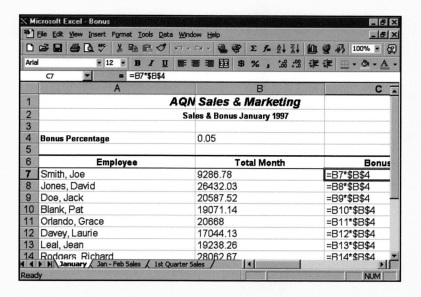

❹ Press Ctrl+Shift **again to toggle back to the normal view of the worksheet.**

January bonuses are calculated in column C. Cell C7 is where you can begin editing the original formula so that its result is rounded.

continues

To Round a Formula's Result (continued)

The formula in cell C7 currently reads like this:

=B7*$B$4

This formula needs to be rounded to –1 decimal points so its value will read $460.00 rather than $464.34.

5 **Click in the formula bar to the right of the equal sign (=) and type the following:**

ROUND(

Excel is in Edit mode, as shown in the status bar. Do *not* press ⏎Enter yet; you aren't finished.

6 **Place the insertion point to the right of $B$4 (in the formula bar) and type the following:**

,-1)

Then press ⏎Enter.

7 **Select cell C7 again so you can view the modified formula in the formula bar. The formula should now read this way:**

=ROUND(B7*$B$4,-1)

The formula result is now rounded to the nearest 10 dollars, as shown in Figure 10.2.

Figure 10.2
The bonus formula in cell C7 now uses the ROUND function to round the bonus to the nearest 10 dollars.

The modified formula as it appears in the formula bar

The new formula result for cell C7

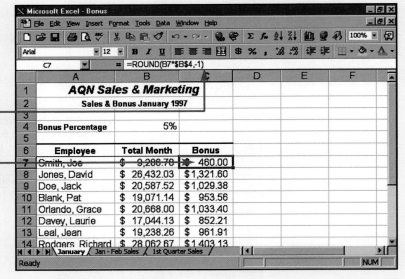

8 **Grab the fill handle in cell C7 and drag it to cell C21.**

9 **Press Ctrl+Home to return to the top of the worksheet, and then select cell C7.**

View the modified bonus results in column C, as shown in Figure 10.3.

Figure 10.3
The original monthly
bonus figures are now
rounded.

The bonus amounts
in column C now
appear rounded

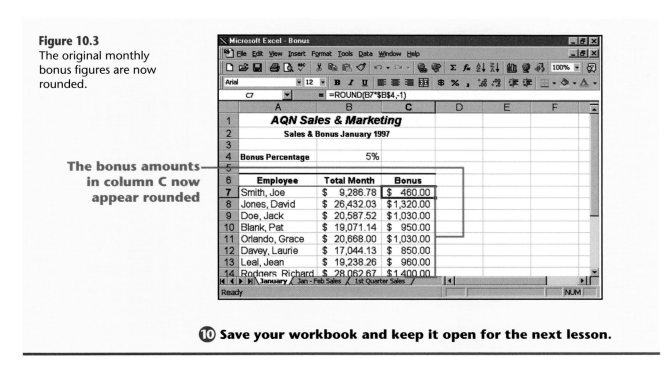

⑩ Save your workbook and keep it open for the next lesson.

Inside Stuff

Why would you round your figures instead of specifying a fixed number of decimal places? If you format your numbers to a fixed decimal place, your totals may not appear to add up correctly. Although you can only see the results of your designated format, the value may have more decimal places than are showing. Anyone reading a printout of the worksheet might question the accuracy of your figures. If you use rounding, your formulas use the actual number shown. Therefore, rounding your figures produces a result that matches the figures shown in the cells of your worksheet. The sum of 10.15, 12.65, and 20.54 when rounded to zero decimal places would appear to be the sum of 10, 13, and 21 with a result of 44. When fixed decimal formatting is used with zero decimal places, the figures appear to be a sum of 10, 13, and 21 but the result shows as 43. The actual result is 43.34.

Excel provides another method besides rounding to change formatted numbers to the actual number shown. Choose Tools, Options, and click the Calculation tab. In the Workbook options area, select the Precision as displayed check box and click OK. An alert message is displayed, warning you that data will permanently lose accuracy because the actual values in the worksheet will be converted to the formatted, displayed values. Click OK if you want to do that. If you change your mind, choose Tools, Options, and click the Calculation tab; then deselect the Precision as displayed check box.

Lesson 2: Creating a Decision-Making Formula

Spreadsheets are terrific tools; they help you analyze data and make decisions based on that data. Often, however, you have to scroll through a worksheet to find an exact piece of data so you can analyze it and make a decision. Excel can help you pare down this process by using functions that not only analyze data for you, but also tell you what decision is appropriate for that data. Of course, you must first set up the function, telling it what data to look for and the best decision for each result.

In this lesson, you modify the bonus formula so only those employees who meet a minimum sales goal during the month receive the five percent bonus. If an employee's sales are equal to or greater than $20,500, he receives the five percent bonus; if his sales are less than $20,500, he does not receive any bonus.

You can use the IF function (from Excel's Logical function category) to create a formula that looks at each employee's sales, determines whether the number is above or below the target amount, and decides whether the employee has earned a bonus. This type of function performs a *logical test*; that is, the function asks "Is this condition true?" (Yes, the employee sold $20,500 or more last month). If the condition is true, the function displays one value (the actual bonus amount); if the condition is false, it displays a different value (for this example, the text No Bonus).

You set up such an IF statement like this:

```
=IF(logical_test,value_if_true,value_if_false)
```

Here's what the statement's arguments mean:

> *logical_test* is a condition that can be evaluated as true or false.
>
> *value_if_true* is the result if *logical_test* is true.
>
> *value_if_false* is the result if *logical_test* is false.

The following table shows comparison operators that can be used in the logical test:

Comparison Operator	Symbol
Equal to	=
Greater than	>
Less than	<
Greater than or equal to	>=
Less than or equal to	<=

To Create a Decision-Making Formula

❶ With the Bonus **workbook open, activate the January worksheet.**

❷ Select cell C7.

Now you will modify the bonus formulas in column C. For each employee, if the employee's sales number in column B is greater than or equal to $20,500, the formula in column C will be positive and will calculate the employee's bonus as being five percent of the amount in column B. If the number in column B is less than $20,500, the formula in column C displays the words No Bonus.

❸ In the formula bar, click to the right of the equal sign (=) and type the following (including the comma):

```
IF(B7>=20500,
```

Do not press ⏎Enter yet; you aren't finished.

❹ Place the insertion point at the end of the formula (following the closing parenthesis) and type the following:

```
,"No Bonus")
```

Then press ⏎Enter.

❺ Select cell C7 again so you can view the modified formula in the formula bar, as shown in Figure 10.4. The formula should now read as follows:

```
=IF(B7>=20500,ROUND(B7*$B$4,-1),"No Bonus")
```

In cell C7, the result is No Bonus because the value in cell B7 is $9,286.78, which is less than $20,500. This makes the result of your logical test false; that is, the value in cell B7 is not greater than or equal to $20,500. Therefore, the formula returns the *value_if_false* argument, which is the text No Bonus.

Figure 10.4
The bonus formula in cell C7 now checks to see whether the sales amount in cell B7 matches or exceeds the target amount of $20,500.

The modified formula now uses the IF function to perform a test

The new formula result for cell C7

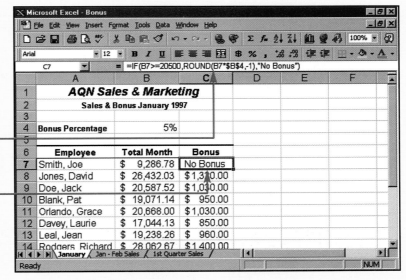

❻ Grab the fill handle in cell C7 and drag it to cell C21.

❼ Press Ctrl+Home to return to the top of the worksheet and then select cell C7.

Look at each employee's record now; your worksheet should look like Figure 10.5. If the value in column B is greater than or equal to $20,500 for any employee, column C shows a bonus of five percent of the month's total sales, rounded to the nearest ten dollars. Otherwise, column C shows No Bonus.

continues

To Create a Decision-Making Formula   (continued)

Figure 10.5
The bonus figures now reflect the result of the IF test, which checks the sales amounts in Column B.

The formulas in column C have been updated to include the IF function

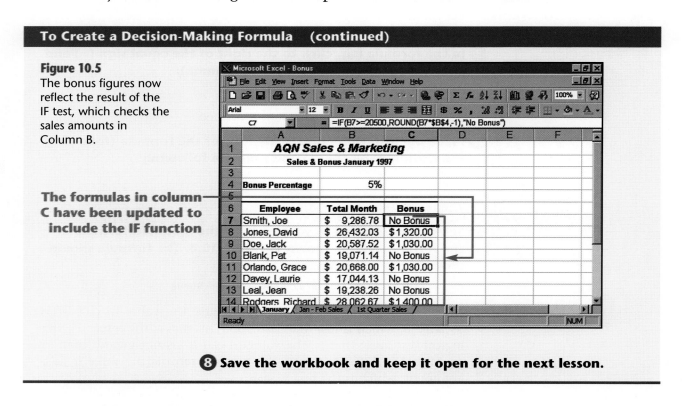

⑧ **Save the workbook and keep it open for the next lesson.**

If you want to include text as part of your formula, you must surround the text with double quotation marks (such as `"No Bonus"`). The quotation marks alert Excel to the fact that you want the text to appear exactly as shown. If you want to include a blank in the formula, use double quotation marks with nothing between them (`" "`).

Lesson 3: Creating a Formula with Nested Functions

At AQN Sales & Marketing, the salesperson gets an additional five percent bonus per month if his or her sales are over $20,500 for both the current month and the prior month. As you calculate bonuses, you need to look at sales not only for this month, but also for last month. Remember: The additional bonus takes effect only if sales for *both* months are over $20,500. If sales for either month are less than $20,500, the extra bonus doesn't apply.

You can create a formula that determines this for you by performing two logical tests. In this case, both tests must be true for the formula to return *value_if_true*. If only one of the tests is true (or if neither is true), the formula will return *value_if_false*.

This formula looks similar to the single-condition formula you created in Lesson 2, but will contain two logical tests, which are *nested* as follows:

```
=IF(AND(logical_test1,logical_test2),value_if_true,value_if_false)
```

Nested formula

A formula that includes multiple functions.

Here's what the arguments mean:

logical_test1 is the first condition to be evaluated as true or false.

logical_test2 is the second condition to be evaluated as true or false.

value_if_true is the result if both *logical_test1* and *logical_test2* are true.

value_if_false is the result if either *logical_test1* or *logical_test2* is false (or if both are false).

The *AND* operator evaluates the combined results of the *logical_test1* and *logical_test2* conditions.

To Create a Formula with Nested Functions

1 **In the** Bonus **workbook, activate the** Jan—Feb Sales **worksheet.**

This worksheet includes January and February sales figures for the sales staff.

2 **Select cell D4.**

Column D is where you will calculate the additional bonuses.

3 **In cell D4, type the following:**

```
=IF(AND(C4>=20500,B4>=20500),(C4*.05)+(B4*.05),"No Bonus")
```

Then press ⏎Enter.

As soon as you press ⏎Enter, Excel calculates the formula and No Bonus appears as the result in cell D4. Although cell C4 is greater than $20,500, cell B4 is not. The formula returns *value_if_false* because only one of the conditions was met—not both.

Now you can copy the formula down the column to test each employee's eligibility for the extra bonus.

4 **With cell D4 still selected, grab the fill handle and drag it down to cell D18.**

This copies the formula into each of the following cells. Excel automatically updates the formula in each cell so it uses the correct cell addresses for its new row.

5 **Adjust the width of column D, if necessary.**

Look at each employee's record now; your worksheet should look like Figure 10.6. If the values in both column B and column C are greater than or equal to $20,500 for any employee, column D shows a bonus of five percent of the combined month's total sales for that employee. Otherwise, column D shows No Bonus.

6 **Save the workbook and keep it open for the next lesson.**

continues

To Create a Formula with Nested Functions   (continued)

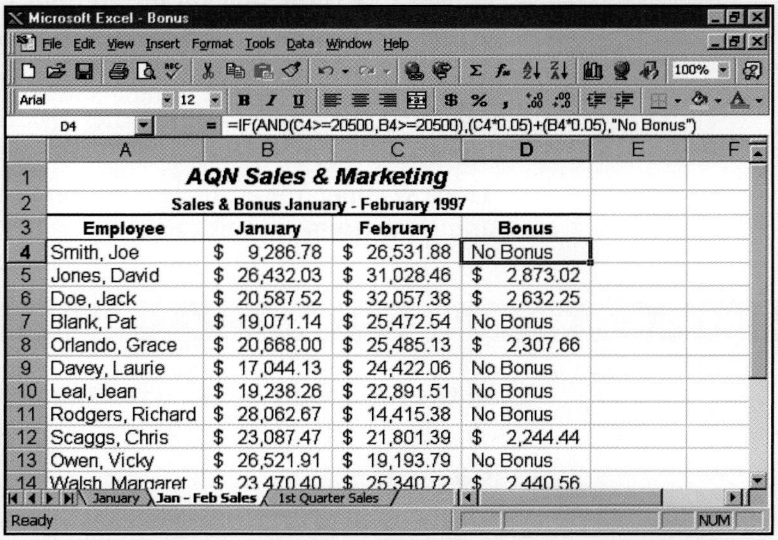

Figure 10.6
The Jan–Feb Sales work-
sheet now includes the
extra bonus calculations
for all employees.

Lesson 4: Creating a Formula with Multiple IF Statements

Imagine that it's time to calculate quarterly bonuses for the AQN Sales &
Marketing sales staff. The company has a graduated bonus scale for quarterly sales, which works like this:

■ Salespeople with sales below $60,000 for the quarter do not receive a
bonus.

■ Salespeople with sales between $60,000 and $69,999.99 receive a five
percent bonus.

■ Salespeople with sales between $70,000 and $79,999.99 receive a 10
percent bonus.

■ Salespeople with sales of $80,000 and above receive a 15 percent
bonus.

As you can see, a formula for this job could require a lot of tests. For example, you could use five different columns, put a different IF statement in
four of them, and then add them together in the fifth column. But there's a
simpler way. You can write one formula that contains multiple IF statements, like this:

```
=IF(logical_test1,value_if_true1,IF(logical_test2,value_if_true2,IF(
logical_test3,value_if_true3,value_if_false)))
```

Here's how the arguments will be set up:

logical_test1 checks to see whether the quarterly sales are less than
$60,000; *value_if_true1* is No Bonus.

logical_test2 checks to see whether the quarterly sales are less than

$70,000. This works for sales between $60,000 and $70,000 because if sales were less than $60,000, the formula would not have passed *value_if_true1*.

value_if_true2 is the bonus amount, or five percent of the sales.

logical_test3 checks to see whether the quarterly sales are less than $80,000. This works for sales between $70,000 and $80,000 because if sales were less than $70,000, the formula would not have passed *value_if_true2*.

value_if_true3 is the bonus amount, or 10 percent of the sales.

value_if_false is the bonus amount, or 15 percent of the sales.

This formula includes three IF statements; every time you use a function, you start with an opening parenthesis. For every opening parenthesis you have in a formula, you must have a closing parenthesis. Therefore, your formula ends with three closing parentheses. You do not need to put in a qualifier for sales greater than or equal to $80,000 because the formula already has qualifiers for sales less than $80,000—and anything that is not less than $80,000 must be greater than or equal to $80,000. Therefore, you can assume that if the value is not caught in the three logical tests, it must be greater than or equal to $80,000, and is therefore eligible for a 15 percent bonus.

In this exercise, you create the following formula:

```
=IF(B4<60000,"No         Bonus",IF(B4<70000,B4*5%,IF(B4<80000,
B4*10%,B4*15%)))
```

Although you can type this complex formula in the cell as you did in Lesson 3, Excel provides assistance in using its functions. In this exercise, you use the Formula Palette to create this formula.

To Create a Formula with Multiple IF Statements

① Activate the 1st Quarter Sales **worksheet and select cell C4.**

This worksheet includes the totals for the first quarter's sales figures. Column C is where you calculate the bonuses based on the figures in Column B.

② Click the Paste Function button on the Standard toolbar.

Note: The Formula Palette can be accessed by clicking the Paste Function button on the Standard toolbar, by choosing Insert, Function, or by clicking the Edit Formula button on the formula bar.

The Paste Function dialog box is displayed on your screen, as shown in Figure 10.7. Pick a category and then the function name. This dialog box provides the formula's structure as well as a description of what the function does.

continues

To Create a Formula with Multiple IF Statements (continued)

Figure 10.7
Excel's function categories and their respective functions can be accessed from the Paste Function dialog box.

Help button ——→

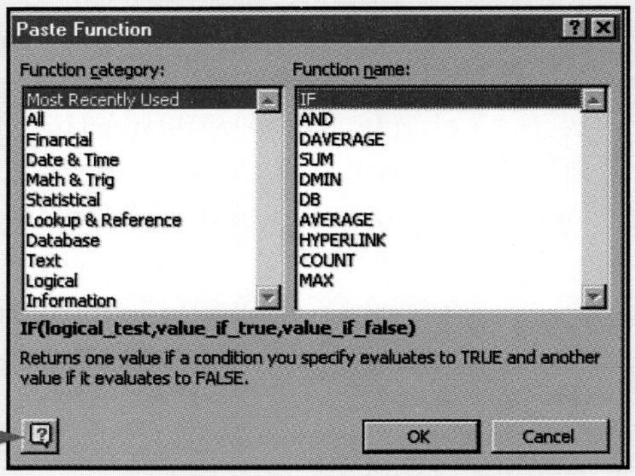

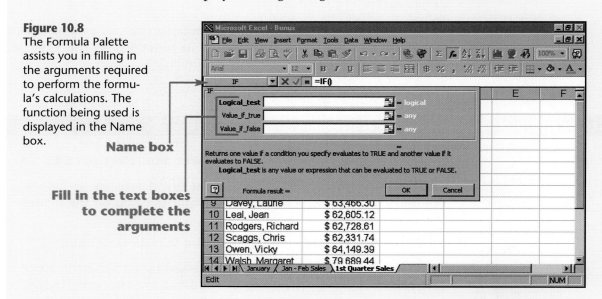

If you have problems...

For help in using functions, you can click the Help button in the Paste Function dialog box to activate the Office Assistant.

③ Select Logical in the Function category list and then IF in the Function name list.

④ Click OK.

The Formula Palette is displayed, as shown in Figure 10.8. Text boxes are provided to complete the function's arguments. Excel displays the beginning of the formula in the formula bar.

Figure 10.8
The Formula Palette assists you in filling in the arguments required to perform the formula's calculations. The function being used is displayed in the Name box.

Name box

Fill in the text boxes to complete the arguments

⑤ Drag the Formula Palette below row 4 on the worksheet.

By moving the Formula Palette, you see the worksheet cells being referenced in the formula you are writing. Now complete the Logical_test text box for the first condition to be tested.

⑥ Type B4<60000 **and press** Tab⭲.

The first test checks to see whether the quarterly sales are less than $60,000. Now complete the Value_if_true.

⑦ Type No Bonus **and press** Tab⭲.

The text is automatically surrounded by double quotes. If the first test shows the value to be true, the employee will not receive a bonus, as shown in Figure 10.9.

If you have problems...

If you pressed ↵Enter instead of the Tab⭲ key to move the insertion point to the next text box, just click the Paste Function button to return the Formula Palette to the screen.

Now complete the Value_if_false, which will be a second IF statement.

Figure 10.9
The Value_if_false text box will contain the second IF statement.

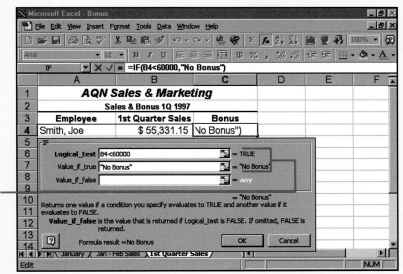

Results of the first test

⑧ Click the Name box displaying the IF function.

The Formula Palette now displays the three text boxes to complete the second condition. When the first condition is false (quarterly sales are greater than $60,000), the second condition is tested. Now complete the Logical_test text box.

⑨ Type B4<70000 **and press** Tab⭲.

The second condition checks to see whether the quarterly sales are less than $70,000. Now complete the Value_if_true text box.

continues

To Create a Formula with Multiple IF Statements   (continued)

⑩ Type the formula B4*5% **and press** Tab↹.

When the condition is true, the employee receives a bonus of five percent of the quarterly sales. Now complete the Value_if_false text box, which will be the third IF statement.

⑪ Click the Name box displaying the IF function.

The Formula Palette displays the three text boxes to complete the third condition. If the first and second conditions are false, the third condition is tested. Now complete the Logical_test text box.

⑫ Type B4<80000 **and press** Tab↹.

When the first two conditions are false, the third condition checks to see whether the quarterly sales are less than $80,000. Now complete the Value_if_true text box.

⑬ Type the formula B4*10% **and press** Tab↹.

When the condition is true, the employee receives a bonus of 10 percent of the quarterly sales. Now complete the Value_if_false text box.

⑭ Type the formula B4*15%.

If the third condition is false (quarterly sales are greater than $80,000), the employee receives a bonus of 15 percent.

⑮ Click OK.

Note the completed formula in the formula bar. When you use the Formula Palette, the proper punctuation marks (commas and parentheses) are added to the formula.

Excel calculates the formula and No Bonus appears as the result in cell C4. This means that Joe Smith's first quarter sales met the condition of the first logical test in the formula; that is, the number was less than $60,000. Therefore, Joe does not receive a quarterly bonus.

Now you can copy the formula down the column.

⑯ With cell C4 still selected, grab the fill handle and drag it down to cell C18.

This step copies the formula into each of the following cells. Excel automatically updates the formula in each cell to use the correct cell addresses for its new row.

⑰ Press Ctrl+Home **to return to the top of the worksheet and then select cell C4.**

⑱ Adjust the width of column C if necessary.

Your worksheet should look like Figure 10.10.

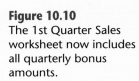

Figure 10.10
The 1st Quarter Sales worksheet now includes all quarterly bonus amounts.

The completed formula with multiple IF statements

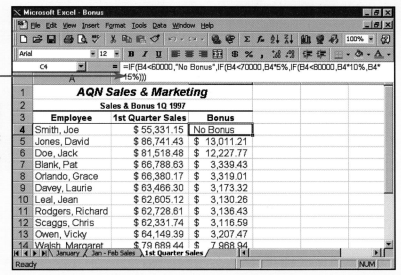

19 **If requested by your instructor, print two copies of the worksheets in this workbook and then save and close your workbook.**

If you have completed your session on the computer, exit Excel and Windows 95 before turning off your computer. Otherwise, continue with the "Checking Your Skills" and "Applying Your Skills" sections.

Remember, when creating an IF statement for a graduated scale (as in this lesson's example), start at the bottom of the scale and work your way to the top or do the opposite. In this lesson, you started at the bottom of the bonus scale and worked your way up.

Project Summary

To	Do This
Copy a formula from one cell to a contiguous range of cells.	Select the cell to be copied; then drag the fill handle to select the range.
Toggle the formulas in all cells on or off.	Press Ctrl+⇧Shift to toggle.
Round off a calculation to a specified number of places.	Use **=ROUND(*value,decimal_places*)**
Set up a logical test.	Use **IF(*logical_test,value_if_true, value_if_false*)**
Include text as part of a formula.	Surround the text with quotes.

continues

To	Do This
Create a formula with nested functions.	Use a logical AND to combine the results of individual tests (true only if both tests are true).
Create a formula with multiple IF statements.	Nest the IF statements so that the next IF statement starts where the previous IF statement's *value_if_false* argument would go.

Checking Your Skills

True or False

For each of the following statements, check *T* or *F* to indicate whether the statement is true or false.

__T __F   **1.** Rounding numbers is more accurate than formatting numbers to a fixed decimal position.

__T __F   **2.** The IF function is used when creating a decision-making formula.

__T __F   **3.** In the nested formula `=IF(AND(B4>=20500,C4>=20500,10%,"No Bonus")`, only one condition must be met to return *value_if_true*.

__T __F   **4.** You can chain a maximum of three IF statements in a formula.

__T __F   **5.** If you create an IF statement with a graduated scale, you must start at the bottom of the scale and work your way up to the top.

Multiple Choice

Circle the letter of the correct answer for each of the following.

1. Which function is used to round off a calculation to a specified number of decimal places?

   a. IF

   b. AND

   c. ROUND

   d. None of the above

2. The Formula Palette can be accessed through the

   a. Paste Function button

   b. Insert menu

   c. Edit Formula button in the formula bar

   d. All of the above

3. A formula that includes multiple functions is called a

   a. statement

   b. nested formula

   c. logical test

   d. none of the above

4. The IF function is found in what function category?

   a. Text

   b. Information

   c. Lookup & Reference

   d. Logical

5. When text is used as part of a formula's argument, surround the text with

    a. commas

    b. asterisks

    c. quotation marks

    d. none of the above

Completion

In the blank provided, write the correct answer for each of the following statements.

1. Use _____ + _____ to toggle the formulas in all cells in a worksheet on and off.

2. In the function, **=ROUND*(value,decimal_place)***, you would write _____ in the argument to round a value to two decimal places to the left of the decimal.

3. For every opening parenthesis you have in a formula, you must have a _____ parenthesis.

4. When you set up an IF statement, the _____ is a condition that can be evaluated as true or false.

5. In a formula with multiple IF statements, the next IF statement starts where the previous IF statement's _____ would go.

Matching

In the blank next to each of the following terms or phrases, write the letter of the corresponding term or phrase.

a. absolute reference

b. IF

c. arguments

d. functions

e. A5

f. nested formula

g. $A$5

h. ROUND

i. AND

j. relative reference

_____ 1. Built-in formulas in Excel that perform simple to complex calculations

_____ 2. The inputs you supply for a function so that it can perform the calculation

_____ 3. A cell reference in a formula that adjusts to the new location when you copy the formula

_____ 4. A cell reference in a formula that doesn't change when you copy or move the formula to a new location

_____ 5. A formula that includes multiple functions

_____ 6. An example of an absolute cell address

_____ 7. An example of a relative cell address

_____ 8. Use this to create a formula with nested functions

_____ 9. Use this to create a logical test

_____ 10. Use this to round off a calculation

Applying Your Skills

Practice

The following exercises enable you to practice the skills you have learned in this project. Take a few minutes to work through these exercises now.

Calculating Selling Prices

Your coffee shop marks up coffee by 75 percent, based on the cost. You want to use an Excel worksheet to help figure the selling price for various coffees.

To calculate selling prices, follow these steps:

1. Open Proj1002 from the Project-10 folder on the CD and save it as Store Markup.

2. In cell B3, enter the markup, 75 percent, as a decimal number.

3. To calculate the selling price for a product, multiply the cost by 1 plus the markup. Be sure to use an absolute cell reference to point to the markup percentage in cell B3.

4. Copy the formula from cell C6 to cells C7 through C12.

5. Change the formula in cell C6 to round the prices to one decimal place.

6. Copy the formula from cell C6 to cells C7 through C12.

7. Change the formatting of cells C6:C12 so that two decimal places display.

8. If requested by your instructor, print two copies of the Store Markup worksheet. Save the workbook and leave it open for the following exercise.

Evaluating Sales

Lately, you have noticed that the more expensive coffees might not be selling as well as the lower priced beans. You want to identify those coffees that sell for $5.50 or more per pound so that you can compare their sales with the lower priced coffees. You want to enter a function that determines if a coffee sells for $5.50 or more per pound. If it does, you want to enter Track Sales into the cells. If it does not, you want the cell to be left blank.

To evaluate sales, follow these steps:

1. Select cell D6.

2. Type the following formula into this cell:

```
=IF(C6>=5.50,"Track Sales","")
```

Because you don't want anything to be entered if the value = false, you have entered empty quotation marks for this argument.

3. Copy this formula to cells D7:D12.

4. If requested by your instructor, print two copies of the `Store Markup` worksheet. Save and close the workbook.

Adjusting Coffee Prices

After additional evaluation, you have determined that some of the higher priced coffees are not selling as well. You decide to reduce the price of these coffees, hoping to boost sales. Instead of a 75% markup, you decide to use a 60% markup. In this exercise, you create a formula that determines if coffee sales are below a certain amount, and if the price is above the certain amount. If both conditions are met, the price is reduced.

To adjust coffee prices, follow these steps:

1. Open the file Proj1003 from the Project-10 folder on the CD and save it as `Price Changes`. The worksheet is the same as the one you worked with in previous exercises, except that it includes a column showing average monthly sales for each type of coffee.

2. You want to enter a function that will check and to see whether the price of the coffee is greater than or equal to $5.30 per pound, and if the average sales are less than $220 per month. If both conditions are true, you want to mark up the price by 60%. If the conditions are not met, you want "No change" to be entered into the cell.

3. Type the following formula into cell E6:

   ```
   =IF(AND(C6>=5.3,D6<220),(B6*$C$3)+B6,"No change")
   ```

4. Copy the formula down to cells E7:E12.

5. If requested by your instructor, print two copies of the `Price Changes` worksheet. Save and close the workbook.

Analyzing Accounts Receivable

Your mail order coffee business has been expanding, and with the expansion have come accounts receivable collection problems. You decide to start offering a discount to those customers who pay their bills promptly.

To analyze accounts receivable, follow these steps:

1. Open the file Proj1004 from the Project-10 folder on the CD and save it as `Accounts Receivable`.

2. You need to calculate any discount in column E. If the customer has paid within 10 days, they get a 15% discount. If they have paid within 20 days, they get a 5% discount. If they do not pay within this time, they are not entitled to a discount.

3. Enter the following formula in cell E6:

   ```
   =IF(D6-B6<=10,C6*.15,IF(D6-B6<=20,C6*.05,0))
   ```

4. Copy the formula down to cells E7:E13.

5. In column F, you need to determine whether the customer took more than 30 days to pay. If so, 2% needs to be added to their invoice.

6. Enter the following formula into cell F6:
   ```
   =IF(D6-B6>30,C6*.02,0)
   ```

7. Copy this formula down to cells F7:F13.

8. In column G, you need to total the invoice. You should take the amount of the invoice, subtract any discounts, and add any additional charges. Enter a formula into cell G6 to perform this calculation.

9. Copy this formula down to cells G7:G13.

10. Save the worksheet and leave it open for the following exercise.

Formatting the Accounts Receivable Worksheet

In this exercise, you use the rounding function to round the discount and additional charge columns in the Accounts Receivable worksheet. You also use formatting techniques you learned in previous projects to improve the worksheet's appearance.

To format the accounts receivable worksheet, follow these steps:

1. Select cell E6.

2. Add the ROUND function to the formula in this cell, rounding the result to 2 decimal places.

3. Copy the new formula down to cells E7:E13.

4. Add the ROUND function to the formula in cell F6, rounding the result to 2 decimal places.

5. Copy the new formula down to cells F7:F13.

6. Format the data in columns E and F to currency, with two decimal places.

7. If requested by your instructor, print two copies of the `Accounts Receivable` worksheet. Save and close the workbook.

Challenge

The following challenges enable you to use your problem-solving skills. Take time to work through these exercises now.

Calculating Retail Prices

Your friend, Larry, owns Larry's Discount Amplifiers. You have shown Larry how using Excel has made running your business much easier. Larry wants you to help him set up several spreadsheets. Larry's Discount Amplifiers marks up all merchandise by 32 percent. Larry adds new merchandise from time to time, and also changes his markup as needed to maintain his competitive edge. Larry wants to use an Excel worksheet to help figure the selling price for various products.

To calculate retail prices, follow these steps:

1. Open Proj1005 from the Project-10 folder on the CD and save it as `Larry's Markup`.

2. In cell B3, enter the markup, 32 percent.

3. Calculate the selling price for each product.

4. Change the formula to round the prices to the nearest ten dollars.

5. If requested by your instructor, print two copies of the `Store Markup` worksheet. Save and close the workbook.

Calculating Commissions

Larry has done so well with his discount amplifier store that he is adding an outbound telephone sales group. To encourage sales, he is going to offer a two-tier commission structure. For selling a lower-priced product (level 1), the commission is 3 percent of the selling price. The commission for a level 2 product is 5 percent of the selling price. Larry reduces his markup to 20 percent and adjusts the selling price to offset the commission costs.

To calculate commissions, follow these steps:

1. Open Proj1006 from the Project-10 folder on the CD and save it as `Commissions`.

2. Compute the loaded selling price first. Because the load (commission) depends on the level of a product, you need to use an IF statement to select the correct commission. To calculate the selling price, add the markup percentage to the commission percentage plus one, and multiply by the cost. If there is a problem with the level in column B, the cell should show `Level ?`. This formula goes in cell D7. (Remember to use absolute references in the formula where necessary, so that the formula can be copied to the other cells in column D.)

3. Copy the formula to cells D8 through D16.

4. In cell E7, enter a formula that computes the sales commission, based on the level of the product. (Remember to use absolute references in the formula where necessary, so that the formula can be copied to the other cells in column E.) If there is a problem with the level in column B, the cell should show `Level ?`.

5. Copy the formula to cells E8 through E16.

6. Save the workbook.

7. Test your formula by entering invalid numbers into column B. If a number other than 1 or 2 is entered, `Level ?` should display in column D and E.

8. Be sure to enter the correct number back into column B.

9. Once you know the formula is correct, print two copies of the `Loaded Markup` worksheet if requested by the instructor and then save and close the workbook.

Analyzing Accounts Receivable

Now that Larry is doing telephone sales and billing customers, he needs to start tracking his receivables. To encourage timely payment, he offers a 5 percent discount to customers who pay in full within 15 days of the date of the invoice. If an invoice is not paid within 30 days, Larry sends the customer a reminder.

To analyze accounts receivable, follow these steps:

1. Open Proj0407 from the Project-10 folder on the CD and save it as `Receivables`.

2. Larry is starting this system as of March 6, 1998. Enter this date as `3/6/98` in cell B3 so that you can see how the worksheet operates as you build it.

3. In cell E9, build a formula that determines how much is due from the customer if he pays Larry today. Your formula must determine the amount due, based on whether less than 15 days have passed since the invoice was sent. A word of warning: Make sure that your formula has equal numbers of opening and closing parentheses and uses quotation marks surrounding text!

4. Copy the formula in cell E9 to cells E10 through E17.

5. In column F, calculate the total amount due today.

6. Save the file and leave it open for the following exercise.

Identifying Past Due Accounts

Now that Larry's Accounts Receivable worksheet is set up to calculate discounts, you want it to identify those accounts that are past due. To do this, use an IF statement to identify those accounts that are over 30 days old.

To identify past due accounts, follow these steps:

1. To help Larry handle each of these outstanding accounts, build a formula in cell G9 that indicates the appropriate action. If an invoice is over 30 days old, the formula should print `Overdue` in the cell; if between 16 and 30 days, it should print `Due`; and if 15 days old or less, `Discount`.

2. Copy the formula in cell G9 to cells G10 through G17.

3. If requested by the instructor, print two copies of the `Receivables` worksheet; then save the workbook.

4. Make Larry's worksheet automatic. Delete the date from cell B3. Enter the formula `=NOW()`. This automatically enters the current date from your computer system.

5. Save and close the workbook and exit Excel.

PinPoint Assessment

You have completed the project and the associated lessons, as well as the Checking Your Skills and Applying Your Skills sections. Now use the PinPoint software evaluation mode to assess your comprehension of the specific exam tasks you have just learned. You can also use the PinPoint Trainer Mode and the Show Me tutorials to practice these specific exam tasks.

appendix A

Working with Windows 95

Objectives

In this Appendix, you learn how to

➤ Start Windows 95

➤ Use the Mouse

➤ Understand the Start Menu

➤ Identify the Elements of a Window

➤ Manipulate Windows

➤ Exit the Windows 95 Program

Why Would I Do This?

Graphical user interface (GUI)
A computer application that uses pictures, graphics, menus, and commands to help users communicate with their computers.

Desktop
The background of the Windows screen, on which windows, icons, and dialog boxes appear.

Icon
A picture that represents an application, a file, or a system resource.

Shortcut
Gives you quick access to frequently used objects so you don't have to look through menus each time you need to use that object.

Microsoft Windows 95 is a powerful operating environment that enables you to access the power of DOS without memorizing DOS commands and syntax. Windows 95 uses a *graphical user interface* (GUI) so that you can easily see onscreen the tools that you need to complete specific file- and program-management tasks.

This appendix, an overview of the Windows 95 environment, is designed to help you learn the basics of Windows 95.

Lesson 1: Starting Windows 95

The first thing you need to know about Windows is how to start the software. In this lesson, you learn how to start Windows; however, before you can start Windows, it must be installed on your computer. If you need to install Windows, refer to your Windows 95 manual or ask your instructor for assistance.

In most cases, Windows starts automatically when you turn on your computer. If your system is set up differently, you must start Windows from the DOS prompt (such as C:\>). Try starting the Windows program now.

To Start Windows 95

Taskbar
Contains the Start button, buttons for each open window, and the current time.

Start button
A click of the Start button opens the Start menu.

❶ Turn on your computer and monitor.

Most computers display technical information about the computer and the operating software installed on it.

If Windows starts, you can skip step 2. Otherwise, you will see the DOS prompt C:\>.

❷ At the DOS prompt, type win and press ⏎Enter.

When you start the Windows program, a Microsoft Windows 95 banner displays for a few seconds; then the *desktop* appears (see Figure A.1).

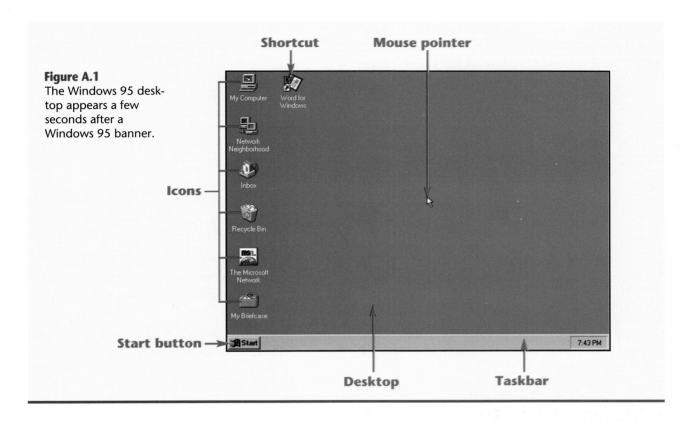

Figure A.1
The Windows 95 desktop appears a few seconds after a Windows 95 banner.

Shortcut

Mouse pointer

Icons

Start button

Desktop

Taskbar

Inside Stuff

Program *icons* that were created during installation (such as My Computer, Recycle Bin, and Network Neighborhood) are displayed on the desktop. Other icons might also appear, depending on how your system is set up. Shortcuts to frequently used objects (such as documents, printers, and network drives) can be placed on the desktop. The *Taskbar* appears along the bottom edge of the desktop. The *Start button* appears at the left end of the Taskbar.

Pull-down menus
Menus that cascade downward into the screen whenever you select a command from the menu bar.

Dialog box
A window that opens on-screen to provide information about the current action or to ask the user to provide additional information to complete the action.

Mouse
A pointing device used in many programs to make choices, select data, and otherwise communicate with the computer.

Mouse pad
A pad that provides a uniform surface for the mouse to slide on.

Lesson 2: Using the Mouse

Windows is designed to be used with a *mouse,* so it's important that you learn how to use a mouse correctly. With a little practice, using a mouse is as easy as pointing to something with your finger. You can use the mouse to select icons, to make selections from *pull-down menus* and *dialog boxes,* and to select objects that you want to move or resize.

In the Windows desktop, you can use a mouse to

■ Open windows.

■ Close windows.

■ Open menus.

■ Choose menu commands.

■ Rearrange on-screen items, such as icons and windows.

The position of the mouse is indicated onscreen by a *mouse pointer.* Usually, the mouse pointer is an arrow, but it sometimes changes shape depending on the current action.

Mouse pointer

A symbol that appears onscreen to indicate the current location of the mouse.

Onscreen, the mouse pointer moves according to the movements of the mouse on your desk or on a *mouse pad*. To move the mouse pointer, simply move the mouse.

There are four basic mouse actions:

- *Click.* To point to an item, and then press and quickly release the left mouse button. You click to select an item, such as an option on a menu. To cancel a selection, click an empty area of the desktop. Unless otherwise specified, you use the left mouse button for all mouse actions.

- *Double-click.* To point to an item, and then press and release the left mouse button twice, as quickly as possible. You double-click to open or close windows and to start applications from icons.

- *Right-click.* To point to an item, and then press and release the right mouse button. This opens a Context menu, which gives you a shortcut to frequently used commands. To cancel a Context menu, click the left mouse button outside the menu.

- *Drag.* To point to an item, then press and hold down the left mouse button as you move the pointer to another location, and then release the mouse button. You drag to resize windows, move icons, and scroll.

If you have problems...

If you double-click but nothing happens, you may not be clicking fast enough. Try again.

Lesson 3: Understanding the Start Menu

Program folder

Represented by an icon of a file folder with an application window in front of it, program folders contain shortcut icons and other program folders.

The Start button on the Taskbar gives you access to your applications, settings, recently opened documents, the Find utility, the Run command, the Help system, and the Shut Down command. Clicking the Start button opens the Start menu. Choosing the Programs option at the top of the Start menu displays the Programs submenu, which lists the *program folders* on your system. Program folders are listed first, followed by shortcuts (see Figure A.2).

Program folder

Figure A.2
Click the Start button to open the Start menu. All your programs are grouped together in the Programs submenu.

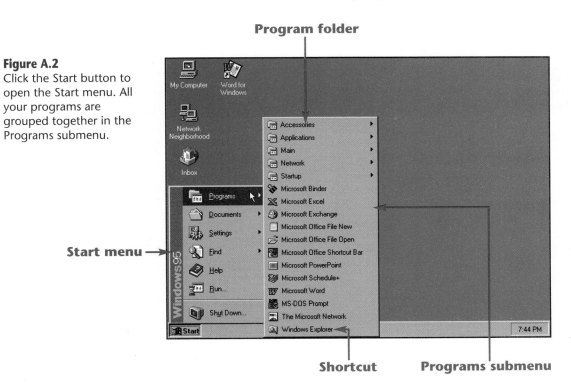

Start menu

Shortcut   **Programs submenu**

When the Start menu is open, moving the mouse pointer moves a selection bar through the menu options. When the selection bar highlights a menu command with a right-facing triangle, a submenu opens. Click the shortcut icon to start an application. If a menu command is followed by an ellipsis, clicking that command opens a dialog box.

Lesson 4: Identifying the Elements of a Window

In Windows 95, everything opens in a window. Applications, documents, and dialog boxes all open in windows. For example, double-clicking the My Computer icon opens the My Computer application into a window. Because window elements stay the same for all Windows applications, this section uses the My Computer window for illustration.

Title Bar

Across the top of each window is its title bar. A title bar contains the name of the open window, as well as three buttons to manipulate it. The Minimize button reduces the window to a button on the Taskbar. The Maximize button expands the window to fill the desktop. The Close button closes the window.

Menu Bar

The menu bar gives you access to the application's menus. Menus enable you to select options that perform functions or carry out commands (see Figure A.3). The File menu in My Computer, for example, enables you to open, save, and print files.

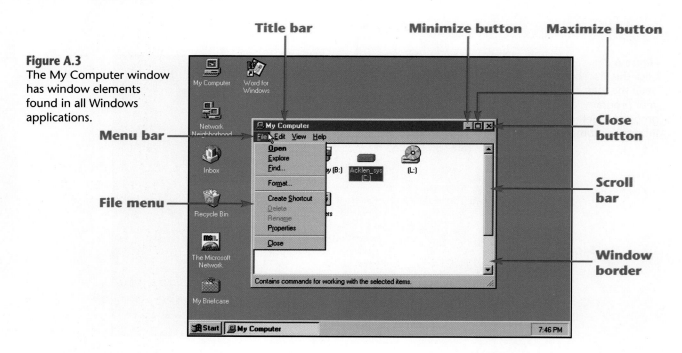

Figure A.3
The My Computer window has window elements found in all Windows applications.

Some menu options require you to enter additional information. When you select one of these options, a dialog box opens (see Figure A.4). You type the additional information, select from a list of options, or select a button. Most dialog boxes have a Cancel button, which closes the dialog box without saving the changes; an OK button, which closes the dialog box and saves the changes; and a Help button, which opens a Help window.

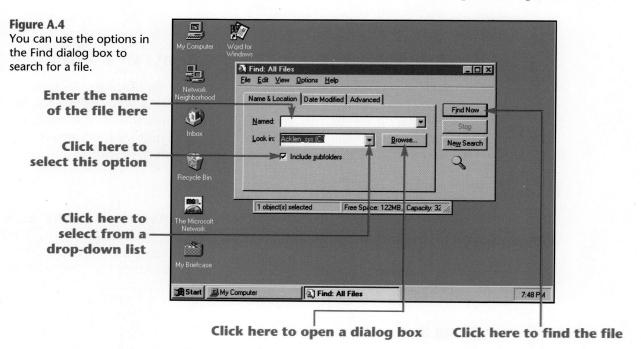

Figure A.4
You can use the options in the Find dialog box to search for a file.

Scroll Bar

Scroll bars appear when you have more information in a window than is currently displayed on-screen. A horizontal scroll bar appears along the bottom of a window, and a vertical scroll bar appears along the right side of a window.

Window Border

The window border identifies the edge of the window. In most windows, it can be used to change the size of a window. The window corner is used to resize a window on two sides at the same time.

Lesson 5: Manipulating Windows

When you work with windows, you need to know how to arrange them. You can shrink the window into an icon or enlarge the window to fill the desktop. You can stack windows together or give them each an equal slice of the desktop.

Maximizing a Window

Maximize
To increase the size of a window so that it fills the entire screen.

You can *maximize* a window so that it fills the desktop. Maximizing a window gives you more space to work in. To maximize a window, click the Maximize button on the title bar.

Minimizing a Window

When you *minimize* a window, it shrinks the window to an icon on the Taskbar. Even though you can't see the window anymore, the application stays loaded in the computer's memory. To minimize a window, click the Minimize button on the title bar.

Minimize
To reduce a window to an icon.

Restoring a Window

When a window is maximized, the Maximize button changes into a Restore button. Clicking the Restore button restores the window back to the original size and position before the window was maximized.

Closing a Window

When you are finished working in a window, you can close the window by clicking the Close button. Closing an application window exits the program, removing it from memory. When you click the Close button, the window (on the desktop) and the window button (on the Taskbar) disappear.

Arranging Windows

Changing the size and position of a window enables you to see more than one application window, which makes copying and pasting data between programs much easier. You can also move a window to any location on the desktop. By moving application windows, you can arrange your work on the Windows desktop just as you arrange papers on your desk.

Use one of the following options to arrange windows:

Tile
To arrange open windows on the desktop so that they do not overlap.

Cascade
To arrange open windows on the desktop so that they overlap, with only the title bar of each window (behind the top window) displayed.

- Right-click the Taskbar and choose Tile <u>H</u>orizontally.

- Right-click the Taskbar and choose Tile <u>V</u>ertically. See Figure A.5 for an example.

- Right-click the Taskbar and choose <u>C</u>ascade. See Figure A.6 for an example.

- Click and drag the window's title bar to move the window around on the desktop.

- Click and drag a window border (or corner) to increase or decrease the size of the window.

Figure A.5
The windows are tiled vertically across the desktop.

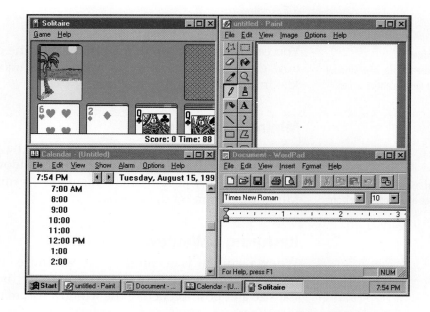

Figure A.6
The windows are cascaded on the desktop.

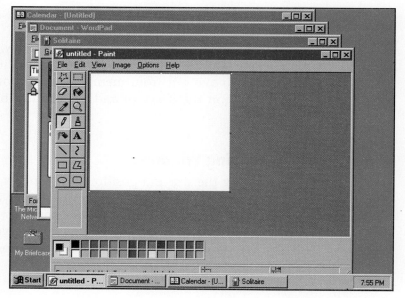

Lesson 6: Exiting the Windows 95 Program

In Windows 95, you use the Shut Down command to exit the Windows 95 program. You should always use this command, which closes all open applications and files, before you turn off the computer. If you haven't saved your work in an application when you choose this command, you'll be prompted to save your changes before Windows shuts down.

To Exit Windows 95

1 Click the Start button on the Taskbar.

2 Choose Shut Down.

3 Choose Shut down the computer.

4 Choose Yes.

Windows displays a message asking you to wait while the computer is shutting down. When this process is complete, a message appears telling you that you can safely turn off your computer now.

appendix B

Glossary

Absolute reference   An absolute reference is a cell reference in a formula that does not change when copied to a new location.

Active cell   The currently selected cell (a thick border appears around that cell when you click in it).

Ascending order   Sorts records from beginning to end, for example from A to Z or 1 to 100. (Records with a blank sort field appear in front of other records.)

AutoFormat   A built-in collection of formats (such as font size, patterns, and alignment) that you can quickly apply to a range of data. Microsoft Excel determines the levels of summary and detail in the selected range and applies the formats accordingly.

Axis   A line that serves as a major reference for plotting data on a graph. In a two-dimensional chart, there are generally two axes: the vertical axis is the y-axis or Value Axis and the horizontal axis is the x-axis or Category Axis (except in bar charts where the Category Axis is the vertical and the Value axis is horizontal). In a three-dimensional chart, the z-axis represents the vertical plane, and the x-axis (distance) and y-axis (width) represent the two sides on the floor of the chart. Pie charts do not have axes.

Browser   A program that translates the HTML codes in a web page to a layout that is viewed by the user.

Category   One item against which Excel plots the data series. It may be a time (month, year, quarter), a product name, a location, and so on.

A chart may only have one category, or it may have several.

Cell   Rectangle formed by the intersection of a column and a row.

Cell address   Each cell (or rectangle) in the spreadsheet has a unique address by which you may reference that cell in formulas. That address consists of the letter of the column the cell is in and the row number.

Clip art   Pictures you can use without copyright restrictions.

Clipboard   A temporary memory holding area where Windows stores items that you Cut or Copy from a document. The items remain in the Clipboard until a different item is cut or copied or until your computer is shut down; the new item then replaces it. As long as an item remains in the Clipboard, you may Paste it into an Excel worksheet. Pasting places a copy of the Clipboard contents into the active cell or selected range.

Comparison operator   A sign used to compare two values, such as = (equal to), > (greater than), < (less than), >= (greater than or equal to), <= (less than or equal to), or <> (not equal to).

Conditional format   A format, such as cell shading or font color, that Microsoft Excel automatically applies to cells if a specified condition is true.

Data labels   Optional labels that appear at the data points on the chart. They may show the value, category, or percentage of the data point.

Data marker   A bar (in column and bar charts), shape (in area or pie charts), dot, or symbol (in line and Scatter charts) that marks a single data point or value. Related markers in a graph represent the same data series.

Data point   A single cell value, representing a single category in a data series.

Data series   A row or column of data used to plot one line, one pie, or one set of bars or columns in a chart.

Database   A collection of related information organized into fields and records. You use a database to store, organize, and retrieve information. A mailing list is a type of database.

Descending order   Sorts records from end to beginning, from Z to A or from 100 to 1.

Dynamic Data Exchange (DDE)   A communications protocol that lets you share data between two open applications.

Embedded charts   A chart that is placed on the same worksheet that contains the data used to create the chart. A chart can also be placed on a chart sheet in the workbook so that the worksheet and chart are separate. Embedded charts are useful for showing the actual data and its graphic representation side-by-side.

Embedding   Places an "object" created by another program directly into your worksheet. You edit the object contents by activating the source application directly from your worksheet. Changing an embedded object does not change the source document.

Field   A piece of information unique for each record in the database. In a mailing list, the name of the city would be stored in a "city" field, and each individual in the database would also have data in that "city" field.

Filter   An action Microsoft Excel performs to select a subset of your list. All the rows in the subset meet specific criteria, and all other rows are "filtered out."

Font   A set of characters that have the same typeface, which means they are of a single design (such as Times New Roman).

Formula   An algebraic expression using numbers, functions, mathematical operators, and cell addresses that tells Excel what operations to perform on numbers or the contents of the designated cells.

Function   Ready-made formula that performs a series of operations on a specified range of values.

Gridlines   Optional lines that extend from the tick marks on an axis through the plot area to make it easier to evaluate data points (*see also Major and Minor Gridlines*).

Histogram analysis tool   Calculates individual and cumulative frequencies for a cell range of data and data bins. It generates data for the number of occurrences of a value in the data set.

Hyperlink   Colored and underlined text or graphics on web pages that you click to go to another location on the current page, another Web page, an HTML page on the World Wide Web, or an HTML page on an intranet.

Hypertext Markup Language (HTML) HTML is a collection of instructions, or *tags*, that tell a browser program how to display a document—when the text is bold, italic, and so on.

Internet   A worldwide conglomeration of computer networks that can talk to each other.

Intranet   A company's computer network working with software that lets it route HTML documents. The documents can be read on the network using a browser.

Legend   A key that identifies the patterns, colors, or symbols associated with the markers of a data series. Shows the data series name that corresponds to each marker.

Linking   Utilizes the Clipboard (via the Cut and Copy commands) to bring data from a source document and place it into your document. Any updates to the source information will also appear in your worksheet. The location of the source file cannot change or the link will fail.

Macro   A set of commands and instructions that are recorded and played back when you command it to run.

Major and minor gridlines   Major gridlines help you pinpoint exact locations in a chart without cluttering the chart. On the value axis, the value labels appear next to the major gridlines. When major gridlines don't provide enough detail, you can use minor gridlines as well. Minor gridlines fall between the major intervals on the axis.

Mixed reference   A reference that is only partially absolute, such as A$2 or $A2. When a formula that uses a mixed reference is copied to another cell, part of the cell reference (the relative part) is adjusted.

Number format   Determines how a number appears in the format, such as a Currency format which adds a dollar sign ($), a comma as a thousands separator, and two decimal places to the number you entered in the cell.

Object Linking and Embedding (OLE) Extends your ability to dynamically share information between programs and program files. Because of OLE, you can embed or link files from another application into your worksheet; or you can embed a new object and use the object's source application to enter data into your worksheet.

PivotTable   An interactive table that summarizes large amounts of data. To see different summaries of the source data, you rotate its rows and columns.

Plot area   The area in which Excel plots the data for a graph. It includes the axes and all markers that represent data points.

Query   A question you ask about data stored in an external database.

Range   A group of adjacent cells joined horizontally or vertically.

Record   An individual set of information consisting of the data for each field in a database that relates to one individual or company or thing. In a mailing list, a record would be one person's name, address, city, state, and zip code.

Relative reference   A *relative reference* is a cell reference in a formula that is adjusted when the formula is copied.

Series names   The names that identify each row or column of data. These names appear in the legend.

Shared list or workbook   A workbook that allows multiple users on a network to view and make changes to the workbook simultaneously. Users who save the workbook can view the modifications made by others.

Style   A collection of formats (such as font size, patterns, and alignment) that you define and save as a group.

Template   A preformatted workbook or worksheet that contains text, formulas, and automating features that help you set up consistent workbooks for specific tasks.

Tick mark   A small line that intersects an axis and marks off a category, scale, or data series.

Tick mark labels   The names that appear along the Category axis where the tick marks are.

URL   The Web uses a type of address called a uniform resource locator (URL) to identify specific documents and locations.

Web   The World Wide Web (or just Web) is a component of the Internet. It's a collection of documents accessible through the Internet.

Workbook   An Excel file. Each workbook consists of three worksheets (although you can add and remove worksheets as needed). The tabs at the bottom of the workbook window (labeled Sheet1, Sheet2, and Sheet3) let you flip through the worksheets by clicking them with the mouse.

Worksheet   Consists of columns and rows that intersect to form boxes called cells into which you enter values (numbers) or labels (text).

appendix C

Student Preparation Guide

The purpose of this appendix is to provide you with information you'll need about the certification tests—how to register, what is covered in the tests, how the tests work, and so on.

Studying for the Tests

Although you aren't required to take a training course to pass the Microsoft Office User Specialist exams, you certainly need to be sure you can successfully complete the tasks that are covered by the exams. Although a training class provides guidance, support, and practice, it may not be convenient or necessary for you.

This book provides the tutorial, review questions, and practice to help you complete your exams successfully. It can be used in a classroom situation, or you can work through the projects on your own. You don't have to work through the book from front to back, as each project stands on its own. The Checking and Applying Your Skills sections at the end of each project give you a chance to become familiar with the tasks. The Kelly PinPoint CBT trainer located on the accompanying CD has end–of-project computer-based training and evaluation as well as a final practice examination.

Levels of Certification

For the Microsoft Office User Specialist exam for Microsoft Excel 97, there are two levels of certification:

- **Microsoft Excel Proficient Specialist** You should be able to handle a wide range of everyday tasks without difficulty.

- **Microsoft Excel Expert Specialist** In addition to the everyday tasks at the Proficient level, you should be able to handle complex assignments involving advanced formatting and functionality.

Microsoft also has a special Office 97 certification, the Microsoft Office Expert. To attain this level, you must be an Expert User in each of the Microsoft Office applications (Access, Excel, Word, PowerPoint, and FrontPage) and have taken the Office Integration Exam to prove you can integrate these applications.

The specific topics covered at each level are listed in the "Required Tasks" section of this appendix. In this book, these tasks are broken down into projects. At the beginning of each project is a list of which tasks are covered and which subject area they fall under in the tests.

Required Tasks

Each exam involves a list of required tasks that you may be asked to perform. The list of possible tasks is categorized by skill area.

Proficient User

A Proficient User should be able to do the following:

- Basic financial statements
- Budgets
- Expense reports

- Invoices and purchase orders

- Marketing and sales reports

- Spreadsheet information for use on the Internet and intranet

The skill areas covered in the exam and the required tasks for those skill areas are listed in Table C1.

Table C.1 Proficient User Skills	
Skill Set	Required Activity
Create workbooks	Open electronic workbooks Enter text and numbers Enter formulas Save workbooks Close workbooks
Modify workbooks	Delete cell contents Delete worksheets Revise text and numbers Rotate and indent text Revise formulas Copy and move data Insert, modify, and delete rows and columns Use references (absolute, relative, and mixed) Sort data
Print workbooks	Preview and print worksheets Print the screen and ranges Print headers and footers
Format worksheets	Modify cell size and alignment Apply general numbers formats Apply font formats Apply outlines
Create and apply ranges	Create and name ranges Clear and format ranges Copy and move ranges
Use functions	Use the AVERAGE, MIN, and MAX functions Use worksheet functions
Use draw	Create and modify lines and objects Create and modify 3D shapes
Use charts	Create, format, and modify charts Preview and print charts
Save spreadsheets as HTML	Save spreadsheets as HTML documents

Expert User

You are not required to pass, or even take, the Proficient User exam before taking the Expert User test. If you feel confident of your skill level, you can take the Expert User exam without taking the Proficient User test and receive the Expert User certification when you pass.

An Expert User should be able to do the following:

- Accounting and other financial statements
- Amortization schedules
- Data Analysis
- Forecasts
- Lists
- Personnel records
- Statistical tables

The skill areas covered in the exam and the required tasks for those skill areas are listed in Table C2.

Table C.2 Expert User Skills	
Skill Set	Required Activity
Format worksheets	Apply formats (accounting, fraction, and scientific)
	Create custom formats
	Use styles and AutoFormats
Use lists	Sort data
	Query from a list
Print workbooks	Preview workbooks
	Print workbooks
Audit a worksheet	Check and review data
	Find cells referred to in a specific formula
	Find formulas that refer to a specific cell
	Find errors
Use advanced functionality	Query databases
	Extract data
	Use filters
	Use data analysis and pivot tables
	Use data map
	Use data validation
	Use conditional formatting
	Perform multilevel sorts
Use macros	Create and record macros
	Edit macros
	Run macros
Import and export data	Import from other applications
	Export to other applications

Skill Set	Required Activity
Use templates	Work with existing templates
	Create templates
	Edit templates
Use multiple workbooks	Link workbooks
	Use multiple workbooks
Use workgroup functions	Cell tips
	Share lists
	Track changes
	Resolve conflicts
	Show history of changes
	Merge workbooks

Registering for the Exams

Microsoft Office User Specialist exams are administered by Authorized Testing Centers (ATC). To find out where the nearest ATC center is, call (800) 933-4493. Contact the ATC center to find out what their test policies and schedules are, whether they accept walk-ins or must register the candidates in advance, how the exams are conducted, and what they are charging for the tests. The estimated retail price of each exam is $50.00 in the United States, but that can vary based on the center's sales policies. Payment for the tests must be paid in advance. There is no refund for missed exam appointments or failed tests.

Exams are currently available only in English, although Microsoft plans to offer the Office 97 exams in other languages as soon as the courseware in those languages becomes available.

Taking the Tests

Microsoft Office User Specialist exams are not multiple-choice or true-false tests. Instead, they are based on the types of tasks you may encounter in the everyday world. When you take the test you sit at a computer that uses Windows® 95 or Windows NT® Workstation, work with a Microsoft Word 97 document, and use the features of Word to perform the tasks outlined for you.

You can't use notes, manuals, laptops, tape recorders, or other aids during the tests. Word Help is available, but using it may cut down on the time you have available to complete the exam tasks.

Exams are one hour or less (some as short as 30 minutes). Your score is based on the number of tasks you successfully perform in the allotted time. This measures your productivity and efficiency, as well as your skill and knowledge.

Each test has a minimum score. If your score meets or exceeds that minimum, you pass the test. If not, you may take the test as many times as you need to until you pass. There is no refund if you don't pass the test.

You see your test results as soon as you complete the exam. Successful candidates receive a certificate a week or two after the testing. Test scores are confidential; only you and Microsoft see them.

To keep up to date on the Certified Microsoft Office User exams, check Microsoft's Web site:

http://www.mous.net

http://www.microsoft.com/office/train_cert/

INDEX